Shelter *from the* Storm

Hope for Survivors of Sexual Abuse

Cynthia Kubetin &
James Mallory, M.D.

Facilitator Guide written by Jacqualine C. Truitt

Search Resources

*As God works through us, we will help and churches know Jesus Christ and seek His kingdom
by providing biblical solutions that spiritually transform individuals and cultures.*

ACKNOWLEDGEMENTS

Shelter from the Storm: Hope for Survivors of Sexual Abuse
Copyright ©1995 Search Resources, Reprint 2004

ISBN 978-1515030232

Subject Heading: SEX CRIMES//VICTIMS OF CRIME

Sources for definitions in *Shelter from the Storm: Hope for Survivors of Sexual Abuse*
By permission. From *Webster's Ninth New Collegiate Dictionary* ©1991 by Merriam-Webster
Inc., publisher of the Merriam-Webster® dictionaries

Unless otherwise indicated, biblical quotations are from the Holy Bible, *New International
Version*, copyright © 1973, 1978, 1984 by International Bible Society (NIV). Other versions
used: the *New American Standard Bible* (NASB) © The Lockman Foundation, 1960, 1962, 1963,
1968, 1971, 1972, 1973, 1975, 1977. Used by permission; the *King James Version* (KJV).

Printed in the United States of America

Table of Contents

4

Beginning Recovery

Case in point

I'VE BEEN BETRAYED!

Terri says that 35 years of her life were extended torment. She remembers little of her childhood—just that her father always seemed to be angry and her mother was frightened and distant. And she had frightening memories of a dark room. Initially she did not remember the episodes of sexual abuse, but she recalled the frequent whippings and the feeling that she was wrong, evil, and somehow different than other girls.

When she was 16, Terri ran away from home with a man who was 22. Her marriage quickly turned from the dream she had imagined into a nightmare of anger, disappointment, and rejection.

The day before her thirty-sixth birthday Terri attempted suicide. After the failed attempt, she went for counsel to a wise and sympathetic Christian counselor. Only then did Terri begin to untangle the web of abuse that had scarred her life and led her to so many bad decisions and so much additional pain. Now Terri is participating in a sexual abuse recovery group. She realizes that she still has a long way to go, but she says, "Life is beginning to make sense. For the first time, I have a reason to live. I can't believe I almost ended it all."

In *Shelter from the Storm*, you will read about many individuals—women and men, children and adults—whose lives have been distorted by the trauma of sexual abuse. You will learn how you can seek the help and support you need, and how you can identify and deal with the pain and the aftereffects of sexual abuse.

In recovery groups, we have a saying, "Only you can do it, but you can't do it alone." Nothing in life so isolates us from healthy human relationships and from a relationship with God as does sexual abuse. Any experience of sexual abuse—but especially child sexual abuse—violates our boundaries and our trust. The experience teaches us not to trust appropriately. It sets us up for a life that combines times of painful isolation interrupted by experiences of blindly trusting, which set us up to be victimized again and again.

Course goal

Shelter from the Storm will help you to understand yourself. You will begin to identify destructive patterns that the abuse began and that other influences and choices have strengthened and in your life. As you identify these harmful patterns, you will be able to make Christ-honoring and life-enhancing changes. It will help you learn how you can experience God's love, forgiveness, and power in all of life's circumstances. *Shelter from the Storm* will help you—with the help of a support group of fellow recoverers—to not only understand the storm of sexual abuse but to move from victim to survivor to thriver.

After you participate in a *Shelter from the Storm* group, you will have the means to identify the ways that your past experience is damaging your present circumstances. You will be equipped to begin a healing process which will bring you a clear sense of identity and a healthy relationship to the lordship of Christ built on positive experiences of His unconditional love.

How this course fits in

Shelter from the Storm is not merely designed for you to understand concepts. The purpose of this material is life change. *Shelter from the Storm* is part of the LIFE® Support Group Series. The LIFE® Support Group Series is an educational system of discovery-group and support-group resources for providing Christian ministry and emotional support to individuals in the areas of social, emotional, and physical need. These resources deal with such life issues as chemical dependency, codependency, recovery from sexual abuse, eating disorders, divorce recovery, and how to grieve the losses of life. LIFE® Support Group Series courses are a form of focused discipleship. The Christ-centered recovery process helps people to resolve painful issues so that they can effectively minister to others.

Shelter from the Storm is a support-group course. A support group studies dysfunctional family issues and other sensitive emotional issues that individuals might face. A carefully selected group facilitator guides discussion of the topics and helps group members process what they have learned during their study. This group is not a therapy group. This is a self-help group in which group members help each other by talking in a safe, loving environment.

Shelter from the Storm is an integrated course of study. To achieve the full benefit of the educational design, you will need to prepare your individual assignments and participate in the group sessions. The principles behind *Shelter from the Storm* represent a lifelong learning process. This is not a course which you will study and then forget. It represents an opportunity to understand the cause of your pain, to learn to grieve and to take responsibility for your healing, emotions, and behavior.

What's in it for you?

Participating in a *Shelter from the Storm* group will be the beginning of a journey. The journey is not always easy, but it leads to a whole new world of healing and usefulness. When you complete *Shelter from the Storm*, we will suggest some possibilities from which you may wish to choose to continue your growth and study.

Study Tips. Because survivors of sexual abuse vary so widely in their experience and present situation, we do not impose any rigid schedule for your study of the book.

Some individuals are stabilized in their personal lives and are highly motivated to deal with their sexual abuse issues. If you are one of those individuals, you will find that *Shelter from the Storm* is divided into five lessons per unit. The basic group plan is for you to cover one unit per week in preparation for your weekly support group meeting. You may be able to study the material and complete the exercises in 30 to 60 minutes of study time each day. Even if you find that you can study the material in less time, spread the study out over five days. This will give you more time to apply the truths to your life. Many other survivors of sexual abuse have extreme difficulty concentrating, or some of the material may be so challenging that you cannot complete a unit in a week, or even in many weeks. Do not shame or pressure yourself for needing to recover slowly. Recovery is a long-term process.

The basic plan we suggest is to participate in three cycles of a *Shelter from the Storm* group. If you follow this suggestion, the first time you go through *Shelter,* you will be learning the basics of recovery from sexual abuse. Then the next time you cycle through the group and through the book, you will apply the recovery process at a deeper level. The third time that you participate in a group and in the study, you will be able to implement some of the recovery actions that seemed completely impossible to you earlier in your recovery.

Study at your own pace. Your group may decide to take a longer time to study each unit. Do not become discouraged if you cannot complete *Shelter from the Storm* in 12 weeks. Remember that the purpose is life change, not speed reading. Take the time necessary to apply recovery to your hurt, anger, and behaviors.

This book has been written as a tutorial text. Study it as if Cindy Kubetin, Jim Mallory, or Jacque Truitt is sitting at your side helping you learn. When they ask you a question or give you an assignment, you will benefit most by writing your response. Each assignment is indented and appears in **boldface type**. When you are to respond in writing, a pencil appears beside the assignment. For example, an assignment will look like this:

✎ **Read Psalm 139:13. Write what the verse tells about God's care for you.**

In an actual activity, a line would appear below each assignment or in the margin beside the assignment. You would write your response as indicated. Then, when you are asked to respond in a non-written fashion—for example, by thinking about or praying about a matter—an ➾ appears beside the assignment. This type of assignment will look like this:

➾ **Pause now to pray and thank God for unconditionally accepting you.**

In most cases your "personal tutor" will give you some feedback about your response; for example, you may see a suggestion about what you might have written. This process is designed to help you learn the material and apply the concepts more effectively. Do not deny yourself valuable learning by skipping the learning activities.

Set a definite time and select a quiet place where you can study with little interruption. Keep a Bible handy for times in which the material asks you to look up Scripture. Make notes of problems, questions, or concerns that arise as you study. You will discuss many of these during your support-group sessions. Write these matters in the margins of this textbook so you can find them easily.

Support-Group Session. You will benefit most from *Shelter from the Storm* if once each week you attend a support-group session. Others in your support group will share your journey with you. They will affirm, encourage, and love you as you do the difficult work of recovery.

As sexual abuse survivors, many of us have experienced broken trust in our families. Our support group becomes the supportive family we may never have experienced before.

If you are not involved in a *Shelter from the Storm* support group, we encourage you to seek out a Christ-centered sexual abuse recovery group led by a trained facilitator. Some of the issues in sexual-abuse recovery are so frightening that we strongly discourage you from doing your recovery work alone.

Shelter from the Storm is written with the assumption that you already have received Jesus Christ as your Savior and Lord and that you have Him guiding you in the healing process. If you have not yet made the important decision to receive Christ, you will find guidance in unit 2. You will benefit far more from *Shelter from the Storm* if you have Jesus working in your life and guiding you in the process.

> # A key decision

The Issue of Professional Counseling

Sexual abuse is the most personal and damaging form of betrayal. Recovery from sexual abuse is the most intense and emotionally challenging form of recovery. Survivors of sexual abuse often struggle with powerful issues such as shame, thoughts of suicide, addictions, and even dissociation. For all these reasons, we strongly recommend that every sexual-abuse support group maintain a link with a professional Christian counselor with experience in the area of sexual abuse recovery. The facilitator can seek counsel and support from the professional and can refer group members who need assistance for further counseling. The ideal situation is for group members to begin the recovery process with a professional evaluation.

Most sexual abuse victims experience profound emotional isolation. Virtually all sexual abuse survivors could benefit from professional care. Ask your facilitator for the names of competent Christian professionals in your area.

UNIT 1

A Foundation for Recovery

Focal passage

I will go before you and make the rough places smooth; I will shatter the doors of bronze, and cut through their iron bars. And I will give you the treasures of darkness, and hidden wealth in secret places, in order that you may know that it is I, the Lord, the God of Israel, who calls you by name.

–Isaiah 45:2-3, NASB

This Unit's Affirmation:
I can find hope
and healing.

A LOAD OF RAGE

When Pam came for counseling, she received a book on sexual abuse. The book contained a list of characteristics of people who had been sexually abused. As she reviewed the list, she slumped into a chair and began to cry. For the first time her life made sense.

Although Pam couldn't remember most of her childhood, she was carrying a big load of pent-up rage, guilt, and shame. When she began to realize the source of her thoughts and feelings, for the first time she saw herself as normal—at least normal for what had happened to her as a child.

In this unit you will learn more about sexual abuse and about recovery. You will begin the process that can result in healing.

Growth goal

This week's goal

You will begin to develop a support system and set goals for your recovery. You will take your first steps toward healing from sexual abuse.

Why a Support Group?	Can I get the Support I Need?	Indications of Recovery	Help in the Storm, Part 1	Help in the Storm, Part 2
Lesson 1	Lesson 2	Lesson 3	Lesson 4	Lesson 5

Memory verse

This week's passage of Scripture to memorize

I said, "Oh, that I had the wings of a dove! I would fly away and be at rest— I would flee far away and stay in the desert; I would hurry to my place of shelter, far from the tempest and storm."

–Psalm 55:6-8

9

LESSON 1

Why a Support Group?

You met Pam in the unit story. She is a survivor of sexual abuse. Like many survivors, she experienced a host of life problems, and like many survivors, she had never connected the abuse to the problems in her life. In fact she had blocked out the very memories of the abuse.

Did you know that many people in our society are survivors of sexual abuse? They are the silent victims of an all too common crime.

- Every fourth woman you see may have experienced sexual abuse as a child.
- One in every five women suffered child sexual abuse by a family member.
- In addition to the children who are sexually abused, many adults have been assaulted by an acquaintance or stranger.

Recent studies indicate that men also frequently suffer sexual abuse, with statistics approaching the same figures previously reported for women. Somewhere between one in four or one in five men suffer silently.

As you can recognize from the statistics above, you are not alone. This book is designed to help you to experience the support of compassionate and caring people as you seek recovery from the effects of sexual abuse. Recovery, however, is a process. Recovery is difficult, but it is possible.

✎ **In the margin read the definition of the word *recover*. Below write your own definition of what the word *recovery* means to you.**

recover–v. to get back: regain (Webster's)

_____

_____

_____

People all seem to have their own definitions of recovery. We explain it this way: when God created you, He had a great plan. He intended for you a life with meaning and purpose. The actions of one or more people damaged that life. Recovery means regaining what God intended for you.

✎ **Can you think of at least one thing you would like to "get back" that the experience of abuse has taken away? Describe it below.**

_____

_____

The answers to the question can be as numerous as are the survivors. Some of us want our sense of safety returned. For some our need is release from the inappropriate shame we have felt or the sense of unworthiness. Whatever you described, God and your group members desire to support you as you follow the path of recovery.

Sometimes you may feel that all hope for healing is lost. You especially may feel that way as you first begin to struggle with the burden of the abuse, its wounds, and its memories. You may have struggled a long time just to survive, to hide your hurt, and to heal the wounds alone and in your own strength. As a member of a support group you will have affirmation from others who understand those times and you will no longer be alone. With the care and support of others you can find shelter from the storm.

Many mental health professionals consider support groups to be one of the most important resources in the recovery from sexual abuse. A group can help you to develop a new and living way out of silence and isolation. Recovery involves learning to enjoy intimacy with God, which includes emotional and psychological health, spiritual freedom, and positive relationships with others.

Like many other survivors you may believe that you cannot trust God since He did not protect you from the abuse. Yet, God offers hope through a relationship with Jesus Christ. As you work through the the healing process in supportive Christian surroundings, you will have the opportunity to find that your sadness can be turned to joy. Christ offers hope and healing from the effects of sexual abuse. Jesus Christ can be your shelter from the storm.

I feel very small—
 very weak
Against a
 powerful monster
Who wishes
 to consume me.

I look outside
 And see people dancing
  Laughing in their own worlds
And I long to join
 In the festival of life
But my world feels dark
 And I've lost the beat.

The Matter of Terminology

Two words often are used to label the people involved in sexual abuse—*victim* and *perpetrator*. These words accurately depict the violence and betrayal of the sexual abuse. At various points in this book we will use these terms, however, we have chosen to use other terms more often. We prefer to use the term *survivor* rather than *victim*. We want to see ourselves as survivors who are strong and who can make life-enhancing and Christ-honoring decisions. Once we were victims, but we can and will be survivors. Similarly, we prefer to avoid over-using the term *perpetrator*. The term de-humanizes the person who committed the crime of sexual abuse. Since those who commit sexual abuse are so often themselves victims of the same crime and since our continued resentment interferes with our own recovery, we most often refer to the *person(s) who committed the abuse.* This term recognizes the full reality of the offense while seeing those who committed the abuse as people.

Inform and Encourage

Most Bible scholars agree that the purpose of the Book of Hebrews is to inform and encourage the discouraged Christians. If you are a survivor of sexual abuse, you probably need to be informed and encouraged—informed about the facts of sexual abuse and encouraged in your recovery process. We encourage you to recognize that you no longer have to be "only a survivor." You now can be an overcomer—even a thriver.

Let us not give up meeting together, as some are in the habit of doing, but let us encourage one another.
–Hebrews 10:25

✎ **Read Hebrews 10:25 that appears in the margin. Below describe what the verse says to you about the importance of your support group.**

_____

_____

_____

Most survivors isolate themselves from others to avoid the risk of being hurt again.

Hebrews 10:25 refers to the church assembling for worship, but it also points to the biblical base and need for support groups. Most survivors isolate themselves from others to avoid the risk of being hurt again. Isolation prevents them from developing the skills with which to encourage one another. In your *Shelter from the Storm* group you will begin to experience encouragement, acceptance, safety, and love, both as a receiver and as a giver.

✎ **When you think about the people in your Shelter group offering you encouragement, acceptance, safety, and love, what feelings do you experience? Below check all the feelings you are experiencing about attending a support group and add any other feelings you can identify.**

❑ excited   ❑ numb   ❑ other _____
❑ afraid   ❑ angry
❑ detached   ❑ hopeful

✎ **What do you hope to gain from attending a support group for survivors of sexual abuse?**

_____

_____

_____

_____

What issues are important to you when you think of attending such a group? What are your concerns or fears?

_____

_____

_____

_____

_____

Survivors later communicate how vital the group experience has been in their recovery process.

Most survivors of sexual abuse find attending their first group meeting a little frightening, some even terrifying. However, most later communicate how vital the group experience has been in their recovery process.

We hope you will experience recovery as you read and complete the exercises, spend time in prayer and Bible study, and share your journey through the storm with the other members of your support group. We hope that you will gain strength, hope, and acceptance as you learn and grow in your support group. Your group is a safe place where you can be yourself.

You may not understand what we mean by a "relationship with Jesus." You may be angry at God for allowing you to be abused. You may even question the existence of God. We encourage you, do not give up. You are accepted in the group. Share your doubts and questions with your group and with your facilitator. Come as you are.

I said, "Oh, that I had the wings of a dove! I would fly away and be at rest— I would flee far away and stay in the desert; I would hurry to my place of shelter, far from the tempest and storm."
–Psalm 55:6-8, NASB

Assignment for the lesson

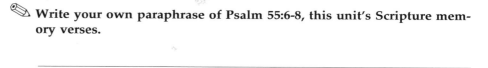 **Write your own paraphrase of Psalm 55:6-8, this unit's Scripture memory verses.**

_____

_____

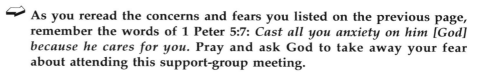 Say aloud this affirmation five times.

I can find hope and healing.

As you reread the concerns and fears you listed on the previous page, remember the words of 1 Peter 5:7: *Cast all you anxiety on him [God] because he cares for you.* Pray and ask God to take away your fear about attending this support-group meeting.

LESSON 2

Can I Get the Support I Need?

In addition to your support group, we encourage you to establish additional support for yourself as you go through recovery. Almost everyone who goes through recovery is reluctant at first to enlist the support of others, but your support system will largely determine the success of your recovery. You need support. You are worthy of support. You can learn to express your needs in healthy ways. You can talk about what happened to you with others who will support you.

What can I expect to happen when I tell?

As other survivors of sexual abuse will tell you, you will find it helpful to be careful and deliberate about who you choose to include in your immediate support system. You will need to supply your supporters with information about how to help you. They will not automatically know what to say or do to help. People who genuinely mean well may say and do some painful and damaging things because they do not understand. You can help them to understand and help rather than hinder your recovery. At your first meeting your group facilitator will provide you with some materials to help you.

As you read the following paragraph, pay particular attention to your feelings. In the margin write any thoughts or feelings you experience. Then after the paragraph describe your reaction to what you have read.

Try not to accept responsibility for the reactions of others.

Friends may respond in one of many ways when you tell them about your experience. Learning about your abuse may be difficult for your family and friends. They will experience many feelings. They may feel angry, sad, or afraid. They may not know what to say to you. Try not to accept responsibility for the reactions of your friends and family. Your friends and family may be intense in their feelings about what happened to you. Some may react by "shutting-down" their feelings, or telling you to "just forget it." If the rule in their family was to avoid talking about painful events, their first reaction may be to turn off their feelings. This reaction is not due to a lack of concern for you. Some may react by trying too hard and smothering you with care and concern. This is your journey. Your supporters will help you, but they cannot go on this journey for you. Know in advance that your family and friends have limitations. Acknowledge to yourself the reality of those limitations. They may not know what you need. Your support group facilitator will help you know how to tell them your needs.

✎ **In the margin describe your reaction to what you have just read.**

Many survivors respond with panic to the assignment of sharing their story with another person. People commonly respond to sexual abuse with silence and secrecy, however, telling your story is an important part of the recovery process. You control how much you tell, to whom, and when. Your support group facilitator will show you how to start slow, make wise choices, and move forward at a pace that is comfortable for you. You can observe the following guidelines for selecting a support person and preparing to share.

Guidelines for Selecting Supportive People

1. Pray for God's wisdom as you choose a supportive person.
2. Choose a person unrelated but sympathetic to the situation surrounding your abuse. You may want to consider someone who has been in recovery for a year or more, a professional counselor, a pastoral counselor, or a lay caregiver.
3. If you tell a family member, do not blame them for not helping sooner.
4. Determine how much of your story you want to tell. You might want to try writing an outline ahead of time. Remember that you do not have to tell anything you do not want to tell.
5. Pray for the person you will enlist for support.

Some survivors have difficulty with the reactions of others when they tell their stories. Remember to allow your supporters room to struggle with their feelings. Remember they need for you to tell them what you need. They also need the freedom to decide if they can provide what you need. They have to consider their own emotional needs and time limitations.

↪ **Do you have a friend or family member that you could trust enough to say:**

"I am a survivor of sexual abuse. I am going to join a *Shelter from the Storm* support group. Will you agree to pray for me while I take this important step in my life?"

✎ **Write that person's name in the space below.**

_____

**When I think
of enlisting support,
I feel...**

_____

_____

_____

_____

Positive
_____
_____
_____
_____

Negative
_____
_____
_____
_____

✎ **In the margin describe both your positive and negative feelings as you think about enlisting this person's support.**

Managing Crisis

Participants in sexual abuse support groups sometimes struggle with anxiety or panic attacks. As you face the pain, perhaps for the first time, you may be overwhelmed by your emotions and memories. For many, the emotions produce a sensation of being trapped. Most survivors of sexual abuse have had suicidal feelings at some point. You may experience such feelings as you go through the healing process.

It is critical for you to develop a relationship with other members of the support group. We highly recommend that the names and phone numbers of all members of the support group, the phone number of your pastor, and of a sexual issues hotline be available to you.

A form like the one below has been found to be of invaluable help at times. We encourage you to copy it, fill it out, and keep it beside the telephone. You may also wish to carry a copy in your wallet or handbag, since crisis is almost always a part of the healing process in facing the pain of sexual abuse.

MY PLAN FOR MANAGING CRISIS

I must learn to ask for help and be willing to accept help when it is offered. When I feel overwhelmed with my emotions, anxiety, depression, or suicidal thoughts I will contact the following individual(s):

I will call _____ at
_____.

If that person is not available, I will call _____
at _____ as backup.

I may also call my pastor at _____ or my counselor at _____.

Others who have agreed to be a support for me—

_____

_____

Life is worth living because . . .

_____

_____

_____

If you can't think of any reasons why life is worth living, ask your group facilitator or some other person you trust to help.

Remember that God says:

I will go before you and make the rough places smooth; I will shatter the doors of bronze, and cut through their iron bars. And I will give you the treasures of darkness, and hidden wealth in secret places, in order that you may know that it is I, the Lord, the God of Israel, who calls you by name.

–Isaiah 45:2-3

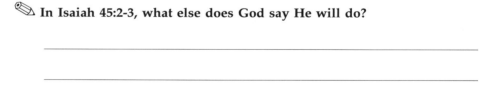 **What do the verses say God will give you out of the darkness?**

_____

What will God give you from the secret places?

_____

Why does God want to give you these things?

_____

"I have discovered a wealth of information about who I am as a person and as a creation of God."

Jacque said, "I have found as I have been willing to open the doors on those secret places in my life that I have discovered a wealth of information about who I am as a person and as a creation of God." God calls you by name also. He created you and wants to restore to you that which was taken from you. Though sexual abuse will always be a part of your past, your future can be brighter than you now may be able to imagine because of His love for you. As you learn and grow, God will reveal to you that those dark places in your life contain treasures.

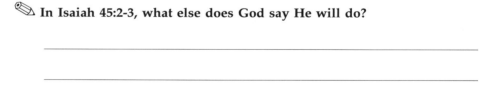 **In Isaiah 45:2-3, what else does God say He will do?**

_____

_____

God says He will go before you. He will remove the barriers and you will find shelter and healing. God's healing power can still the storm created by sexual abuse.

You may already have told one or more people about your abuse, or you may feel that you can never tell anyone. You may have chosen this book because you have been in recovery and want to take one step further on your journey. You may have just picked this book up off the shelf because you are wondering if what happened to you was sexual abuse and you want to find out. Whatever your reason, we encourage you to continue your journey toward recovery. You can do so at your own pace.

I said, "Oh, that I had the wings of a dove! I would fly away and be at rest— I would flee far away and stay in the desert; I would hurry to my place of shelter, far from the tempest and storm."
–Psalm 55:6-8, NASB

Assignment for the lesson

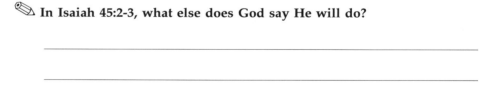 **Write on a card Psalm 55:6-8, the Scripture memory verses for this unit. Carry the card with you and regularly review the verses.**

↪ **Say aloud this affirmation five times.**

I can find hope and healing.

↪ **Remember 1 Peter 5:7 from the previous lesson? Ask God to help you overcome your anxiety to share you story with the person or people He has helped (or will help) you to chose.**

LESSON 3

Do not be anxious about anything, but in everything by prayer and petition, with thanksgiving, present your requests to God. And the peace of God, which transcends all understanding, will guard your hearts and your minds in Christ Jesus.

–Philippians 4:6-7

Indications of Recovery

Indications of Recovery

Many of us are afraid of the past. We do not want past events to hurt us any longer. As we consider facing the events and effects of the past, we feel anxious and afraid. The apostle Paul's approach to finding peace involved making his anxieties known to God. See Philippians 4:6,7 which appears in the margin below. His statement demonstrates that Paul dealt with anxiety. He also had to learn to be honest with God. Our hope in Christ focuses upon God's promise of a life to come without pain and suffering. Life this side of heaven will never be free from pain; but we can experience healing in this life as a foretaste of the life to come.

Recovery from the effects of sexual abuse does not follow a precise path. You will find that the experiences and responses of those in your support group will vary widely. Do not expect that each member of the group will reach all of the goals listed below at the same time. You may anticipate that you will have accomplished some of the goals before other members of your group are even well under way. But as you advance in your recovery from abuse, be assured that God will equip you with the ability to function in meeting life's inevitable challenges and surprises.

Remember, recovery is an ongoing process. The following list describes a person who has worked through and recovered from sexual abuse. Be honest in comparing your behavior to the characteristics of a recovered survivor, but also be patient with yourself as you work toward the goals that are the most difficult for you.

✎ **As you review this list mark the items as follows: Place an * beside those that you believe you are already experiencing, a ? by those that you do not understand, and place a ✓ by those that you believe will be particularly difficult for you.**

___ I am willing to face the abuse and acknowledge the hurt and the pain.
___ I understand that the abuse was a violation.
___ I have an increased awareness of my value and worth.
___ I can list significant others I can trust.
___ I can share thoughts and feelings about the abuse with others if I choose to do so.
___ I recognize relationship tendencies that avoid honesty and intimacy.
___ I am overcoming feelings of shame and false guilt.
___ I recognize that I was a victim even though I may have experienced physical arousal during the abuse.

✎ **Below in the appropriate space write those items from the list that you marked:**

I am already experiencing recovery in these areas.

_____

_____

I don't understand this.

_____

_____

I believe this will be very difficult for me.

_____

_____

When Jacque responded to this list she was already recognizing that the abuse was a violation of her body and her personhood. She didn't understand, however, why she needed to share with others her thoughts and feelings about the abuse. She felt confused and frightened. The idea that she could actually overcome the feelings of shame and false guilt seemed impossible. Eventually Jacque discovered that she could make the journey from victim to survivor to thriver. Admittedly, the process was slow. It included pain, setbacks, and frustration; however, with the leadership and guidance of God, she found she could experience hope and healing.

With the leadership and guidance of God, Jacque found she could experience hope and healing.

☛ **Review that list again and ask God to lead you to experience each item on the list. Recognize that recovery is a process and over time God will answer your prayer.**

Assignment for the lesson

✎ **Below write the unit Scripture verses from memory. To check your work refer to page 9.**

_____

_____

_____

_____

☛ **Say aloud this affirmation five times.**

I can find hope and healing.

☛ **Ask God to help you realize He is with you during every step of this difficult process.**

LESSON 4

Help in the Storm, Part 1

The last two lessons of this unit will help not only you, the survivor of abuse, but also your friends (including relatives of all degrees of closeness) and helpers (including therapists and other caregivers). By the time many survivors have reached maturity, they have been revictimized many times. Some survivors have abused others, at least by being overly angry. Accordingly, the most precious gift of this book would be to impart truth to all readers—truth that would produce life for each individual.

What not to say

The list below contains "The Don'ts." The 15 statements in this list are all words that family members, close friends, or well-meaning Christians might say to a sexual abuse survivor. These words and phrases are not helpful. Sometimes people make these statements because they have absolutely no understanding of sexual abuse issues. Other times the speaker may be mentally exhausted with the survivor or the recovery process. Still other individuals simply may not wish to deal with this difficult situation, because it is threatening to them and consumes too much time.

The Don'ts

Don't say to the survivor—
- "Why are you making such a big deal of this? You were very young at the time it happened."
- "What did you do to make this happen?"
- "You're the problem. You're just using this as an excuse to get your way."
- "Why didn't you stop it from happening?"
- "You mean you didn't tell anybody when it happened? So why tell now?"
- "Why can't you just forget it?"
- "You should just forgive and forget. God won't be there for you unless you forgive."
- "I don't believe you were ever abused."
- "What is past is past. Let's just not bring it up again."
- "Just pray about it. God will take care of it."
- "Why can't you just hurry up and get over this?"
- "I'm so sick of hearing about *your* needs. What about *my* needs?"
- "You are just feeling sorry for yourself."
- "Can't you just let go of it? Nothing is happening to you now."
- "It is a sin to think about this. God says to focus on what is good."
- "The Bible says to forget the past and to press on to the future."

 In the list above, underline the statements that others have said to you when you have revealed your abuse to them.

We can never understand fully why others do or say the things they do.

We can never fully understand why others do or say the things they do. Possibly they have made painful statements because they do not understand sexual abuse issues. Sometimes those who care become mentally exhausted with the survivor or with the recovery process. Others may refuse to deal with the issue because it threatens them or because it takes too much time.

✎ **Review the list of "don'ts" again. Beside each statement that someone has said to you, write the feelings you experienced when this was said.**

You will have an opportunity to share your statements and feelings with your group. This will be a way to begin getting acquainted with your support group.

✎ **While we cannot fully understand or control others' reactions, we can learn more effective and appropriate ways to respond to their statements. Review the list of statements one more time. Select two of the statements that trouble you most. Below write an appropriate response to those two statements. We have given you some examples.**

I didn't tell anyone then because I was afraid; now I'm learning not to be afraid.

I don't choose to bring up the past and think about it so much. It surfaces sometimes when I don't want to think about it.

I cannot forget the past, but I am trying to let God help me put it to rest as I learn from it.

_____

_____

_____

_____

Whatever the reasons others have for making any of these "don't" statements, you need to recognize the statements for what they are: statements that bring darkness—a kind of death—to you and to other survivors. In time you will be ready to leave the past, but premature advice to forgive and forget can be very destructive. All too often people make these statements when they learn of the abuse or during the difficult days of the healing process.

The most important gift your friends and family can give you is the time to heal.

The most important gift your friends and family can give you is the time to heal; however, you will need to tell your friends and relatives what you need from them. The *Supporter's Packet* your group facilitator will give you includes this list of statements. This list will aid you as you share with the people that you choose to support you during your recovery. Remember this is new to them too, and they need help to know how to help you.

Of course this list of "don'ts" could be longer. The important thing is that you and your friends and helpers be able to work on the "don'ts." You may have difficulty, but it will help you to write down unhelpful words and phrases that others say.

✎ **If you can identify some words and phrases to add to the list of "don'ts," write them in the space below.**

_____

_____

You might have added "Just stop thinking about it!" or "You know they—the abusers—didn't mean to hurt you." Continue to add to your list.

Most individuals do not understand that they are hurting you with their "helpful" advice and comments. They think they are helping. The scars of sexual abuse are deep and emotionally painful. Others cannot know you hurt unless you tell them. Choose your helpers carefully and be honest with them. Continue to think about your list of supportive people and be ready to list them at the end of this unit.

Assignment for the lesson

✎ **Below write the Scripture verses for this unit from memory.**

_____

_____

⇨ **Say aloud this affirmation five times.**

I can find hope and healing.

⇨ **Ask God to help those who help you.**

LESSON 5

Help in the Storm, Part 2

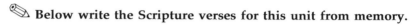

You are dealing with an injury people cannot see. Recovery takes time. If you had a broken arm or leg, friends would rush in to help. Most people—even casual acquaintances—would be willing supporters during your healing process. But if recovery were to take a long, long time, even a willing participant might grow weary.

The brokenness of a bone is evident, by x-ray if not by outward appearance, however, a real problem for you will be that your friends—even friends who want to help—can't see the brokenness of your heart. Your heart may be truly shattered, but unfortunately, you have no x-ray to show friends. They will have to depend on you to help them understand that the pain is real to you even though they can't see it.

The Requirements of Giving

For some of you one of the most difficult struggles of recovery will be to rely on others.

For some of you one of the most difficult struggles of recovery will be to rely on others. You may have used giving, kindness, and serving to maintain control. As long as you were serving or giving to others, you were in charge. Now in the recovery process others may be giving more than you are. Sometimes you may feel like you are incapable of giving. One husband and wife came to the counseling office because the wife did not want to have sexual intercourse with her husband. She was in denial as a result of the abuse, and he was very angry because she refused to have sex with him. To his dismay, the counselor suggested abstinence from sex for a period of time so the wife could begin to deal with past sexual abuse. He agreed only because, as he said, "That's what's happening anyway—so it couldn't be any worse." Fortunately, in spite of his initial reluctance, the husband was able to reach deep inside himself to help his wife. God was able to touch their lives, although during the early part of the wife's recovery, she simply was not functioning. This story ended in a great victory for both husband and wife.

She said, "For the first time, sex is good. I never knew or understood the intimacy that God intended for me through sex. How distorted it was for me in the past, but now the most beautiful part is how tenderly my husband sees me. I want to say it is a miracle, but I realize this is really just how God meant it to be."

Your sexual abuse is not just your problem.

This husband chose to support, accept, and understand. He and his wife certainly had good days and bad days in the process of recovery, but they chose to forgive and try again to continue on their long journey through the storm. You can also find shelter in the midst of the storm through friends, family, your spouse, and your relationship with Christ. The important thing is to recognize that if one partner has a problem, both of you do. Your sexual abuse is not just your problem. Both of you can choose to recover.

If you are not married, you need to develop a caring, supportive group of friends that will provide support for you. Whether married or single you can choose to recover. Your friends can help by refraining from the "don'ts" you studied in the last lesson and by following the list of "do's" recorded below.

The Do's

Friends and family can be helpful by standing ready to give—

- Support
- Acceptance
- Love
- Time
- Understanding

- Interest
- Forgiveness
- Help
- Belief
- Prayer support

- Encouragement
- Hope
- Honor
- Trust
- Validation

✎ **All of us have different needs. Some things feel more supportive than others. Which items on the "do" list seem most important to you?**

_____

_____

_____

What would you like to add to your list of "do's"?

_____

_____

_____

One person wrote on her list: "Invite me to lunch sometime." Another wrote, "to have a friend to talk to." You could have added many things to your list of "do's."

✎ Do you have people in your life who already practice some of these items on the "Do" list? Write their names beside the item. These people may be ideal candidates for your support network.

✎ Take some time now to pray again. Ask God to bring to mind the people for your list of potential supporters. In the margin box list those people.

✎ Write a letter that you can give to these family members and friends requesting the support you need. Be specific. Include in your letter the items on the "do" list that are important to you.

You can attach this letter to the packet of information your group leader will give you. This packet together with your letter will help your family and friends be more prepared to respond to you in a helpful manner. Remember they need for you to educate them. They have no way to know what to do unless you tell them. Right now you may not know what to tell them. Your group leader and your group will help and encourage you to discover what you need.

Candidates for my support network
_____
_____
_____
_____

Unit Review

✎ Look back over this unit. What statement or activity was most meaningful for you?

_____

_____

✎ Can you remember any statements or activities with which you were uncomfortable? Write those below.

_____

_____

✎ Write a prayer asking God to help you in your areas of struggle.

_____

_____

_____

_____

_____

UNIT 2

Discovering Hope

This Unit's Affirmation:
I accept God's love and kindness toward me.

Focal passage

Who redeems your life from the pit; Who crowns you with lovingkindness and compassion; Who satisfies your years with good things, so that your youth is renewed like the eagle.

–Psalm 103:4-5, NASB

MY STORY: BY CINDY KUBETIN

Cindy tells her story of sexual abuse and of eventual healing. "God promised healing, but it took many years before I felt His comfort or received wholeness. As a very young child, I began to isolate myself from others because of sexual abuse from someone I loved and believed was there for me. My memory is too sketchy for me to be sure of the extent of the abuse prior to age seven. I don't know if more than one person abused me in those early years. I do know that at least ten people had sexually abused me by the time I reached adulthood."

In this unit you will learn about the hope God extends to those who have been abused.

Growth goal

This week's goal

You will recognize and accept that if you have been sexual abused your life includes personal and relational tendencies that are similar to those of other survivors of sexual abuse.

Recovery is Possible	What is Abusive?	Symptoms of Abuse, Part One	Symptoms of Abuse, Part Two	Restoration is Possible
Lesson 1	Lesson 2	Lesson 3	Lesson 4	Lesson 5

Memory verse

This week's passage of Scripture to memorize

Who satisfies your years with good things, so that your youth is renewed like the eagle.

–Psalm 103:5, NASB

LESSON 1

Recovery Is Possible!

Life for a survivor of sexual abuse resembles living in a storm. The feelings can be devastating. They range from hopelessness to the drive to prove ourselves and be in control, from inappropriate guilt and shame to rage. Sometimes the symptoms are intense and overwhelming. Other times survivors experience no feeling at all. Christ provides hope and healing. He is the shelter from the storm. We pray that you will allow Him to be your shelter as you go on your journey through the storm, that you will find calm and peaceful seas and a life that is whole and complete. We begin by walking with one person as she traveled through her experience of the storm.

 The next three paragraphs begin to tell Cindy's story. Circle any words or phrases that describe your experience too. Underline any part of Cindy's recovery that you would like to have in your life.

"From personal experience, I know that healing from sexual abuse is possible. The process may be slow and will include pain, setbacks, and frustrations. The awesome power of God is available to overcome these obstacles. Isaiah 57:18 describes how God restores, heals, and gives comfort. Many years elapsed before I felt the comfort or received the wholeness, however. As a very young child, I began to isolate myself from others because of sexual abuse from someone I loved and believed was there for me. My memory is too sketchy for me to be sure of the extent of the abuse prior to age seven. I don't know if more than one person abused me in those early years. I do know that at least ten people had sexually abused me by the time I reached adulthood.

"To fix vividly in my mind that I had been a victim took many years. Somehow the abuses just seemed like something that happened to me. I felt devastated when I actually recognized that I had been a victim of childhood sexual abuse. I felt more shame than ever. My flashbacks became more frequent, and I felt despicable and worthless. As God's restorative power began to take hold of me, however, I not only saw myself as a victim but I began to see that to become a survivor was possible. I even began to feel a joy in having survived so much. I saw more positive things about myself than I ever had, and even learned to risk myself a little more. I liked this stage, but there was still too much pain inside, too much anxiety and fear. Also, I continued making grave mistakes in my life. It seemed so obvious to me that I didn't yet have it all together !

"By this time, I had begun to seek God in my life. I wanted the mental torment to stop, not just for a day, but for a lifetime. But when I read the Bible's wonderful promises, I was sure that they applied to someone else; surely this book couldn't have been written to help me. I couldn't yet see the Bible as a resource for me. I hadn't begun to understand the way of Jesus—that He wanted me to have good things in life, not just bad things. I didn't understand that God wanted to redeem my life. But I kept reading, and for me verses 4 and 5 of Psalm 103 explained the Lord's way quite well. As I read these words my heart pounded with hope. A real and personal God was still difficult to believe, but I knew that even a little faith was better than none.

 In the margin read Psalm 103:4-5. Underline the words that provide hope for you.

I have seen his ways, but I will heal him; I will guide him and restore comfort to him.

–Isaiah 57:18

Who redeems your life from the pit; Who crowns you with lovingkindness and compassion; Who satisfies your years with good things, So that your youth is renewed like the eagle.

–Psalm 103:4-5, NASB

God said He would renew your youth "like an eagle" and satisfy "your years with good things." God said He would crown you with loving kindness and compassion, redeem you and therefore make your life different.

What Is Sexual Abuse?

A complete definition of sexual abuse must be as broad as the range of human sexual activity.

Many people think that sexual abuse is limited to intercourse, but other behaviors can result in the same damage to the victim. Any sexual activity carried out in an inappropriate context is abusive. A complete definition of sexual abuse must be as broad as the range of human sexual activity. With a narrow definition both victims and perpetrators tend to minimize the harmful results or even deny that sexual abuse has occurred. Therefore, we use the definition that sexual abuse is *any sexual activity—verbal, visual, or physical—engaged in without consent, which may be emotionally or physically harmful and which exploits a person in order to meet another person's sexual or emotional needs. The person does not consent if he or she cannot reasonably choose to consent or refuse because of age, circumstances, level of understanding, and dependency or relationship to the offender.*[1]

✎ **Below write the key words and phrases to this definition in the blanks.**

Sexual abuse can be defined as "any _____—verbal, visual

or physical—engaged in without _____, which may be

emotionally or physically _____ and which _____

a person in order to meet another person's _____

or _____ needs. "

In the next lesson we will more fully examine this definition of sexual abuse.

Assignment for the lesson

Who satisfies your years with good things, So that your youth is renewed like the eagle.
–Psalm 103:5, NASB

✎ **Write your own paraphrase of Psalm 103:5, this unit's Scripture memory verse.**

_____

_____

_____

_____

☞ **Say aloud this affirmation five times.**

I accept God's love and kindness toward me.

☞ **Pray for yourself and for each member of your *Shelter from the Storm* group.**

LESSON 2

What is Abusive?

Sexual abuse can happen to anyone. Victims can be young or old, male or female, rich or poor. Victims can come from Christian homes and are sometimes abused in those homes. Victims of sexual abuse tend to minimize the abuse in order to hide the emotional pain. You may have heard or said things like "it's no big deal" or "he/she didn't mean anything by it" or "that hasn't affected my life." Regardless of the duration or nature of the sexual abuse, it is a big deal! Sexual abuse does affect lives negatively. We need to know what it is and how to deal with it.

Freedom to Choose

Consent is a key issue in the definition of sexual abuse. A person does not consent if he or she does not have the ability either to choose or to refuse the sexual activity. Age, circumstances, level of understanding, dependency, and relationship to the offender are all factors that can limit a person's ability to choose.

 In the following examples, identify and describe the factor that limits the person's ability to choose. Write your answer in the space provided.

1. A 67-year-old man staying in a nursing home describes being exposed, viewed, and fondled. He keeps reassuring the listener that he is not crazy or drugged. "It really happened," he says, as he looks to the floor in despair.

_____

_____

His lack of strength and mobility have caused this man to be vulnerable, and his freedom to choose was limited.

"I began to feel uneasy when Daddy would come into the bathroom, but I didn't understand."

2. "I was about eight, maybe nine years old. Mother had started working nights, so now it was Daddy who put me to bed. I began to feel uneasy when Daddy would come into the bathroom, but I didn't understand. One night he said he needed to look at me all over to see if I was growing all over. I felt funny, but when he began to hold me, it felt good to be so close. I didn't even mind too much when he touched me down there."

_____

_____

This little girl had a normal desire for attention from her father. Because of her age and level of understanding she did not know how to say no to the unwanted sexual advances without losing that attention.

3. Another victim in her early twenties shares that when she was 16 she was sexually involved with her 40-year-old employer. "He would buy

me presents and tell me I was his princess. When he began to hug and kiss me, I felt confused. I decided not to tell my parents. I had gotten the job because he was the husband of my mother's best friend. I thought, *If I tell, mother will blame me and it might even cause a divorce. He won't do it again.* But he did, and the next time I thought, *they won't understand why I let him before.* He told me it only happened because I was so pretty. He said he couldn't help it, so it must be my fault!"

"He said he couldn't help it, so it must be my fault!"

This is an example of the offender manipulating the victim. This was not an affair. Sex with a minor is legally recognized as rape because of the age of the victim. In some situations the victim technically is not a minor, but the age or power differences create the same result.

Sometimes in the repeated sexual abuse of a child by a family member or friend of the family, the person who does the abusing seeks to get the "consent" of the child, though the child is too young to offer genuine consent. If this happened to you—if you gave this kind of permission out of guilt, childlike loyalty, fear, or any other reason, recognize that you were not capable of making an adult decision. This "consent" does not render guiltless the person who abused you. You were only responding—in perhaps the only way you knew how. You were a child. Even adolescents are not adults.

✎ **Think about your own abuse situation and identify the factor or factors that prevented you from being able to choose. Check all the factors that apply.**

❑ Age
❑ Level of understanding
❑ Dependency/relationship to offender
❑ Fear of consequences
❑ Physical strength or intimidation
❑ Other _____

✎ **Write any insights or feelings you experienced as you completed this exercise.**

_____

_____

_____

_____

Some survivors become very angry when they realize that they have been blamed for something another person did. Other survivors continue to blame themselves. You may have felt any emotion from complete numbness, to anger, to a sense of relief. Remember that your feelings are your own. Recovery will result in some painful emotions, but only by facing and feeling your emotions will you gain freedom and healing. You can make this journey at your own speed.

Only by facing and feeling your emotions will you gain freedom and healing.

Types of Sexual Abuse

Most people have difficulty understanding healthy sexual boundaries. As a result they have doubt and confusion about the nature of sexual abuse. The tendency to minimize or deny the abuse causes further pain for both adults and children that have been abused. Everyone needs to know what constitutes sexually abusive behavior. Technically, not all of these are crimes, but they certainly constitute offensive and damaging behaviors.

✎ **As you read the following list of abusive behaviors, check those that happened to you, underline those that you were not aware were abuse. In the margin, add any behaviors that you have experienced that are not on the list.**

Examples of physical sexual abuse:
❑ Touching or fondling a child or an adult without consent
❑ Excessive tickling and physical restraint
❑ French kissing a child
❑ Excessive enemas or excessive concern about genital hygiene
❑ Intercourse/oral sex or sodomy with any child or with an adult without consent

Examples of visual sexual abuse:
❑ Exposure of a child to pornography
❑ Exposure of pornography to an adult without consent
❑ Force, manipulation, or coercion of another to observe masturbation or the sexual activity of another
❑ Exposure of genitals to non-consenting party or to a child

Examples of verbal sexual abuse:
❑ Exposure of a child or non-consenting adult to sexual jokes, teasing, or graphic sexual descriptions
❑ Exposure of a child to repeated remarks about the child's developing body
❑ Refusing to allow a child privacy for bathing or dressing
❑ Name calling of a sexual nature—calling a child a *slut* or *whore* is sexual abuse

Examples of covert—without the immediate knowledge of the victim—sexual abuse:
❑ Observing another person nude without their consent
❑ Videotaping, without their consent, people having sex

Examples of ritualistic sexual abuse:
❑ Forcing a person to participate in religious activities that include sex
❑ Sexual activity that involves chants or incantations

Sexual abuse does not have to involve physical contact.

Sexual abuse does not have to involve physical contact. Sexual abuse often begins with non-contact types of abuse that invade the emotional and psychological boundaries of the victim before the abuser makes any attempt to cross physical boundaries. Most sexual abuse does not involve intercourse or force. The abuser is rarely a stranger.

Sometimes victims are confused about the reality of the abuse. Vague memories from so long ago can seem unreal. One victim describes her memory of abuse as "pictures and frames like in a film—dark and shadowy and only a moment of something bad happening." Sometimes a person may remember a situation and view it as sinful or morally wrong but fail to recognize that it was also abuse. Memory blocks are often a symptom that abuse has occurred. Jan Frank in *A Door of Hope*, her book on sexual abuse, encourages every victim of abuse to pray verse 6 of Psalm 51.

Behold, thou dost desire truth in the innermost being. And in the hidden part Thou wilt make me know wisdom.
–Psalm 51:6, NASB

☞ **Stop now and take time to read Psalm 51:6 as a prayer to God. God has already begun the recovery process in your life or you would not be reading this book. Tell God that you want to join Him in the process and ask Him to make your thoughts clear and to lead you to accurately separate fact from fiction in your life.**

✎ **Below describe what this passage means to you. What are your thoughts and feelings?**

_____

_____

_____

_____

Assignment for the lesson

Who satisfies your years with good things, So that your youth is renewed like the eagle.
–Psalm 103:5, NASB

✎ **On a card write Psalm 103:5, this unit's Scripture memory verse. Carry the card with you and regularly review the verse.**

☞ **Say aloud this affirmation five times.**

I accept God's love and kindness toward me.

☞ **Pray for yourself and for each member of your *Shelter from the Storm* group.**

Symptoms of Abuse, Part One

LESSON 3

Lack of Healthy Boundaries
Headaches
Addictions
Low Self-esteem
Rage
Over-reacting
Spacing out
Sexual Differences
Sleeplessness
Memory Block

If I stop
For just a moment
And lay my head
on your lap,
I know I could
Forget all my pain.
But I find it hard
To get that close,
So I just keep moving.

Trust is a difficult issue for survivors, but we encourage you to trust God as much as you can. The Bible tells us that He understands when you can't. God responds to faith the size of a mustard seed! Don't become bogged down in trying to force yourself to remember things from the past. Allow God to bring about insights and memories according to His will and timing so you are not overwhelmed and can deal with them one by one.

In this lesson and the next you will find many tendencies that are common to victims of sexual abuse. Information about the day-to-day struggles of other survivors may help make it easier to understand and accept yourself. Many survivors criticize themselves for these tendencies. Recognize that in some way these behaviors allowed you to survive. As you review these tendencies we will ask you to identify the ones that apply to you. Seek to understand and accept others in your group that may have a different combination of tendencies. Most of all recognize that valuing yourself and your ability to cope is the first step in choosing to make positive changes in your life.

✎ **Read the following list of tendencies of survivors of sexual abuse. Check those symptoms that describe your past or present feelings and behaviors. In the space that follows the example, write a short sentence describing the effect of that tendency on you and your relationships.**

❑ Headaches

"My headaches started very early. People would say to me, 'Marcy, you're too young to have headaches.' The headaches stopped for awhile, but now they last for days and often I am sick at my stomach."

_____

_____

❑ Sleeplessness

"I am 19 and healthy, but a sleep-aholic. Everyone teases me because I can sleep in any position, or at any time. What they don't know is that every night is torture. I can't go to sleep. I hate the night. I will read any book, clean the house, do anything just to stay awake."

_____

_____

❑ Sexual Difficulties

"I want so much to be able to tell people I will not have sex with them. I can't seem to stop."

or

"I know I confuse my husband, how could I not? One moment I am all affectionate and romantic; I even want flowers and candlelight. But in a flash, everything can change for me."

_____

_____

❑ Low Self-esteem

"No, I don't feel good about myself. How could I? I was told again and again that I was no good. What I wanted never mattered—only what he wanted. I didn't matter. Why should I? I really am nothing."

_____

_____

❑ Lack of Healthy Boundaries

"I guess it would be funny if it weren't so sad. I can't say no to anyone. I can't say no when they want me to keep their kids. When someone says no to me, I always feel rejected. I can't seem to say no or accept a no from others."

_____

_____

❑ Rage

"People have told me I act like I have a terrible rage within, and you know what, what they're saying is true. I look at my children and I see the fear in their eyes. It breaks my heart. I never wanted to yell and scream like I did. Like I do. I hate myself for it."

_____

_____

❑ Over-reaction to People and Situations

"I was fifteen years old and we had moved across the country again. It was about 5 a.m. when we arrived in Los Angeles. We had stopped for breakfast. I needed to use the restroom, but once I was inside, I panicked when I heard someone about to come in the door."

_____

_____

❑ Addictions

"I drink when I'm down so that I can forget everything for a while."

"I drink when I'm down so that I can forget everything for a while. It seems I am always medicating my feelings with compulsive behaviors—overeating or not eating at all, using chemicals such as alcohol or other drugs, working/busy-ness, overspending, religious activity."

_____

_____

_____

❑ Spacing Out

"Sometimes I feel like I'm not really there. I have this fuzzy feeling in my head. I don't pay attention to where I am going or what I am doing."

_____

_____

❑ Memory Block

"I used to get so angry when people would talk about their childhood. Where was mine? There aren't even any pictures! When I try to think back, I only remember a dark house and a dark room. I can't even remember holidays."

_____

_____

Major Issue Alert

This list alone does not mean that you were sexually abused. Some of these symptoms can be caused by other circumstances. Keep the big picture in mind. This list may be a confirmation to you along with other evidence such as memories. This list alone cannot be used to point to sexual abuse.

🖉 **What are you feeling after reading this list of tendencies?**

❑ Angry
❑ Sad
❑ Confused
❑ Relieved
❑ Ashamed
❑ Afraid
❑ More normal
❑ Lonely
❑ Guilty
❑ Other _____

🖉 **List those tendencies that have been the greatest struggle for you.**

_____

_____

Assignment for the lesson

🖉 **Below write the unit Scripture verse from memory. To check your work refer to page 24.**

_____

_____

☞ **Say aloud this affirmation five times.**

I accept God's love and kindness toward me.

☞ **Pray for yourself and for each member of your** _Shelter from the Storm_ **group.**

LESSON 4

Symptoms of Abuse, Part Two

In this lesson you will examine more tendencies that are typical of survivors of sexual abuse. These tendencies may help you to understand better yourself and your situation. Remember that these tendencies do not, in themselves, indicate sexual abuse.

✎ **As you continue to read, check any of the tendencies below that fit your experience. In the space below each example write the effect of that tendency on you and your relationships.**

❏ Perfectionism

"I guess I am overly critical. I really criticize everything, but most of all my husband. It's true I want people to give me a break, and really, I want to give them a break. I'm not as picky as people think. I just want everyone and everything to be in order."

_____

_____

❏ Performance/Need for Achievement

"I always feel driven to succeed. Being good isn't enough. I have to be the best. I feel that I have to earn the right to be happy or worthy while, at the same time I'm afraid the (real) person inside will be exposed."

_____

_____

❏ Repeatedly Feeling Betrayed

"Well, all I can say is, if you have been abused, you have been betrayed."

"Well, all I can say is, if you have been abused, you have been betrayed. But why am I so angry now? I believe everyone betrays me, even when they don't. My son forgets to turn out the light in the kitchen and I think he did it on purpose just to hurt me. I test everybody to see if they will betray me."

_____

_____

❏ Fear

"I fear almost everything—being alone, being abandoned, going to sleep. Once, I couldn't take a job because it was across town. My mind is full of all kinds of things that might happen!"

_____

_____

❑ Withdrawal

"I go places and stand in the corner. I have stayed in the bathroom as long as I could without embarrassing myself. I have all sorts of ways to isolate myself."

_____

_____

❑ Anxiety/Sense of Doom

"Sometimes I become anxious for what appears to be no real reason. I sometimes feel if I move, I'll bump into something—something bad. I'm afraid if I try to do anything I'll make a mistake."

_____

_____

❑ Repeated Victimization

"I think the first one who abused me was my step dad. It only happened once, I think. Then a couple of years later I was abused by an uncle and then by one of my brother's friends. Nothing ever seemed to change in my life. I decided something about me must be causing this to happen."

_____

_____

❑ Seductive Behavior

"All my life they said I dressed sexy. I didn't know what they were talking about. I just dressed like everyone else. I liked the attention I got from boys. It somehow proved that I was pretty."

_____

_____

❑ Anger and Depression

"I realize now that I have been depressed most of my life. I go through periods when I have no energy. I don't want to do anything but lie down. I feel angry when people expect me to want to be a part of things. All I want to do is go to my room and close the blinds."

_____

_____

❑ Codependency

"In my relationships I am either controlling or being controlled. I am a legalist. If you were to be there at 3 p.m., you better be there! I am jealous when my friends have other friends. I want people to need me. When I help them I feel like I'm somebody."

_____

_____

❏ Self-destructive Behavior

"I don't know why but I can't seem to stop setting myself up. I go from one conflict to another with friends and family. I know when I lie that I will get caught but I don't feel like I deserve any better. I also eat when I'm not hungry. I seem to have accidents all the time."

_____

_____

(Note: Some people's self-hatred surfaces in suicidal thoughts or physically hurting themselves. If you have problems with self-destructive thoughts or behaviors, please talk to someone.)

✎ **Take some time to write down the feelings you experienced as you read this list of tendencies. In the margin write a prayer telling God exactly what you feel. Remember your memory verse. God desires to renew your youth. The honesty that helped the psalmists through some difficult times can help you too.**

These exercises have given you a powerful start on your journey to recovery. Hopefully some of your feelings and behaviors have begun to make more sense to you. Identifying the symptoms in your life will help you to set specific goals for recovery. Hope does exist. Begin to experience it by reading the following list of overcomer's hopes.

Dear God,
_____
_____
_____
_____
_____
_____
_____
_____
_____
_____

The Overcomer's Hopes

In Christ I can—
- live without fear controlling me.
- live without being controlled by others.
- live without needing to control others.
- live without condemnation or condemning others.
- live without shame and guilt.
- live where I know the difference between what is safe and what is not safe.
- live without rage, hate, and depression.
- live with stable emotions.
- live with joy and happiness—even in the midst of trials.
- live with peace and love.
- live without helplessness.
- live understanding my value in Christ.
- live where I can be intimate with others.
- live where I can trust others who are trustworthy.
- live with a deep relationship with God.

✎ You might want to copy the list of overcomer's hopes on a card to keep with you so you can read them when you are discouraged. Add to the list your own personal list of hopes. You need to know that people do recover from sexual abuse.

Assignment for the lesson

✎ Below write from memory this unit's Scripture verse. You may check your work on page 24.

_____

_____

↪ Say aloud this affirmation five times.

I accept God's love and kindness toward me.

↪ Pray for yourself and for each member of your *Shelter from the Storm* group.

Restoration Is Possible

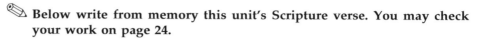

In the first lesson you read about Cindy's story. This lesson continues the story of Cindy's healing process. Cindy shares how God used the Bible story of Joseph to give her hope for restoration.

You Can Be a Survivor

LESSON

5

More of Cindy's story

"God provided assurance that He was involved in my healing process."

"God had provided assurance that He was involved in my healing process. Even with this assurance in my heart, the recovery years were a struggle, with little evidence of progress. Surely there had to be more to life than I was experiencing. In anger one day, I cried out to God, 'Help me!' He responded by making clear to me the journey through the storm to restoration. He used Joseph in the Book of Genesis as a role model. I pray that gripping story of Joseph and his 12 brothers found in chapters 37-50 of Genesis will be helpful to you as well. The story is long, but take time to read these chapters from the Bible."

Joseph experienced massive betrayal. His brothers tried to kill him, then sold him into slavery. While Joseph was a slave, his master's wife tried to seduce him. When Joseph refused to be seduced, he was falsely accused and thrown into prison. In prison he helped others, but when they got out, they forgot about Joseph. But Joseph did an amazing thing. He kept believing God. Eventually God delivered Joseph from prison and made him second-in-command over all Egypt.

God made Joseph forget the pain, the anger, the loneliness, and all the other distressing emotions he must have felt. My journey was not completed, but now I knew where I was headed. God was leading me to restoration—restoration from all the hurt! I was, over a period of time, to become whole; I was to live again.

Cindy continues, "Now I understood that I couldn't run away from the darkness of the storm, and I realized that I couldn't fix the storm. I saw that God would shine His light right into the darkness of the storm. That light meant there was hope for me. Like the apostle Paul in 2 Corinthians 4:8-9 I had been afflicted, but I wasn't crushed. I was perplexed, but not desolate and void of hope. I had been persecuted, but not forsaken; struck down, but not destroyed. For the first time I realized that I was a survivor."

Like Cindy, you can be a survivor too!

This may be difficult, but allow yourself to experience hope. Begin to speak the truth about yourself even though you may not feel it.

✎ **Write the following sentences in the space provided.**

I am a survivor!

_____

Restoration is possible for me too.

_____

God loves me.

_____

I will allow God to be my shelter from the storm.

_____

✎ **Describe how you feel as you read the sentences you have just written.**

_____

_____

_____

In the early stages of recovery most survivors have a difficult time doing this exercise. Sometimes writing positive statements causes a feeling of freedom, but more often the person feels angry, afraid, phony or just plain numb. It may take time for you to believe the truth of those statements and feel the freedom. Writing them down is one step toward *feeling* like a survivor.

You Can Be an Overcomer

"I wasn't satisfied with just being a survivor," Cindy continued. "I wanted more. I was disturbed when I would sometimes revert back to being a victim, although my hope was real by this time and the treasure I had was inside.

We are hard pressed on every side, but not crushed; perplexed, but not in despair; persecuted, but not abandoned; struck down, but not destroyed.
–2 Corinthians 4:8-9

Even when I was afflicted and struck down again, I knew I wasn't destroyed. I knew I was different.

"I took heart in Romans 12:2. I knew that God was renewing my life! And I knew that this Scripture would also be a part of my healing process."

> Do not conform any longer to the pattern of this world, but be transformed by the renewing of your mind.
> –Romans 12:2

✎ **Below describe what God is saying to you through Romans 12:2 about your healing process.**

_____

_____

_____

The responses of others to Romans 12:2 may have been similar to Cindy's. This passage helped her in the following way:

"This passage was telling me not to be fashioned or shaped by my own experiences of sexual abuse. I realized that my abuse experiences caused me to be unstable. God wanted to make me new again. God wanted to renew my mind and heal me of what an abuser had done to me.

"Sexual abuse is not in the will of God. I knew then that God had not used sexual abuse to 'teach me some lesson.' He was showing me that His will was to restore my life from that which had been stolen by the abuse. I began to be restored.

"I had believed all my life in the lies I had heard, and now I was trying to believe in the truth; that Jesus was the son of God; that I was born of God; and that God had victory over the evils of the world.

"I know now that courage came from God, because even when I thought I couldn't go on with my recovery, I did. Even when I thought I couldn't deal with one more memory, I did. Even when I thought I couldn't pray one more prayer, I did.

"The more I overcame, the more peace I experienced in my life. Sometimes it would seem that nothing was happening in my recovery process, but then I would notice that I could sleep peacefully at night, or that I didn't say I hated myself so often. I was being restored to life. God truly was healing my hurts, my disappointments, my failures, my wounds, and I was no longer an outcast.

"I didn't feel dirty anymore. I did not allow myself to feel dirty in response to what others would say or do. God had restored my dignity. I had changed. How could I now be affected by what people said, when I knew what God said? I was an overcomer! I was no longer broken. I felt no shame, no condemnation. God had given me back my innocence concerning the abuse.

"I was excited. There was a joy inside me that had never been there before, a belief that even when victory was delayed, I still had hope in God. Although I was uncertain about what was actually happening, I knew it was something wonderful and that I could now focus completely on getting along with my journey."

Just as the effects of abuse become evident without prior awareness of how the abuse was affecting you, God's restoration happens without your awareness of His work. One day, you are surprised by the joy of realizing that you have been changed! You are better!

Can you believe that restoration is possible for you? Our prayer is that you will let God begin to restore your life.

✎ **You might want to stop here and write a prayer thanking God that you survived and ask Him to give you hope for your recovery.**

_____

_____

_____

_____

You Can Be Restored

"I had come far enough to know that the road to recovery was one that I must walk by myself. I read everything that I thought would help lift the state of depression that still hung over me. When I got impatient, thinking my progress was taking too much time, or discouraged about my ability to make it any farther, I would tell myself, 'Tomorrow is another day' or 'I will feel better, tomorrow I will feel better.' Saying the words again and again somehow always seemed to help me get through the day.

"God has restored me and He can also restore your life. I have taken the risk of placing my recovery in His hands, and I can assure you that God does bring healing and restoration from the pain and hurt of loss and abuse.

"Hope does exist. God took me through my pain to recovery."

Stop now and respond to what God did in Cindy's life. Is it your desire for God to do that in yours? In Christ you can be an overcomer too.

If you are not a Christian, let us introduce you to Jesus Christ. Giving your life to Christ means letting go and allowing Jesus to have control of your life. It means that you trust Jesus to lead you and heal you. You may express your desire by praying the following prayer.

> _Jesus, I have been trying to live life by my own power and I realize now that I can't do that anymore. You said that You came to redeem me and crown me with Your lovingkindness and compassion. I am willing to let You do that. I realize that I cannot save myself. I accept You as my Savior and commit my life to You as much as I know how right now. In Jesus name, Amen._

If you prayed that prayer, asking Jesus Christ into your life, congratulations! As a confirmation and reminder, we encourage you to sign your name and write the date of this decision below.

_____ (signature) _____ (date)

Trusting in Christ does not mean you will be delivered instantly from the storm of sexual abuse or from any other problem in life. It means that you are forgiven of all your sins and restored to a relationship with God that will

God will keep His promise to be with you and to lead you and guide you.

last throughout eternity. It means that you will receive His unconditional love and acceptance, as well as His strength, power, and wisdom, as you grow. God will keep His promise to be with you and to lead you and guide you. We encourage you to tell your group facilitator and your group about your decision.

Unit Review

✎ Look back over this unit. What statement or activity was most meaningful for you?

_____

_____

✎ Can you remember any statements or activities with which you were uncomfortable? Write those below.

_____

_____

✎ Write a prayer asking God to help you in your areas of struggle.

_____

_____

_____

_____

UNIT 3

Tell Yourself the Truth

Focal Passage

Do not conform any longer to the pattern of this world, but be transformed by the renewing of your mind, then you will be able to test and approve what God's will is—his good, pleasing, and perfect will.

–Romans 12:2

This Unit's Affirmation:
The truth
will set me free!

THE POWER OF FALSE BELIEFS

A ten-year-old child describes the power of false beliefs in action. She is a beautiful child who is slightly underweight. She said, "I can't figure out why I'm so fat, because some days I don't eat at all. Each time I look in the mirror, I think I am so ugly. I can even have a new dress and get my hair fixed, but when I look into the mirror all I see is this fat, ugly person.

"I never do anything right! I know something is wrong with me, or this wouldn't have happened. Even God really hates me. I know it wasn't me that wanted to have the sex, so it must have been my body and that's why it happened. I hate me, I hate my body, and I hate everybody."

In this unit you will read more about the false beliefs that complicate recovery from sexual abuse.

Growth goal

This week's goal
You will recognize and begin to replace the false beliefs you have about yourself and your abuse. You will learn five steps for letting go of false beliefs.

Lies Versus Truths, Part One	Lies Versus Truths, Part Two	Consequences of False Beliefs	The Truth Will Set You Free!	Getting Rid of False Beliefs
Lesson 1	Lesson 2	Lesson 3	Lesson 4	Lesson 5

Memory verse

This week's passage of Scripture to memorize
You will know the truth, and the truth will set you free.

–John 8:32

LESSON 1

Lies Versus Truths, Part One

The experience of being sexually abused almost always leaves its victims with a damaging set of false beliefs about their value and worth. Held as absolute truths, these false ideas create mistaken guilt, destroy self-esteem, and assign undeserved responsibility for what has happened to those who have already suffered devastating emotional and physical trauma.

Christians who are survivors often struggle with the contrast between what they know to be scriptural truth and the overwhelming emotions they experience as a result of the abuse. They long to believe all God tells them in the Bible, yet they have difficulty bringing the truth into their hearts and living it out every day.

Sexual abuse victims struggle with four major false beliefs about the abuse. These are—
   1) It's my fault.
   2) I must be a terrible person for him/her to do this to me.
   3) I wanted him/her to do this to me.
   4) It didn't happen! I must have made it up.

In this lesson and the next we will explore examples and causes of each of these false beliefs.

Lie # 1 - It's my fault!

This is the BIG ONE. Almost every victim of sexual abuse struggles with this misconception. "It was my fault. I should have…."

Five-year-old Lisa was describing the horror of an abuse situation by making a distorted face and whining. "It was my fault," she said during a counseling session. "It was not your fault," her counselor responded. "You are only five years old. Your father is the adult, and he was the one who decided to do this thing to you. In fact, as you've told me before, you didn't want to do it, but your father made you do it. Many times you've told me how you hated it. Do you understand that it's your father's fault and not your fault?" "Oh, yes," she said, "I know it's my daddy's fault. He always told me it was both our fault. He would say what we were doing was my fault and his fault."

"He said what we were doing was my fault and his fault."

Lisa's understanding of the relationship between herself as the victim and her father is typical. The sexually abusive person establishes in the child's mind the concept of "we." "We" are doing this; therefore, "we" are responsible. As children mature, this concept of "we" becomes more and more firmly cemented in their minds because they begin to think of all the times they could have asked the abuser to stop the abuse but didn't. The reality, of course, is that a child rarely, if ever, could have stopped the abuse.

Victims—whether they are adults or children at the time of the abuse—typically accept total responsibility for the abuse. They will say such things as "If I hadn't been there…." "If I hadn't answered the door…." Often rapists yell filthy accusations at their victims as the rape is in progress. During and immediately after this time of great fear and despair, the victim is more psychologically open to the false message. Adolescents and children have even less ability to comprehend the truth of the situation.

Incested

She learned real young in life,
In order to get by
She must do what is expected
And never question why...

It didn't seem to matter
How she felt—or why she cried...
Each time she was incested
More child-likeness died.

Too young to understand
Why she deserved this thing—
She buried her emotions
And the torture it would bring.

He said that she must never
Tell another living soul—
Too small to know the reason,
Yet...she knew...she wasn't whole.

She felt it was imprinted
For all the world to see—
I am dirty...I am ugly...
Please...don't look...at...me.

She'd never heard of shame
Yet she knew its symptoms well...
The harder that she tried, it
* seemed,*
The harder then, she fell...

She knew she was responsible
For everybody's pain—
So she tried hard to fix it
Over... and over... again.[1]

Most victims blame themselves for the abuse! Have you ever heard yourself saying something like this?

> "But I was drunk and I didn't know what was going on. I should have known better and should not have gotten in that situation. It was my fault."

> "We were kissing and he got excited. He couldn't help himself. It was my fault for leading him on."

> "My uncle said he did it because I was pretty. He said he couldn't help it. It must be my fault."

In the following exercise identify the self-blaming statements you have made. These statements are false beliefs about yourself and the abuse. Write the first thoughts that come to your mind.

✎ **Below write self-blaming statements you have made. For now, ignore the blanks for the truth statements. If you need help, review the preceding paragraphs. We have done the first one as an example.**

FALSE BELIEF: "It is my fault because I enjoyed the attention he gave me!"

FALSE BELIEF: "It is my fault because _____

_____

TRUTH: _____

_____

FALSE BELIEF: "It is my fault because _____

_____

TRUTH: _____

_____

FALSE BELIEF: "It is my fault because _____

_____

TRUTH: _____

_____

FALSE BELIEF: "It is my fault because _____

_____

TRUTH: _____

_____

✎ Now go back to the TRUTH lines on the exercise. For each self-blaming statement write a positive statement that is opposite of the false belief. Write the statement even if you don't believe it! If you can't think of any opposite statements, read your false beliefs to your group and let them help you with the truth statements. Another possible aid is to pretend someone else said the first statement to you. What would you say to them? We have done the first one as an example.

FALSE BELIEF: "It is my fault because I enjoyed the attention he gave me!"

TRUTH: Attention is a healthy human need. It is normal to enjoy attention. I wanted attention—I didn't want sex.

We encourage you to share your false beliefs and your truths with your support group. Encourage each other to speak the truth.

Lie # 2 - I must be a terrible person for him/her to do this to me!

Children have difficulty accepting the idea that an adult would do something wrong.

Most children want to believe, or do believe, that adults can do no wrong. They view parents as almost God-like. To children, adults are all-powerful and all-knowing. Children have difficulty accepting the idea that an adult would do something wrong. Generally, when children think an adult has done something bad, they feel as if they somehow caused the adult to do it.

Adults who are abused also experience this tendency. Frequently victims accept this false belief because the abuser is someone they admire spiritually. For example, a church secretary knew she must be causing her pastor to have these sexual fantasies about her!

Laura believed that somehow she caused her Sunday School teacher to lead her into a sexual encounter. The woman who witnessed to her and led her to Christ also sexually abused her. Laura assumed that she must have done something to tell this woman she wanted sex with her. She felt dirty, guilty, and uncomfortable throughout the relationship with this woman, often daydreaming or just floating to avoid the discomfort. Laura was trapped by her false beliefs. "It must be my fault. I must be a terrible person for her to want to do this to me."

When a person accepts lie number one, the next lie follows closely behind.

✎ As a response to the false belief that you are a terrible person because you caused this person to do this to you, write two truth statements in the space below.

TRUTH: _____

_____

TRUTH: _____

_____

Just in case you couldn't think of any, here are several true statements which counter this false belief. 1) The responsibility for the abuse belongs to the abuser. 2) I am a special person, created by God. 3) I was vulnerable, but I am worthy of respect and love. If you continue to have difficulty writing truth statements for this false belief, ask your *Shelter* group facilitator for assistance. Sometimes we all need the objectivity of an understanding person to help us see the truth about our situations.

Victims often try to hold on to the positive aspects of relationships with the abusers by viewing themselves as dirty and undeserving of respect. Speak the truth. Allow the shame and guilt to fall on the people who committed the abuse. By doing so you will not be making them guilty, you will be recognizing the truth of their guilt. They are responsible for what was done to you.

Assignment for the lesson

You will know the truth, and the truth will set you free.

–John 8:32

✎ **Below write your own paraphrase of John 8:32, this unit's Scripture memory verse.**

_____

_____

☞ **Say aloud this affirmation five times.**

The truth will set me free!

☞ **Pray for yourself and for each member of your group.**

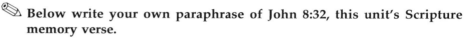

LESSON 2

Lies versus Truths, Part Two

In lesson one you explored the first two false beliefs with which sexual abuse survivors almost always struggle. In this lesson you will consider two more.

Lie # 3 - I wanted him/her to do this to me.

Survivors commonly believe that: "I wanted him or her to do this to me." Eleven-year-old Kevin described his uncle as someone who always took him places. One day his uncle said to him, "I know how to make you feel real good. You're getting interested in girls, and I can show you how they can make you feel real good. Do you want to try?" "Sure," Kevin agreed. Just like his uncle said, what happened did feel good. "But I knew it was wrong and I never wanted to do it again. But whenever we went anywhere, he always did it. I always let him, and the worst part is that it always felt good."

Natalie, a ten-year-old, explained she must have wanted her step daddy to sexually abuse her because she loved sitting on his lap. She really loved her birth father, but he had to work long hours and couldn't come see her. Her new dad made her feel special and gave her lots of attention. "He told me he was going to make me feel really good and I would really like what he was going to do. At first it just kind of tickled. One day it really hurt ,but he said it would feel good after awhile. And it did feel good. I must have gotten so I really wanted it."

Confrontation

You say that I imagined
All those years of agony—
You say it isn't true
That you forced yourself on me.

How can a child imagine
The details that I know.
You're afraid I'll tell it all
And the real you will show!

You say I am a liar
You say I want attention—
But the truth that crowds my
mind
Is too sick for me to mention!

You forget that I was there
When you filled my heart with
fear.
I remember how you whipped
me
If you saw me shed a tear.

How sad it is to think
How different life would be—
If you'd have loved me then
And been a Dad to me...[2]

Both stories you have just read describe normal emotional and physiological responses. As a matter of normal physiology these two children and thousands of other victims sometimes enjoyed a part of the stimulation that occurred during their abuse. Often survivors speak with total disgust toward themselves because they have had a healthy physiological reaction to an unhealthy and illegal act committed upon them.

✎ **Below write two truth statements to replace the false belief that:** *I wanted him or her to do this to me because it felt good.*

Truth: _____

_____

Truth: _____

_____

God created the human body for healthy sexual interaction. He created sex for our enjoyment in marriage. You are not a terrible person if your body responded to sexual stimulation. You may have written something like: "the human body naturally responds to stimulation," "the person who abused me is responsible," or "a child cannot be responsible for the actions of an adult."

The false belief that you wanted the abuse because of the natural responses of the human body traps your mind and holds it captive. Begin to accept your body as it was created. Let go of the belief that you wanted the abuse.

LIE # 4 - It didn't happen! I must have made it up.

Sometimes memories of sexual abuse come in fragments and are unclear. What we remember confuses and puzzles us so we have difficulty believing it ourselves. We have even more difficulty accepting that anyone else will believe us.

Most victims are violated by someone they know, most commonly a significant other, such as a parent, stepparent, family friend, or neighbor. The victim may make an attempt to disclose the abuse to a parent or other adult. Often children assume that parents know what is happening, since they so often view parents as God-like. They may ask, "Do you know what Daddy is doing to me?" or "Do I have to do everything Suzie says?" Unfortunately the adult may not always recognize the child's attempts to disclose.

The need to deny the abuse makes recognition of the problem even greater.

Parents, particularly, are not likely to believe that a spouse is engaging in such destructive behavior. The need to deny the abuse makes recognition of the problem even greater. To complicate the situation further, children often attempt to disclose bad things that are happening to them through their behavior rather than tell someone about it. They may display sexual behavior inappropriate for their age, or school grades may begin to drop. They may engage in stealing or in some form of self-abuse. All of these behaviors can be methods of attempting to show that something is wrong. If no one picks up on their attempted disclosures—whether verbal or behavioral—children begin to feel that no one cares what is happening, and the belief that no one cares reinforces the idea that they must truly be worthless.

Be Kind to Yourself—Don't Rescue Others by Minimizing!

Survivors often minimize sexual abuse. The person who abused you may interpret the situation as harmless. Do not minimize the abuse. One way we block the pain of the past is to deny or minimize the effects. We say things like "That happened so long ago. It really wasn't such a big deal. I really shouldn't let it bother me any more." Consider the following story of an adult survivor:

"I just never felt safe around my Dad. He never did touch me, but it seemed that he was always watching me and finding excuses for being around when I dressed. He would get mad if I told him he couldn't come in my room or the bathroom stating that he had changed my diapers, so he wouldn't see anything he hadn't seen before. He teased me about the size of my breasts and accused me of letting the little boys play with them or they wouldn't be growing so fast. I started to wear big shirts to cover up my body so he wouldn't notice; then he would tease me about hiding myself. I felt ugly and dirty and wanted to cover myself up, so I ate and gained weight so my girl-hood wouldn't be so noticeable."

Regardless of the form the abuse takes it is still sexual abuse and affects the life of the victim.

This woman continues to dress in ways that hide her body, and she still struggles with overeating. Both were methods the child used to cope with the abuse but are not necessary or functional in the life of the adult. Therefore, regardless of the form the abuse takes or how mild it may appear, it is still sexual abuse and affects the life of the victim.

✎ **Have you ever thought you might be making all of this up or that your situation was "no big deal"? If you have, your thoughts are normal. Below describe the things that have caused you to ask yourself "Is this real? Was I abused? Was what happened to me really abuse?"**

_____

_____

✎ **Rewrite the following false belief into a truth statement that acknowledges your experience of sexual abuse.**

False Belief: It didn't happen! I must have made it up.

Truth: _____

_____

You may have written something like the following statements from other survivors—

Truth: "I can only remember parts of the abuse. That's normal and I can accept what I remember as real."

Truth: "It happened only once but I know it was real!"

These memories are evidence that something was wrong. Whatever memories you have provide the signals you can investigate further. Do not let go of what is true even if others respond with angry feelings or non-supportive attitudes. For you to tell your story is appropriate, especially for you to tell your story to someone who can help. You need to find supportive people who will listen and believe you. You need support. Share your feelings with your group, especially when it is difficult! To share details and identities in the group is not always important. Focus on your own feelings.

Assignment for the lesson

 On a card write John 8:32, this unit's Scripture memory verse. Carry the card with you. Whenever you do some routine task like getting a drink of water, review your memory verse.

 Say aloud this affirmation five times.

The truth will set me free!

 Pray for yourself and for each member of your *Shelter from the Storm* group.

LESSON 3

Self-esteem helps us see both our strengths and our weaknesses as people with value and meaning.

Consequences of False Beliefs

The false beliefs victims of sexual abuse hold result in feelings of low self-worth, guilt, and undeserved responsibility for the abuse. Survivors still look to family to fix the brokenness within them—especially if the abuser was a family member. Survivors try to resolve the beliefs and feelings about the person who abused them through various behaviors such as caretaking, people-pleasing, and continued conflict.

Low Self-esteem

Sometimes victims think they do not deserve respect. They often feel dirty. These feelings prevent them from protecting themselves and set them up to be abused again and again. Sometimes survivors think they do not deserve to have their needs met in healthy ways. Self-esteem provides the ability to acknowledge both our strengths and our weaknesses and to see ourselves as people with value and meaning.

Many children, teenagers, and adult survivors have problems with body image. They look into the mirror and tell themselves they are fat or ugly. They often feel hatred toward their bodies. Many times these individuals are thin, attractive people.

A ten-year-old describes her dilemma. She is a beautiful child who is slightly underweight. She said, "I can't figure out why I'm so fat, because some days I don't eat at all. Each time I look in the mirror, I think I am so ugly. I can even have a new dress and get my hair fixed, but when I look into the mirror all I see is this fat, ugly person. I never do anything right! I know something is wrong with me, or this wouldn't have happened. Even God really hates me. I know it wasn't me that wanted to have the sex, so it must have been my body and that's why it happened. I hate me, I hate my body, and I hate everybody."

Everyone struggles with some feelings of inadequacy and low self-worth but those who have been sexually abused have a greater struggle with these issues. Low self-esteem may be experienced in the following ways.

✎ **In the following list of symptoms of low self-esteem, place a check beside any of the characteristics that you experience.**

❑ A constant feeling of worthlessness
❑ Persistent thoughts that you didn't do it right
❑ Broad swings in negative and positive attitudes about yourself
❑ Self-doubt
❑ One mistake destroys feelings of accomplishment or success
❑ Negative self-statements
❑ Over-responsible—feeling that everything is always my fault
❑ Under-responsible—being unable to acknowledge that I was wrong
❑ Difficulty making decisions

You may have checked only one or two responses, or the entire list may apply to you. Consider sharing what these have been like for you with your support group this week.

We need to realize that low self-esteem is a mind-set, not a state of being. Low self-esteem is an attitude about ourselves, therefore it can be changed! We are not vain, self-centered, or egotistical when we view ourselves as God views us. We can allow Christ to lead us as we change our mind-set from one of inadequacy to one of competency and fulfillment. He can transform our feelings from helplessness and hopelessness to affirmation and determination, from condemnation and self-hatred to self-affirmation and love.

Guilt/Self-blame

People who have been sexually abused have a feeling that somehow they caused the abuse.

People who have been sexually abused have an absolutely awful feeling inside that somehow they caused the abuse. Adults believe they should somehow have prevented the abuse from happening. Adolescents and children who have been sexually molested rarely have the emotional maturity to deal with what is happening to them. Physical and mental maturation is not reached until the late teens. When children are violated, however, the normal maturation process is severely damaged.

✎ **Can you identify with guilt and self-blame? Below describe any effects you have experienced from accepting blame or guilt about the abuse.**

_____

_____

One of the results of accepting blame and guilt is the fear of success. You may believe you do not deserve for good things to happen. You may think you do not deserve healthy relationships. Some survivors call themselves names such as "stupid" or "dumb."

Shame

Children lose their rightful identities as loved and valuable human beings.

In addition to self-blame, survivors experience a deeper feeling that something was terribly wrong with them or the abuse never would have happened. That feeling is called shame. Even adults suffering the same victimization have difficulty understanding the situation with which sexually abused children must cope. Children lose their rightful identities as loved and valuable human beings. They must try to mature in life with a foundation based on confusion and betrayal.

Many factors enter into the healthy development of children. The false beliefs of shame and undeserved blame, established as children grow, devastate their emotional stability as adults. Whether we experienced sexual abuse as children, as adults, or both, we need to let go of the shame and undeserved responsibility.

✎ **Have you been shaming yourself? Read the shaming statements below. Then list any shaming statements you say to yourself.**

I don't deserve to be happy.
I am a freak. I am not worth loving.

_____

_____

_____

➥ **Take some time right now to pray about each one of these three major consequences of sexual abuse. Tell yourself the truth by reading the statement listed beside each consequence. Begin to recognize that God wants you to be free of these consequences. We encourage you to write your prayer so that you can be reminded of this moment.**

Low self-esteem *(God loves me and I can love me too.)*

_____

_____

Guilt/Self-blame *(Responsibility belongs to the abuser.)*

_____

_____

Shame *(I am worthy of respect and love.)*

_____

_____

Our prayer for you is this:

> *God, grant these readers the experience of knowing Your love, Your freedom from undeserved guilt, from self-blame, and from shame. May they know that they can love and respect themselves. Help them to believe, to accept, and to feel the truth of Romans 8:1, that there is "now no condemnation for those who are in Christ Jesus." In Jesus' name we pray. Amen.*

Assignment for the lesson

✎ In the margin write John 8:32, this unit's Scripture verse.

⇨ Say aloud this affirmation five times.

The truth will set me free!

⇨ Pray for yourself and for each member of your *Shelter from the Storm* group.

The Truth Will Set You Free!

The false beliefs result from experiencing the trauma of sexual abuse. They begin in what happened to you during the abuse, what the abuser said to you about the abuse, and what others said and did at the time of and after the abuse. Other factors, such as the number of abusers involved and the frequency of the abuse all play a role. You need to understand that these false beliefs are learned and therefore can be unlearned. You can begin to correct these beliefs and stop their effects.

You've heard those "good news and bad news" stories. The bad news is this, every time you repeat a false belief you reinforce it. But the good news is that you can choose to repeat a different message. Think of the negative beliefs as an old coat that has worn out and needs to be replaced, as remnants of an old garment that needs to be discarded. Think of it! You get to pick out a new coat, with a different style and flare. It may not feel like you at first but wear it a while and soon it will fit. You will adjust to it!

The Bible says the way we think in our hearts is the way we are (Proverbs 23:7). What we tell ourselves becomes our reality. If we believe that we are unworthy and unlovable we will only allow into our minds the information that reinforces that belief. The same is true about the way we think of others.

We can solve this problem by changing what is in our minds! We can change the way we interpret and perceive things. We can identify our feelings and give expression to them. Then we can look further to identify the source of those feelings in our beliefs about ourselves and our interpretation of the events and people around us. Then we need to adjust our belief systems to the present by putting off the old patterns of behavior that we learned as a way of coping with the abuse. The false beliefs produce feelings and behaviors that are sabotaging our present, therefore, we must learn to speak and believe the truth about ourselves.

✎ In the margin read Romans 12:1-2 then complete the exercises that follow to identify how you can apply this passage to your life.

What does this passage say we are to *do*?

_____

_____

LESSON 4

For as he thinks within himself, so he is.
–Proverbs 23:7

Therefore, I urge you, brothers, in view of God's mercy, to offer your bodies as living sacrifices, holy and pleasing to God—this is your spiritual act of worship. Do not conform any longer to the pattern of this world, but be transformed by the renewing of your mind, then you will be able to test and approve what God's will is—his good, pleasing, and perfect will.
–Romans 12:1-2

Others have taken your body and abused it. God asks us to allow Him to remove the effects of that abuse by allowing Him to renew our minds. He desires to restore us. God waits for us to offer ourselves to Him.

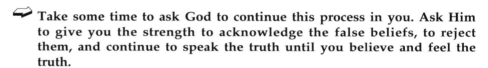 **What does offering our "bodies as living sacrifices" imply that we are to do with our minds?**

_____

_____

As a result...

_____

_____

_____

_____

In the margin describe what the passage says will happen as a result of being transformed by the renewing of your mind?

Since the passage says we are to offer our bodies, that suggests that we must choose to do God's will with our minds. When we seek to obey God with our minds and bodies, we will know the truth about ourselves, then we will be transformed. Renewing our mind is a process that involves the following four steps. We must—

- Recognize the false belief
- Reject the false belief
- Speak the truth
- Repeat the process until our mind is reprogrammed to believe the truth

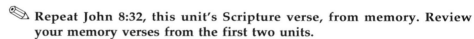 **Take some time to ask God to continue this process in you. Ask Him to give you the strength to acknowledge the false beliefs, to reject them, and continue to speak the truth until you believe and feel the truth.**

Assignment for the lesson

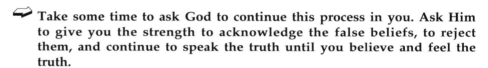 **Repeat John 8:32, this unit's Scripture verse, from memory. Review your memory verses from the first two units.**

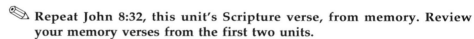 **Say aloud this affirmation five times.**

The truth will set me free!

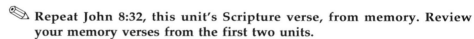 **Pray for yourself and for each member of your _Shelter from the Storm_ group.**

LESSON 5

Getting Rid of False Beliefs

As strange as it may seem, getting rid of false beliefs is difficult. These beliefs seem normal and natural to you. Your feelings and actions make sense because of them. Some of the false beliefs may seem as true and obvious as the statement that the sky is blue! To declare them as untruths will feel strange and phony. As you learn to take a stand on the truth, you will find freedom from the old negative feelings and actions.

Tears bloomed in my eyes
Traffic lights splintered
Creating eerie images
Distorted, disturbing

Memories came crashing in
Unbidden, unwelcomed
Afraid to feel it on the spot
Afraid to cast it away

Yet somehow I know
In feeling there is healing
Or so they say
I know the opposite is true

No feeling—no healing
Only postponed pain
Now my time has come to feel
My time to heal

For victims to recover, they need to discover what false beliefs they hold and then rid themselves of them, permanently. *Telling Yourself the Truth,* a book by William Backus and Marie Chapian, discusses the necessity of telling yourself the "real" truth. If whatever you are thinking about yourself has been distorted by abuse, they emphasize, you must solidly determine not to agree with those thoughts or statements. The real battle is lost if you begin to agree with the negative attitudes caused by the abuse. Naturally, at the start you have no one who will stand up and say, "Oh, that isn't right! You're not worthless, you are special!" You must therefore develop the skill of standing up and saying that for yourself. You must choose diligently to seek God's help so that you will believe the truth.

Five important steps can help you let go of the false beliefs. You have already used them as you completed the exercises in this unit.

1. Identify the False Belief

As you identify the false beliefs, write them down. Then for each one write a scripturally-based truth statement to counter the false belief. At the bottom of page 224 you will find a list of the four false beliefs and contrasting scriptural truths from *Search for Significance.* As a way to begin to identify false beliefs and biblical truths, search this list to see how many of these negative statements you may have said or thought about yourself.

2. Look for the Root of the False Belief

Identify the underlying factor that is causing you to maintain the false belief. Which of these may have been introduced into your thinking by authority figures in your life—parents, teachers, employers, pastors, spouse, or other adults—or suggested by the abuser or significant others in your life?

3. Recognize that the False Beliefs Are Lies

Identify the false beliefs and the experiences or influences that gave life to the false belief. Then with the encouragement of your support group, you can become more objective in your thinking. Seek to recognize intellectually and to accept emotionally the fact that these false beliefs are lies.

4. Relinquish Your False Beliefs

Pray. Ask God to help you let go of your false beliefs and help you believe the truth about yourself. Record your actions and progress. Begin to keep a journal or notebook. Write your thoughts, feelings, and prayers in your journal or notebook. Keep your journal in a private place.

5. Use Scripture as the Source of Truth

Learn to take a stand, even argue against yourself, in order to develop a belief system based on truth and not rooted and grounded in sexual abuse. Learn not to be so harsh and critical of yourself, but rather to love yourself.

The consequences...
_____
_____
_____
_____
_____
_____
_____

Your group facilitator will give you a set of cards that contain affirming statements. Read them every day, and use them to reinforce your determination to overcome your false beliefs.

✎ **Select one false belief that you have held and that has affected your life. In the margin describe as fully as you can the consequences of that belief.**

You may have written something like, "I never join in conversations because I don't believe I have anything worth saying," or "I believe no one will listen to me." Never joining into conversations can lead to loneliness and isolation. As you move toward recovery you will experience less and less of these negative consequences.

This part of your recovery is difficult. You may only now be beginning to discover the full extent of the harm sexual abuse has caused in your life. You may be experiencing feelings that seem more overwhelming than those you experienced at the time of the abuse. You may be starting the process of experiencing those emotions and feelings that you began to hide while your abuse was taking place. Because of the possibility of experiencing overwhelming flashbacks we strongly urge you to seek professional evaluation and assistance if you have not already done so.

A Prayer to Keep You Going

Dear Lord,
Thank You for making me a prized treasure with a special plan for my life. Thank You that You have equipped me with everything I need to achieve the goal that has been set before me. Thank You, Lord, that when I stumble, You lift me up; when I try to run away, You come after me; when I am defeated, You cause me to persevere and to triumph. Thank You, Lord, for Your perfect love for me.

Unit Review

✎ **Review this unit. What statement or activity was most meaningful for you?**

_____

_____

✎ **Can you remember any statements or activities with which you were uncomfortable? Write those below.**

_____

_____

✎ **In the margin write a prayer asking God to help you in your areas of struggle.**

Notes
[1]Shannon L. Spradlin, *Does God Know About This?* (Henderson, Nevada, 1993), 56.
[2]Ibid., 22.

Out of the Darkness into the Light

This Unit's Affirmation:
I am worthy to have God lead me and comfort me...and He wants to.

This Unit's Focal Passage

The Lord is my shepherd, I shall not be in want. He makes me lie down in green pastures, he leads me beside quiet waters, he restores my soul. He guides me in paths of righteousness for his name's sake. Even though I walk through the valley of the shadow of death, I will fear no evil, for you are with me; your rod and your staff, they comfort me. You prepare a table before me in the presence of my enemies. You anoint my head with oil; my cup overflows. Surely goodness and love will follow me all the days of my life, and I will dwell in the house of the Lord forever.

–Psalm 23

MISPLACED RESPONSIBILITY

Sherry told her counselor that her Dad was really lonely. Her Mom was mean and always griping about everything. For as long as she could remember, she and her Dad would escape together.

"He always said he was sorry for what happened, and I believed him," Sherry explains. "I really wanted to go with him every time he asked. We had so much fun—well, all except the sex. I hated it when he touched me, but I never hated him. I could've not gone, but I just learned to live with it. He gave me lots in return, money and special gifts. But most of all I felt sorry for him. It seemed to make him happy. Sometimes we'd have sex three times a day, but I just couldn't tell him no. So you see it was also my fault."

In this unit you will consider the issue of responsibility and how it affects recovery.

This week's goal

Growth goal
You will be challenged to confront the issues of responsibility, betrayal, and denial and to give yourself permission and time to heal. You will be encouraged to allow God to lead you to restoration.

I'm not Responsible!	I've been Betrayed!	The Trouble with Denial	From Death to Life	Help from Psalm 23
Lesson 1	Lesson 2	Lesson 3	Lesson 4	Lesson 5

This week's passage of Scripture to memorize

Memory verse
I will turn the darkness into light before them and make the rough places smooth. These are the things I will do; I will not forsake them.

–Isaiah 42:16

DAY 1

I'm Not Responsible!

Every victim of sexual abuse must deal with the issues of responsibility, betrayal, and denial. First and foremost, each must give total responsibility for the abuse to the perpetrator of the abuse. Unfortunately from the moment of the first abuse incident, victims almost always become confused, losing their objectivity and normal reasoning abilities. When victims describe their first incident of abuse they typically include such statements as "I was so confused"; "I don't know what I've done to deserve this"; or "if only I hadn't done this or that, it wouldn't have happened."

Many rape victims take the responsibility for the rape, at least in part. One 15-year-old victim said she had drunk too much.

"It was a wild party. I knew when I went that there would be sex and alcohol. It is partly my fault. I just kept drinking and drinking. A couple of guys pushed me into this van. A couple more held me down—I'm not sure how many. Somebody told me there were eight."

When she complained to friends, many of them told her, "If you hadn't gone to that party, it wouldn't have happened to you."

✎ **Below describe what is wrong with the reasoning that the abuse is the victim's fault.**

_____

_____

_____

Responsibility for the abuse belongs to the perpetrator, not the victim.

If this girl had not been the victim that night, someone else probably would have been. She was responsible for making a wrong and sinful choice about attending the party. However she was not responsible for the abuse. Responsibility for the abuse belongs to the perpetrator, not the victim.

Survivors must begin to understand that they were victims of a crime. *Webster's New Collegiate Dictionary* defines victim as "one who is injured, destroyed or sacrificed under any of various conditions," including rage, desire, ambition. The victim described above was injured mentally and physically. She was sacrificed for the pleasure of her attackers.

✎ **In the past, did you consider yourself the victim of a crime?** ❑ Yes ❑ No

Do you now consider yourself the victim of a crime? ❑ Yes ❑ No

Describe why or why not. _____

_____

_____

_____

Also For My Mother

How much did you hurt?
Did you hurt like me?
Did you feel afraid?
Did you have a safe place?

I hurt for you
If you never heal
For you'll carry that anger
And fear forever
Without really feeling it
Or knowing why.

I hurt for you
If you ever heal
For you'll have to remember
Not only how you were hurt
But how you hurt me.

"Most of all I felt sorry for him. It
seemed to make him happy."

✎ **Describe the responsible person(s). You may wish to use a description instead of names so that your story does not get out before you are ready. How and why are these persons responsible?**

_____

_____

_____

What feelings do you experience when you think of yourself as the victim of another person's sexual sin?

❑ Anger   ❑ Fear
❑ Grief   ❑ Sadness
❑ Resentment   ❑ Pain
❑ Relief   ❑ Other _____

But what if the victim benefits?

Sherry told her counselor that her Dad was really lonely. Her Mom was mean and always griping about everything. For as long as she could remember, she and her Dad would escape together.

"He always said he was sorry for what happened, and I believed him," Sherry explains. "I really wanted to go with him every time he asked. We had so much fun—well, all except the sex. I hated it when he touched me, but I never hated him. I could've not gone, but I just learned to live with it. He gave me lots in return, money and special gifts. But most of all I felt sorry for him. It seemed to make him happy. Sometimes we'd have sex three times a day, but I just couldn't tell him no. So you see it was also my fault."

Sometimes victims received so-called "benefits" from the abuser, and Sherry's story certainly described some healthy ingredients for a relationship between a father and daughter. A father-daughter relationship should include good times, presents, and love. It should not include a role reversal between mother and daughter, and it absolutely should not include any sex. At some point, the victim must give the total responsibility to the perpetrator for the sexual offenses.

✎ **Did you experience some benefits from the person who abused you? If so, describe those benefits.**

_____

_____

_____

_____

Some benefits that you may have received include attention, gifts, protection from others, and compliments. The person who abused you, however, is responsible for the abuse regardless of any benefits you have received.

👉 **Repeat the following statements aloud three times. We encourage you to say the words whether or not you want to accept or believe them.**

1. No child at any time, *under any circumstances,* can consent to sexual activity with an adult.

2. Because of the differences in maturity and power, adults always are responsible for their conduct with children—children cannot be held responsible.

3. Regardless of the circumstances, no person has the right to force or coerce another person into sexual activity against his or her will.

After repeating the three statements aloud three times, below describe your reaction to the statements.

_____

_____

_____

_____

What about others who were around?

The responsibility of a parent as the enabler of the abuse must be recognized and dealt with.

The survivor also must give responsibility to any co-perpetrator; that is, any person who knowingly aids or allows the person who commits the abuse to perform an abusive act. Certainly in a family setting with another parent present, the responsibility of that parent as the co-perpetrator or enabler of the abuse must be recognized and dealt with.

Victims sometimes express their greatest anger toward the parent who enabled the abuse. Often the victim has to deal with the question of whether or not the "other parent" really knows. The child has learned at an early age that parents are to take care of children. Understanding the role of the enabler is especially difficult if the mother is the person who aided or allowed the abuse. Mother is usually the person who puts bandages on children's scrapes and bruises. She usually dresses the children, prepares meals, puts them to bed, and so on. So why is she not doing something about what is happening?

All victims need to place an appropriate share of the responsibility on the person who allowed the abuse. Most co-perpetrators are not actively involved in the sexual abuse. They just all seem to have come to the same decision—to ignore or discount what they saw or felt was happening. Many times in family counseling sessions, mothers and fathers will weep over the fact that they noticed little things that weren't quite right. They just felt something was wrong but didn't know what it was.

Other primary caretakers might have been too busy, too troubled, or victims themselves. The main issue here is for the survivor to acknowledge that others are responsible for not protecting them. Survivors need to assign appropriate responsibility to all who could have been accountable rather than to continue to take responsibility for the abuse.

Assigning responsibility does not mean blaming.

Assigning responsibility means speaking the truth in love.

Blaming is about holding on to the need to punish.

I cannot blame the abuser for my choices as a survivor.

✎ **In what ways have you avoided acknowledging the role played in your abuse by those who aided or allowed the abuse?**

_____

_____

_____

_____

_____

Other pieces to the problem

Along with dysfunctional or selfish caretakers who failed to protect their children, many other pieces to the problem of responsibility exist. For example, sometimes survivors rationalize the responsibility of the person who committed the abuse because of our society's attitudes toward women, children, sex, and pornography. Whatever may be involved, the person made the choice to abuse. For healing to take place, victims must let go of responsibility for the abuse and acknowledge that responsibility for the abuse belongs to the person who committed the abuse.

✎ **In the paragraph above, underline the sentence that tells what a victim must do for healing to take place.**

The key for healing is to let go of responsibility for the abuse and give that responsibility back to the person who committed the abuse. It was that person's sin.

Assignment for the lesson

I will turn the darkness into light before them and make the rough places smooth. These are the things I will do; I will not forsake them.

–Isaiah 42:16

✎ **Write your own paraphrase of Isaiah 42:16, this unit's Scripture memory verse.**

_____

_____

_____

_____

☛ **Say aloud these affirmations five times.**

I accept God's love and kindness toward me.
The truth will set me free!
I am worthy to have God lead me and comfort me.

☛ **Pray for yourself and for each member of your _Shelter from the Storm_ group.**

LESSON 2

I've Been Betrayed!

According to *Webster's Dictionary*, *betray* means "to lead astray, to seduce by false promise, to desert in time of need." Truly a victim is often led astray by the effects of the abuse. Seduction is frequently a part of victimization. Most importantly, a victim is deserted in time of need. A child in need of a healthy relationship with a parent is abandoned in the world of incest. The youth in need of a spiritual leader is betrayed by her minister when the relationship becomes sexual.

✎ **Describe your feelings toward those people who betrayed you.**

_____

_____

_____

_____

What about God?

Victims must also deal with the issue of God's responsibility. Almost everyone who has been abused asks in one way or another: "What about God? I cried out to Him again and again, 'Where were You when this was happening to me? You weren't there for me then, and I don't feel You are here for me now.'"

"Why did God even let me be born?"

Many victims describe a feeling of profound despair. "Why did God even let me be born? I would have been better off dead. Now this has happened. I didn't do anything to deserve this. Why didn't God help me? Why didn't He kill my abuser? Where was God?"

Consider these biblical teachings that relate to sexual abuse—
* God considers sexual abuse so serious that in the Old Testament the penalty for sexual abuse was death. Leviticus 18 clearly sets forth the rules God intended for humankind's behavior. Sex with a child, with a blood relative, or rape all carried the death sentence.
* God has granted the freedom of choice to people. They can choose right or wrong. Psalm 115:16 tells us that "the heavens are the heavens of the Lord; but the earth He has given to the sons of men."

✎ **Why do you think God gave earth to humankind, when He knew we have the capacity for great wickedness?**

_____

_____

In God's master plan He wants a true relationship with us, and apparently this can only come about if we have free will to love Him or reject Him. If God forced us always to do right or be loving, there would be no true love relationship—we would merely be robots and slaves who automatically act a certain way.

- God did not cause the abuse. He refuses to treat us the way those who commit sexual abuse treat their victims—by imposing their will on their victims. God does not force people to do what He wants them to do.
- Horrible suffering does occur on this planet because people use their free will to do terrible things to each other. God's unfailing promise in this setting, however, is to bring us through all abuses or problems triumphantly as we commit our lives to Him.

All people are accountable for the choices that they make on this earth.

God also promises to bring justice to perpetrators. All people are accountable for the choices that they make on this earth. God gave people a manual that told how to relate to others. That manual is the Bible. Every victim's path has been crossed by an individual who chose the path opposite to God's direct instructions. You were betrayed, but you were not betrayed by God.

The word *betray,* in the Hebrew, occurs in a verb form that means "to cause to fall" or "to deceive, in order to betray." God does not deceive humankind, and no word in the Bible suggests that God betrays people. The Bible is given to instruct us, lead us, and cause us to rise up and be blessed. Abuse is not a blessing, nor is it a way for God to "teach us a lesson." It is a betrayal by people. God is the One who redeems and restores.

✎ **Check the feeling(s) you have had toward God about your abuse.**

❑ Angry
❑ Betrayed
❑ Confused
❑ Alone
❑ other _____

Are you willing to allow God to lead you to recovery?
❑ Yes ❑ No ❑ Not sure

Can you identify any barriers, especially beliefs or ideas, that keep you from reaching out to God for help in your recovery? Plan to share these with your *Shelter from the Storm* group.

_____

_____

_____

O house of Israel, trust in the Lord—
   he is their help and shield.
O house of Aaron, trust in the Lord—
   he is their help and shield.
You who fear him, trust in the Lord—
   he is their help and shield.
                           –Psalm 115:9-11

All of us struggle with questions about God, but at some point, we must understand, as the psalmist says in Psalm 115:9-11, "He is our help." Give people their responsibility and give God His. We live in a fallen world that will always have affliction, but God promises He will never forsake us or leave us. God will rescue us.

Georgie, a beautiful woman in her forties, was ready to give up on God before she experienced the truth of God's promise of restoration. Now she is able to smile as she relays the anger she once felt toward God. "I would have choked Him if I could have. I felt totally betrayed. I would read all those passages and ask God to help me. Nothing happened. I even prayed to die. Still, nothing happened. Finally I decided God was just a fantasy that weak people needed in order to get through life. Regardless of what I called God—Jesus, Allah, Buddha—no god anywhere heard anything. Then one day I really needed help and I prayed for God's help. Something happened that day. Not much, but something. So I decided I would try to believe in God, as if He really lived and worked. I began to pray for things in my life. Weeks, days, months, and yes, even years have passed and God does work. I also found a psalmist who agrees with me—

> *I love the Lord, because He hears*
> *My voice and my supplications.*
> *Because He has inclined His ear to me,*
> *Therefore I shall call upon Him as long as I live.*
> *The cords of death encompassed me,*
> *And the terrors of Sheol came upon me;*
> *I found distress and sorrow.*
> *Then I called upon the name of the Lord:*
> *"O Lord, I beseech Thee, save my life!"*
>
> —Psalm 116:1-4, NASB

Georgie ended her statement by saying, "... and He did! God saved my life. He did not betray me; He saved me from the affliction of this world. I love the Lord because He healed me from my past."

 Read Psalm 27:10 that appears in the margin. Pray and tell God how you feel about the verse.

Assignment for the lesson

 On a card write Isaiah 42:16, this unit's Scripture memory verse. Carry the card with you. Whenever you do some routine task like getting a drink of water, review your memory verse.

 Say these affirmations five times.

> I accept God's love and kindness toward me.
> The truth will set me free!
> I am worthy to have God lead me and comfort me.

 Pray for yourself and for each member of your *Shelter* group.

The Trouble with Denial

LESSON 3

You may have struggled with the issues of responsibility and betrayal. You may also have refused to recognize any of the effects of the abuse in your life. A young adult male told his counselor that he had been molested from the time he was six years old until he was fourteen. He knew he was coming to see a counselor for marriage counseling, but he assured his counselor that being molested had nothing to do with his inability to be sexually intimate. Besides, a long time ago he had worked through what had happened to him when he was a child.

"When my father and my mother forsake me, then the Lord will take me up."
—Psalm 27:10, KJV

I will turn the darkness into light before them and make the rough places smooth. These are the things I will do; I will not forsake them.

—Isaiah 42:16

When we as victims of abuse deny our abuse, we are actually lying to ourselves.

The Hebrew word in the Bible most often translated as *deny* means, in its strictest sense, "to lie." If we apply that meaning, when we as victims of abuse deny our abuse, we are actually lying to ourselves. Often victims will say that they don't want to dig up the past, that they really are doing fine. Some will even quote Paul's statement in Philippians 3:13 to explain what they mean: "But one thing I do; forgetting what lies behind and reaching forward to what lies ahead...." This is a great verse, but it does not mean that we should deny our problems. In fact, Paul spoke more about his past than any other person in the Bible. Moreover, in the earlier part of this same chapter of Philippians, Paul draws a most effective comparison between his past and what he later gained as a true servant of Christ.

In an individual counseling session, a woman was talking about her sexual relationship with her husband. "It can't be my sexual abuse. Before we married, I loved having sex. We had it all the time. It's that I don't love him anymore. I really hate sex with him. In fact, that's how I know I don't love him. No, I haven't ever thought about sexual abuse. It doesn't affect me now. I got over that a long time ago."

Have you ever said anything like this: "It doesn't affect me now. I got over that a long time ago"?

 Describe several ways you have protected yourself through the use of denial.

_____

_____

_____

The truth is that we can't put ourselves, God, or anyone in a box and close the lid on it. Perhaps some persons do exist whose earlier experiences of abuse have caused them few problems in their continuing life. We suspect, however, that those persons are very rare.

For most survivors, one primary reason force feeds denial. They have detached themselves from their feelings. Victims of the violent crimes of rape and incest, regardless of their age, often shut down their emotions. This reaction is similar to the shock of physical trauma, in which victims often recall that they felt no pain at first. Abuse victims understandably suffer an emotional shutdown as well as a shutting down of the physical pain. The body and the mind both have protective overload devices to be used in crisis. These are, however, intended for temporary use only. The longer they remain in place, the more damage they do.

 Shannon, an incest survivor, wrote the following poem about denial. As you read the poem, look for clues that indicate that Shannon was denying reality. Underline words or phrases that show her denial.

I know I once was young, but I don't remember much
About my childhood times with toys, and dolls and such.

I remember Dad was angry, Mom nervous and low keyed—
OUR family was quite healthy... that is, all of them, but me.

I got a lot of whippings, but they weren't all that bad.
I'm sure that I deserved them when I made my parents mad.

When mom was really tired, I would babysit—
I didn't mind—it was my job to help her out a bit.

I remember how she loved to go to bed and read—
And Dad would keep me up, in case there's something he would need.

Their patience would wear thin 'cause they had so much to do.
So I tried to keep things easy… that was my job, I knew.

I remember when my Dad found his way into my bed—
I didn't like what happened… but I couldn't tell, he said.

Confused, hurt, and scared, I must have made him mad—
The whippings kept on coming… but… I guess they weren't that bad.

I don't remember much throughout my childhood years—
So often when I try… my eyes well up with tears.

I wish that I'd been better, when I was a little child…
Then instead of anger, my parents could have smiled.

The memories that I have seem to make me sad—
But… I was just a child… and I guess they're not that bad.[1]

You could have underlined major portions of the poem. The girl/woman was taking on herself the responsibility for the parents' behaviors. Then she was denying her own pain with the refrain that "it wasn't really that bad."

✎ **In the margin beside the poem write what you would like to say to the girl in the poem.**

✎ **Below describe how, if at all, Shannon's denial compares to your denial. Do you minimize the pain you have suffered? Do you continue to accept the responsibility that properly belongs to others? Did or do you feel responsible for the emotions of others?**

_____

_____

_____

_____

Dissociation is different than denial

A more complicated form of not remembering comes from dissociation. Victims sometimes store fragments of memories in bits and pieces in order to protect themselves from the overwhelming experience produced by the complete recall of shattering events. A significant aspect of healing is to recall gradually the fragments and make appropriate connections. It is like putting

A significant aspect of healing is to recall gradually the fragments and make appropriate connections.

a puzzle together. If this is your experience you can be free from the domination of unwanted feelings and behaviors caused by dissociated memories. You cannot simply decide to remember, because the process is mostly unconscious. However, in a safe environment, such as your support group or with a counselor, and with the direction of God, you can gradually put together the fragmented memories of reality. Once you know from where the feelings and behaviors come, you can work through the traumatic memories and deal directly with the hurt, anger, grief, helplessness, and other painful emotions.

✎ **Have you felt detached or dissociated from your memories and your feelings? If so, describe any sensations you felt when you were detached.**

_____

_____

_____

✎ **Describe how and when you shut down.**

_____

_____

_____

_____

It's Time to Heal

Most survivors don't just get over the effects of sexual abuse. The results certainly do not go away just because the abuse happened a long time ago. Your tendency to deny the effects of the abuse in your life affects not only you but also your spouse, children, and friends.

The thief comes only to steal and kill and destroy; I have some that they may have life, and have it to the full.
–John 10:10

John 10:10 tells us that the thief (Satan) comes to kill, steal, and destroy. One of the most effective ways evil can destroy an individual is through sexual abuse. If you take the responsibility that belongs to the person who committed the abuse, you will be consumed with shame, anger, and destruction that are not yours to suffer. If you believe God has betrayed you, you will not seek Him. If you stay in denial, the enemy will have stolen the deepest peace and blessings that God has for you. The enemy will have stolen self-love and self-respect.

If you are the victim of sexual abuse, the time has come for you to give responsibility to the perpetrator, accept your betrayal, come out of denial, and begin the process of dealing with very painful memories. The process of healing has many ups and downs, and proceeds at varying rates. If you were to remember all past events at once, then you might be overwhelmed, but to begin is important. If memories and feelings become too hurtful or tend to promote destructive behavior, seek professional help. In the introduction to this workbook you wrote a plan for staying safe. Go back and read it and keep the commitment you made to yourself.

A Final Caution

Be careful not to use denial as a way to avoid the truth.

We need to give a caution before closing this lesson. Be careful not to use denial as a way to avoid the truth. Yes, Christians are supposed to forgive our enemies. Yes, God intends for us to be victorious. But forgiveness and victory do not arrive instantly. Wounds must be treated, and they take time to heal. Healing from the effects of sexual abuse does not occur until the survivor begins to face the truth. Please don't deny the facts any longer or hide in false responsibility. Allow God to take you beyond betrayal to hope, peace, and healing.

Assignment for the lesson

 Below write Isaiah 42:16, this unit's Scripture memory verse. Continue to work to memorize the verse.

_____

_____

↪ **Say aloud these affirmations five times.**

I accept God's love and kindness toward me.
The truth will set me free!
I am worthy to have God lead me and comfort me.

↪ **Pray for yourself and for each member of your *Shelter from the Storm* group.**

LESSON 4

From Death to Life
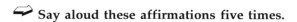

Survivors suffer a mental and emotional death from the experience of sexual abuse. God created you to live in the wholeness of body and soul. Sexual abuse severely damages that ability. Your first need is to have your mind and emotions restored to life and health.

Now that you have started your restoration from sexual abuse, you can understand the biblical pattern of restoration. One of the Hebrew words for *restoration* means "to live" or to "be restored to life." Restoration from the abuse means to live, perhaps for the first time in your life.

This specific word for restoration can be found only in chapter 8 of 2 Kings, in a passage dealing with a woman who lived in Shunem. In 2 Kings 4, this Shunamite woman befriended the prophet Elisha, and she and her husband build a room for the prophet of God in their home. Elisha, wanting to do something for her, prayed that she should conceive a son. The Shunamite woman gave birth to a son the next year. Later in chapter 4, the son, a grown man, died, but God restored him to life. This story vividly demonstrates the principle of restoration. God gives life and even when circumstances cause death, God can restore life.

God will Restore

God will restore the life that has been stolen from you.

Sexual abuse causes its own kind of death. Your next step is to begin to risk and to believe that God will restore the life that has been stolen from you. The Shunamite woman appeared again in chapter 8, where she lost all her land holdings due to a famine. She appealed to the king, who had just learned from Gehazi, the servant of Elisha, that this is the woman whose son Elisha restored. The king then appointed an officer whom he commanded, "Restore all that was hers and all the produce of the field from the day that she left the land even until now" (2 Kings 8:6, NASB).

Through the king, God restored what the Shunamite woman had lost. Our caring God is in the restoration business. As you continue to pray, learn, and grow, God can restore you to a life of meaning, purpose and joy. Begin your appeal to the King, Jesus Christ, and allow Him to restore you to life.

✎ **Below list your dreams and desires that have died because of sexual abuse.**

_____

_____

_____

Some responses given by other survivors to this question have been "a sense of innocence, the ability to trust, spontaneity." If you had a difficult time making your list, these suggestions may help you get started.

Do you think the Shunamite woman ever asked, "Why me?" or, "If only things could have been different"?

✎ **Describe any thoughts like these that you may have had, including the circumstances when they occurred.**

_____

_____

_____

Your responses may indicate that you are beginning to let yourself feel some grief and loss about the consequences of the abuse. That is good recovery work! Keep it up.

✎ **In the spaces below write your feelings about the losses you have suffered due to sexual abuse.**

_____

_____

_____

_____

Assignment for the lesson

 Below write from memory this unit's Scripture verse. You may check your work on page 56.

_____

_____

 Say these affirmations five times.

> I accept God's love and kindness toward me.
> The truth will set me free!
> I am worthy to have God lead me and comfort me.

Pray for yourself and for each member of your *Shelter from the Storm* group.

LESSON

5

Help from Psalm 23

Another Hebrew word for *restore* is found in Psalm 23. This may be the most familiar passage in all of Scripture to Christians and non-Christians alike. The Hebrew word for *restore* in verse three is used in a verb form that means "to cause someone or something to return and to restore someone or something to a former condition." This Scripture can be a powerful part of your restoration. God desires to cause you to return and to restore to you those things that sexual abuse has taken away.

In his book *God's Psychiatry*, Dr. Charles Allen recommends reading Psalm 23 five times a day for one week to help with a distorted attitude about God, particularly that of viewing God as a remote, all-powerful judge. He explains the relationship between shepherd and sheep as the relationship between God and humankind.[2]

Janice's Story

When Janice, an exceptionally thin blonde, first came into the office, she had very long, bouncy hair. She wore thick glasses and was always pushing them up, as they would frequently slip down on her nose. Once during that session, to the reference to God as Father, she retorted very angrily. "This is what I think of my father." She acted as though she were going to spit. She stated clearly that she couldn't stand thinking of God as "father." Every time she went to church as a child, she told me, she would think that God the Father was mean, just like her father. How she hated that word in any form!

She disappeared for a while, and one day she came to the office again. She had quite a different look about her. She had gained a little weight, and her glasses didn't seem to slip as much. She began to share a fascinating story. "One day, I decided to give God one last chance," she said, laughing. "I knelt down and cried out, 'God, I really need You; please help.' Something happened that was very special. I didn't know exactly what and certainly couldn't explain it. I still had a problem trusting this God—this father—so I didn't do anything like go to church or read the Bible. A few months later, I read a story in a magazine about a woman who had been in a car accident and who prayed Psalm 23 during her two years of recovery. This woman's story was so loving toward the Shepherd and so grateful for how He had helped her in all the physical and financial challenges brought on by the accident. She spoke of her victories with the Shepherd.

"Some time after this, I was asked to go to church with a friend. I went to her church three times, and all three times they taught Psalm 23. My friend was completely embarrassed. But I knew in my heart it was just for me. Something happened to me that day when I knelt down and asked God to help me, but I couldn't do anything because even then the word *father* made me sick to my stomach. Now I see God as Shepherd, as Jesus. One day, perhaps soon, as my Shepherd continues to restore me, I will really see God as my Father."

Psalm 23 is a powerful chapter for restoration from abuse.

The Lord is my Shepherd...

The Lord is my shepherd, I shall not be in want.
He makes me lie down in green pastures,
he leads me beside quiet waters,
  he restores my soul.
He guides me in paths of righteousness
  for his name's sake.
Even though I walk
  through the valley of the shadow of death,
I will fear no evil,
  for you are with me;
your rod and your staff,
  they comfort me.
You prepare a table before me
  in the presence of my enemies.
You anoint my head with oil;
  my cup overflows.
Surely goodness and love will follow me
  all the days of my life,
and I will dwell in the house of the Lord
  forever.

✎ **Read this psalm five times a day this week then come back to this space and describe how the Shepherd has ministered to you.**

_____

_____

_____

God does restore the soul, mind, feelings, and emotions. Often survivors can't relate to God, and especially God the Father, during the early part of their recovery. Psalm 23 can help you to start a new relationship with God. The Shepherd will restore your heart, mind, and soul in spite of the scars that

Survivors' Psalm
(based on Psalm 23)

God is my Father
  I have all that I need.
He's healed me from shame
  From guilt I am freed.

He gives me His strength
  For all I'm to do.
Early each morning
  His mercies are new.

He's called me to rest
  Close to His heart
He's available always
  He'll never depart.

Refreshing, restoring,
  And leading each day
He's promised to faithfully
  Show me His way.

When life is hard
  And I'm tempted to fear
I run to my Father,
  and He wipes each tear.

He comforts and holds me,
  As long as I need.
He welcomes me there,
  So I need not plead.

His unfailing love
  Will always be mine.
I'm precious to Him,
  I'm His special design!

I dwell in His presence
  Like a hand in a glove.
I 'm living in peace, and
  Immersed in His LOVE.[3]

remain. Under Christ's lordship, even the scars can help you become more compassionate, understanding, and resilient from having successfully survived such abuse.

You met Shannon through her poem called *Denial* in lesson 3. Later in her recovery journey Shannon wrote her own paraphrase of Psalm 23. That paraphrase appears in the margin. As you read the poem, note the difference between *Denial* on pages 64-65 and *Survivors' Psalm*.

 Take a prayer break. Talk to God about how you feel about Him as Father. Share your feelings with Him about Psalm 23—even if those feelings do not seem acceptable. Ask Him to lead you to restoration and healing.

More about Restoration

The Hebrew word for *restore* found in Joel 2:25 means literally, "to make whole." God promised He would make the people in Joel's day whole after a devastating loss. He is still in the restoring business today. He can restore to you those things that betrayal has taken away. God will restore the time you have lost by making the time you have now more meaningful. Most survivors have had part or all of their childhood stolen. Often when victims survey the past, they cannot see anything that is good.

No human could give back what was taken from you. Only God can do that. If every person who abused you came and asked you for forgiveness, none could give you back the loss that you have experienced. You may feel better, but only God can give a life with meaning and purpose. He can make a beautiful mosaic of the broken pieces of your life.

In the Book of Job, Job suffered devastating losses. He lost his wealth, his health, and he suffered the deaths of his children. At the end of the story, God restored Job. Job received far more than he possessed in the beginning. He regained his health, greater wealth than before, he even had more children. But Job did not gain his dead children. Satan had caused their deaths, and they were not restored to Job—at least not then.

God can restore you in the same way that He restored Job. You can feel clean again. The love and grace of God can cleanse and replace the feelings of shame and filthiness, and the stain of abuse. Allow God to touch those areas where you need restoration. Life will not return to exactly the way things were before the abuse, but God can give you a life with meaning and purpose. You may even come to the place that you see that God has given you more than the abuse took away.

✎ **Below describe the hope that understanding God's process for restoration brings to your life.**

_____

_____

_____

Unit Review

✎ Look back over this unit. What statement or activity was most meaningful for you?

_____

_____

✎ Can you remember any statements or activities with which you were uncomfortable? Write those below.

_____

_____

✎ Write a prayer asking God to help you in your areas of struggle.

_____

_____

_____

_____

[1]Shannon L. Spradlin, *Does God Know About This?* (Henderson, Nevada, 1993), 5.
[2]Charles Allen, *God's Psychiatry* (Old Tappan, NJ: Fleming H. Revell Co., 1953).
[3]Spradlin, 92.

UNIT 5

The Family in the Storm

Focal passage
Do not be afraid; you will not suffer shame. Do not fear disgrace; you will not be humiliated. You will forget the shame of your youth.

–Isaiah 54:4

This Unit's Affirmation
I am clean.

BETRAYED BY MOM AND DAD

Gretchen describes many bizarre incidents of abuse by her babysitter. Sometimes she had to watch the sitter and her boyfriend have sex. Sometimes the babysitter would fondle Gretchen or would stick straws, pencils, and other such objects into her vagina or anus. She would tell Gretchen that she was bad and ugly.

Gretchen tried many times to tell her mom and dad about the abuse, but they did not believe her. They were so busy with their own problems that they didn't seem to care or even pay attention to her. They scolded her for making a fuss about nothing.

In this unit you will examine how the family affects and is affected by the experience of sexual abuse.

Growth goal

This week's goal
You will take steps to remove any barriers to recovery that are a result of your family of origin.

The Dysfunctional Family, Part 1	The Dysfunctional Family, Part 2	The Dysfunctional Family, Part 3	Believing the Truth	A Biblical Example
Lesson 1	Lesson 2	Lesson 3	Lesson 4	Lesson 5

Memory verse

This week's passage of Scripture to memorize
You will forget the shame of your youth.

–Isaiah 54:4

LESSON 1

The Dysfunctional Family, Part 1

Family issues tremendously affect recovery from sexual abuse. In some families, parents or family members may be abusers, while others parents or family members are unaware that the abuse occurred. In other families the abuse may occur outside the boundaries of the family system. The family may or may not know about the abuse, or may not realize that something has happened to the victim. Whatever your case, with God's help you can understand the role your family played in your sexual abuse and the role they can play in your recovery.

If the father abused an incest victim, the victim must also deal with anger toward the mother. A child molested by an uncle may feel unprotected by both parents. A victim of rape may feel she cannot disclose that fact to her family if the family is emotionally shut down and incapable of giving support. In families where the child is abused by a babysitter, the child, as we would expect, has been told to obey the sitter. Often this victim has a great deal of anger toward both parents; the child believes the parents must know what is happening and therefore they must approve of it.

Many reasons contribute to a family's inability to cope with sexual abuse. No families are perfect and most families lack the tools necessary to weather the storm that sexual abuse creates. How well they survive the trauma will depend on how well the family has learned ways of functioning as a family. In recent years, counselors have identified the common characteristics of a *dysfunctional family*. A knowledge of these characteristics helps us to understand sexual abuse and to recover from it.

dysfunctional family–n. a family in which some behavior such as alcoholism, drug abuse, divorce, an absent father or mother, excessive anger, verbal or physical abuse interferes with the ability of the family to do its job effectively.

In most of the families where sexual abuse occurs, the family clearly is dysfunctional. But this does not mean that all dysfunctional families are sexually abusive. The term *dysfunctional* is used to express the inability of family members to meet the God-given needs for nurture. These families are unable to communicate their feelings, both positive and negative, in a consistent and caring way. They are unable to respond to the needs of each family member.

 Think about your family. List all the primary members of the family. What does each individual represent to you? For example, who in your family represents comfort, or expectations, or abuse, or peace, or rescuing, or neglect? How do you feel about each one?

Family members	This individual represents...	My feelings toward this person...

Review the following list of the characteristics of a dysfunctional family. You will then study each one individually. We encourage you to decide how each one relates to you and to your sexual abuse experience.

Characteristics of a Dysfunctional Family

1. Needy family members receive an inappropriate proportion of the family's time, attention, and energy so that members learn to be overly-responsible toward needy people and irresponsible about themselves.
2. A dysfunctional family promotes denial and secrecy.
3. A dysfunctional family has either repressed emotions, explosive emotions, or both.
4. A dysfunctional family does not teach effective living skills to the children. Children do not learn to touch, feel, or trust. They learn to expect rigidity and emotional or physical abandonment.
5. A dysfunctional family squeezes the members into rigid, inappropriate roles.

1. Needy family members receive an inappropriate proportion of the family's time, attention, and energy.

An emotionally needy family member may be one who is addicted to alcohol or drugs, or one who demonstrates other obsessive-compulsive behaviors. The energy and attention of the family is directed toward caring for the emotional needs of this family member. As a result, all of the family members become emotionally needy.

Families with addictive family members have an increased potential for sexual abuse.

Families with addictive family members have an increased potential for sexual abuse. In a family where the focal person is an alcoholic, the unspoken rule in the family may be "Make Dad happy, then maybe he won't get drunk." In a family where there is a rage-aholic, the rule may be "Whatever you do, don't make Mom mad." In a dysfunctional family the family members operate according to these spoken and unspoken rules and not according to personal need.

✎ **Can you identify a member of your family who was emotionally needy? What effect did living in the family with this person have on you?**

_____

_____

_____

Did a relationship exist between this family member and the way your family dealt with the abuse? If so, describe that relationship.

_____

_____

Jean's mother was an alcoholic. Jean would cook and clean and take care of the other children because mom was either drunk or hung-over. When Jean's father began to sexually abuse her, she blamed her mother because he said he wouldn't need her if mom was available. He said that if Jean would have sex with him he wouldn't have to have an affair.

2. A dysfunctional family promotes denial and secrecy.

A monster lived inside my mother
He was always there.
My mother was not the monster.
She was not a nice person who turned into a monster
A monster lived inside her.

Sometimes the monster was very loud and scary
And swung his heavy tail
Knocking out everything in his path.
Roaring and stomping and fiery in his eyes
Not to be controlled or understood.

And sometimes the monster was silent and evil
Sneaking around and hiding in closets.
When you least suspected, you were poisoned
By words that cut like knives and stung like bee stings.

But sometimes the monster fell asleep
and my mother loved me very much.

Gretchen describes many bizarre incidents of abuse by her babysitter. Sometimes she had to watch the sitter and her boyfriend have sex. Sometimes the babysitter would fondle Gretchen or would stick straws, pencils, and other such objects into her vagina or anus. She would tell Gretchen that she was bad and that she was ugly. Gretchen tried many times to tell her mom and dad about the abuse, but they were so busy with their own problems that they didn't seem to care or even pay attention to her. They scolded her for making a fuss about nothing.

Finally Gretchen screamed and yelled the whole gruesome story. Both parents were shocked. They couldn't believe it. Gretchen had been very irritable, but they never dreamed what was happening while they were gone.

Although Gretchen's parents were supportive of her in general, the abuse had come at a very troubled time for the family. Once aware, however, the parents brought Gretchen to counseling and participated in family counseling as well as individual counseling. In counseling, Gretchen expressed her appropriate anger toward her parents. The parents accepted the responsibility for their seeming lack of interest, selection of the babysitter, and failure to recognize Gretchen's attempts to communicate.

Conflict is a normal part of healthy family living. Healthy families expect problems and have healthy ways of coping with them. Family members talk about issues even though someone may feel embarrassed or hurt. Family members take responsibility for their own behavior. Problems can be discussed and solutions found. In a dysfunctional family the "don't talk" rule keeps the victim of sexual abuse bound in silence, even if the crime is committed by a stranger.

✎ **Describe how your family solved problems when you were a child.**

_____

_____

Families solve problems in many ways. Healthy families recognize that they have choices. If one method doesn't work, they try another. Unhealthy families often use the same dysfunctional methods over and over. Maybe your family refused to recognize problems. Often the rule is "don't rock the boat." Other dysfunctional families overreact to things so strongly that everyone is afraid to mention a problem or an issue.

✎ **What effect has your family's method of responding to problems had on your abuse recovery?**

_____

_____

Some dysfunctional families look perfectly normal on the surface.

Some dysfunctional families look perfectly normal on the surface. The father and mother do most of the things that parents should do. They keep an orderly house, a nice yard, food on the table, and clothes in the closet. However, the family may still be dysfunctional because the parents are not emotionally present for their children.

Consider the example of Beatrice, a volunteer for a local rape crisis center. She became a victim herself. She was raped at knife point. The rape occurred one morning when Beatrice, after breakfast with friends, returned to her apartment. Hearing a knock at the door, she peeked out and saw a man she knew, although not very well. She asked what he wanted. "I need to talk to someone," he said. One rule most crisis centers teach is never to open the door under such circumstances. Unfortunately Beatrice did open the door and was raped. Then she decided she didn't want to press charges.

When asked why she, of all people, didn't press charges, she replied that her parents told her it was her fault for opening the door and if she were to follow through on the charges, it would be an embarrassment for the family. She said it was just like when she tried to tell them about her grandfather. Her body was covered with bruises from the beating he gave her. All her parents could say was, "He didn't mean what he did," and, "What did you do to cause it?"

More of Cindy's Story

Cindy shares that even when she was a very young child, she felt she could tell absolutely no one what was happening to her.

"I knew it would be useless to tell. Besides, I loved my perpetrator."

"Everyone around me had so many problems that I knew it would be useless to tell. Besides, I loved my perpetrator. When he would come home from work, I would run out to meet him. Caught in this impossible situation, I chose to keep the abuse to myself and hide from others. I never played with children in the neighborhood. To stay away from everyone seemed the safest choice. Trying to figure out if the people around me were 'good' kept me too confused.

"I also remember always feeling sad, dirty, and completely alone. People frightened me. Once I lived in a place where the mothers in the neighborhood tried to be friendly and talk to me. I would run from them, wondering, 'What do they want from me?' One in particular would leave me cookies, showing me from a distance that they were at her door, then going back inside her house. When I was sure she wasn't coming back outside, I would run as fast as I could to get them. I was so afraid and anxious, it seemed like miles down her walkway."

A dysfunctional family keeps the secret of sexual abuse. Other family members may or may not actually know about the abuse but everyone is aware that something is wrong. The family members work together to keep secret the fact that something is wrong especially from non-family members. Those who are allowed access to the home are screened carefully. The family acts as though all is well and the visitor only sees the performance.

✎ **Was your family open to the outside world? Were you free to talk about your family to others?** ❏ **Yes** ❏ **No**

How does this characteristic relate to your sexual abuse experience?

_____

_____

Many survivors keep their abuse a secret to protect the family from having to deal with the fact that the abuse is occurring. Sometimes they keep the secret because the victim fears that someone will get hurt physically or emotionally or that the family will not survive. The victim will endure the pain of the abuse rather than risk losing the family.

✎ **How and what did you do to protect the family?**

_____

_____

_____

Assignment for the lesson

You will forget the shame of your youth.
–Isaiah 54:4

✎ **Below write your own paraphrase of the Scripture memory verse for this unit.**

_____

_____

↬ **Say aloud these affirmations five times.**
I accept God's love and kindness toward me.
The truth will set me free!
I am worthy to have God lead me and comfort me.
I am clean.

↬ **Pray for yourself and for each member of your _Shelter from the Storm_ group.**

LESSON 2

Dysfunctional Family, Part 2

In this lesson you will study more characteristics of a dysfunctional family. As you better understand your family, you will better understand yourself and your reactions.

3. A dysfunctional family has either repressed emotions, explosive emotions, or both.

A healthy family both permits and models how to express emotions. Children learn how to identify and deal with their feelings. In a dysfunctional family certain or all emotions are forbidden.

Many families transmit messages that say, "Don't express your feelings. Don't cry. Don't get upset. Don't get angry. Don't betray the family. Don't ever tell outsiders about the family secrets." These messages, as well as ones more directly stated toward you, affect your recovery. You may have been told that you are a failure, or shamed by any number of derogatory statements—all of these are characteristic of a family based in shame. You will be invited to focus on the issue of shame in detail in a later chapter. For the moment, however, evaluate how you learned to feel shame about your feelings and responses in your family.

✎ **As a child, did you learn any of these beliefs? Circle those with which you identify.**

Good children honor their parents.
My parents had their faults, but they loved me.
If I say or think bad things about my family, I will betray them.
If I say or think bad things about my family, I will feel ashamed.[2]

The first two beliefs are positive and healthy. The last two are sick rules that serve to maintain the secrecy in a dysfunctional family system.

✎ **Describe how these beliefs affect your life and your recovery.**

_____

_____

Survivors of sexual abuse are sometimes unable to express the feelings necessary for recovery because they learned in their family of origin that feelings were not acceptable. This is especially true if the feelings are negative and if the feelings concern a family member.

You can make wise choices.
You can to reject false messages.

Each family member sends us messages about ourselves. The person who sexually abuses says, "You're worthless. You are no good and you are guilty." Sometimes parents send the same message, not by sexual abuse but by their words and attitudes. Maybe a sister told you that you were stupid. Possibly you had a granddad who said you were special—a badly needed positive reinforcement. You can evaluate the messages that each person who supported and each person who abused gave you. Then you can make wise, godly, and informed choices. You can choose to reject false messages.

✎ **How do you feel when you talk about the abuse? Check all that apply.**

❏ Scared ❏ Shame
❏ Disloyal ❏ Guilt
❏ Relief ❏ Other _____

How have you responded to or compensated for the way your family expressed feelings?

_____

_____

_____

Bill was taught that good children honor their parents. He did not understand that one way to honor a relationship is to make it real by being honest when situations are painful or difficult. As a result, he was afraid to talk about his abuse. Negative thoughts were bad things in his family so he felt guilty and shame-filled for having normal thoughts and emotions.

How would you like to respond now?

_____

_____

Assignment for the lesson

You will forget the shame of your youth.
–Isaiah 54:4

✎ **Write on a card Isaiah 54:4, the Scripture memory verse for this unit. Carry the card with you and regularly review the verse.**

☞ **Say aloud these affirmations five times.**
I accept God's love and kindness toward me.
The truth will set me free!
I am worthy to have God lead me and comfort me.
I am clean.

☞ **Pray for yourself and for each member of your group.**

LESSON 3

Dysfunctional Family, Part 3

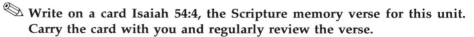

In this lesson you will examine more characteristics of a dysfunctional family. The purpose is not to assign blame or even to determine if your family was dysfunctional. The purpose is to understand how your past affects your recovery.

4. A dysfunctional family does not teach effective living skills to the children.

A healthy family provides an environment that allows children to grow according to their own developmental needs. Children then learn to love themselves and others and to trust that the world can be a friendly place. A child needs a fairly consistent and stable environment.

An example of the dysfunctional family is one that never stays the same. Some victims of sexual abuse report living in more than one family, perhaps first with mother and father and next with grandmother and grandfather. Cindy shares that in her childhood she attended 19 different schools, including five during her high school years.

"I lived with my mother, my grandmother, my mother and stepfathers, my sister's father, and with several other family systems. Each one presented different issues that I had to work through as a part of my recovery. I had to deal with emotional abuse, chaos, and the aftermath of my sexual abuse, all of which made me think that I was profoundly inadequate as a person, since I was unable to alter or control what was happening. The lesson I learned from all of this was that I could do nothing about my life. No matter what I tried to change, it didn't work. No matter what I did to bring order, chaos always resulted. I could not make sense out of chaos.

"I carried the outside shame of moving so many times and the inside shame of sexual abuse. When I left for school in the morning, I didn't know if things would be the same when I got home. I trusted no one because if outsiders knew my story, my pain would be worse. I not only acted toward others as if I didn't care, I began to shut down so I wouldn't care. I would say to myself, 'Only breathing matters, and I am breathing.' But, of course, breathing is not all there is to living. Also, several of the people in my care were alcoholics, which added to my confusion and lowered my self-worth."

Each family system teaches us something very deep about ourselves, and that message is not always positive. The sexual abuse and the chaos in Cindy's family taught her that she was profoundly inadequate. But she also experienced positive learning. Her mother said again and again, "Don't do as I have done, I've done it all wrong. You can do it better."

Cindy says, "She taught me that I was smart, that I could do it. She taught me that a better way exists. She didn't know that better way, but she taught me that if I searched diligently enough, I could find that better way of living. She was right. I found it with God."

Appropriate touch: a living skill

Building a healthy self-image in a recovering sexual abuse victim requires daily reinforcement in terms that demonstrate that person's value. We all need positive statements and healthy physical contact. God created us to give and receive healthy physical love, such as hugging, holding hands, and kissing. Unfortunately sometimes in a dysfunctional family the only touches we may have experienced were bad touches. The result is extremely confusing.

We all need positive statements and healthy physical contact.

If you wanted to be held but the only time you received physical attention was during abuse, you may have felt guilty. This is a double tragedy. However, you can begin to understand that you were not wrong for having basic human needs. God intended for you to have these needs met in a healthy manner.

✎ **What role did touch play in your family of origin?**

_____

_____

_____

Describe how you react when you are touched by someone now.

_____

_____

Touch has to do with personal power and control. If you were touched when you didn't want to be and not touched when you did, you may have a difficult time accepting touch. You may not even know what is appropriate or inappropriate touch. Survivors are often re-victimized because they are not aware that they can say no to touch.

5. A dysfunctional family squeezes the members into rigid, inappropriate roles.

Children in dysfunctional families develop survival roles. These roles are either assigned by the family or unconsciously chosen by the child.

Some examples of survival roles include:

Survival roles

Scapegoat—usually blamed for family problems
Hero—works hard to bring respect to the family name
Surrogate Spouse—often takes the place of the emotionally absent spouse and becomes the child counselor for a troubled adult parent
Lost child—never gets in the way or causes trouble because this family already has enough problems
Surrogate parent—takes over responsibility of parenting tasks
Clown—avoids the pain by being the center of attention

✎ **In the list above, underline any of the roles above that would describe your behavior in your family. Your role may have changed over the years as the family changed.**

✎ **What effect did your role(s) in the family have upon how you coped with the sexual abuse?**

_____

_____

Can you identify roles that others played? What was the effect of their role on your feelings and behavior?

_____

_____

How do you feel after identifying your family role/roles? Check all that apply.

❏ Sad ❏ Afraid
❏ Lonely ❏ Guilty
❏ Ashamed ❏ Other _____
❏ Angry

M.J. describes how her sister was assigned the role of surrogate mother. "All my life I would remember how my sister and I were best friends, how she was always there for me. I would remember how she cooked for me. She dressed me in the mornings for school. She loved me." M.J.'s sister was in the role of the parental child.

Sometimes in situations like M.J.'s, the child develops a fantasy bond with the sibling that is the surrogate parent. "I couldn't understand why, now that we are adults, my sister never has come to see me. I was always the one who went to her house. I always called her on the phone.

"It took a long time, but I finally realized it was all make-believe. This 'bonding' was a way I had learned to cope in my loneliness as a child. My mother had made my sister take care of me. I realize now that she didn't even want to. As my sister and I sat on the porch holding hands, I would fantasize that she loved me. This love, this relationship, was only in my mind; it never really existed. The reason she never called now was because she didn't want to. She never came to my house because she didn't want to."

"This love relationship, was only in my mind; it never really existed."

You may need to seek God's wisdom to become aware of fantasy bonding. We urge you to do so, for this knowledge can set you on the path to have real relationships with these relatives. Even if they are not what you thought or even what you wanted, they will be authentic relationships that you can understand and predict. Your efforts may even lead to loving and intimate relationships, if your relatives are willing to consider honestly all the factors affecting your former situation.

✎ **Describe in detail any fantasy bonding you may have with family members.**

_____

_____

_____

_____

Brenda had a difficult time recognizing that she had developed a fantasy bond with her much older brothers. Like M.J., she emotionally had replaced her need for a father with a fantasy about her relationship with her brothers. Brenda began to understand the truth when they never called and never came to see her as an adult. Even more painful was the realization that they did nothing to protect her from her alcoholic and abusive father when they were grown men and had the means to do so. Eventually, she realized that she must develop healthy relationships with colleagues and peers instead of holding on to the fantasy.

Sometimes survivors of sexual abuse have difficulty letting go of the feeling of responsibility for the abuse. They cling to a fantasy bond to the abuser or another family member who could have protected them.

✎ **Have you continued to accept responsibility rather than face the truth that your bond to one or more family members is a fantasy? Describe your experience.**

_____

_____

_____

Assignment for the lesson

 Below write three times Isaiah 54:4, the Scripture memory verse for this unit.

_____

_____

_____

> *You will forget the shame of your youth.*
> –Isaiah 54:4

☞ **Say aloud these affirmations five times.**
I accept God's love and kindness toward me.
The truth will set me free!
I am worthy to have God lead me and comfort me.
I am clean.

☞ **Pray for yourself and for each member of your** *Shelter from the Storm* **group.**

LESSON 4

Believing the Truth

As you recover you may be surprised to find that some family members may also pursue recovery from their former behavior patterns. If this happens you may for the first time be able to establish functional and loving relationships with them.

Even so, you need to allow God to become your closest family. You don't have to give up your biological family, but you need to place God at the center of your life. He is the one who will never let you down or abuse you. You can allow God to replace your feelings of unworthiness with His truth about your worthiness. Your hopelessness can be replaced with hope in Christ and your profound feelings of inadequacy with the adequacy found in Him.

Search for Significance explains four common false beliefs created and maintained in part by dysfunctional families. The victim of sexual abuse is almost certain to hold as truths these false beliefs. These false beliefs will create guilt, a false sense of responsibility, low self-worth, and a host of other issues for the victim.

One of these beliefs is: *I must meet certain standards in order to feel good about myself.* Whatever standards you have set are in part based on the messages you heard as you were growing up. The false belief blocks you from realizing that you already are fully pleasing to God. No matter how intense, perfect, or successful you become, meeting falsely motivated standards will not bring you the peace you desire. The fact that you were sexually abused does not have to keep you from feeling good about yourself.

 In the margin describe at least one standard you have held that may be blocking your journey to recovery. Ask yourself, "What do I think I must do to be a good person?"

To be a good person, I must...

_____

_____

_____

_____

Jacque thought that she could never let anyone know she felt inadequate or afraid. Regardless of her accomplishments she never felt adequate because something always remained that she didn't know or understand. Her ability to admit she needed help blocked her recovery.

I must have others' approval is another of the false messages families transmit. This belief will lead you to become consumed with pleasing others at any cost. As a result, the fear of rejection or disapproval can overwhelm you. Even if others disapprove because you have chosen to talk about the abuse, you can feel good about yourself. You do not have to have their approval.

✎ **Have you experienced or feared the disapproval of friends or family members because of how you are choosing to recover? ❏ Yes ❏ No**

If so, how are you reacting to them? Do you need to let go of the need to have their approval? What is their approval costing you?

_____

_____

_____

Your recovery may require that you suffer the disapproval of some significant others. Some people will not understand that you need to tell your secret so that you can heal.

The third negative message is: *Because I have failed, I am unworthy and deserve to be punished*. If someone else doesn't punish us, we will punish ourselves. This sense of unworthiness must be recognized for what it is—false shame and guilt.

✎ **Do you continue to hold to any feeling that you are unworthy, or deserve to be punished because of your abuse? ❏ Yes ❏ No**

If so, describe your feelings. _____

_____

You may already have overcome this roadblock to recovery. Romans 8:1-2 speaks powerfully to those of us who struggle with the feeling that we are unworthy and deserve to be punished.

Therefore, there is now no condemnation for those who are in Christ Jesus, because through Jesus Christ the law of the Spirit of life set me free from the law of sin and death.

–Romans 8:1-2

✎ **Reread the verses appearing in the margin. Underline the phrases that you need to believe and accept about yourself.**

✎ **Take a few minutes to pray. Ask God to help you let go of the feeling of unworthiness. Write your prayer here. Ask Him to help you believe that you will be free of this feeling of condemnation.**

_____

_____

_____

The last of the four false beliefs is: *I am what I am; I cannot change; I am hopeless.* The family in darkness places the victim in an environment that teaches hopelessness.

✎ **Every survivor at times feels hopeless. How did you learn hopelessness from your family?**

_____

_____

What gives you hope now?

_____

_____

The greatest source of hope is God.

Hope comes from many places. The support of your group can give you hope. Family and friends that really care provide hope. If you keep a journal, reread what you have written. What have you learned and where have you grown? The greatest source of hope is God who sacrificed Himself for you and promised He would never leave you.

✎ **Below reread the four negative messages. Then rewrite them as positive statements. We have done the first one as an example.**

1. *I must meet certain standards in order to feel good about myself.*
2. *I must have others' approval to feel good about myself.*
3. *Because I have failed, I am unworthy and deserve to be punished.*
4. *I am what I am; I cannot change; I am hopeless.*

Example: #1. I can feel good about myself because I know God accepts me and I know I am learning and growing.

1. _____

_____

_____

2. _____

_____

_____

3. _____

_____

4. _____

_____

These false messages block recovery from abuse.

✎ **Below describe all the ways you can that the false messages have blocked your recovery in the past.**

_____

_____

_____

Recovery on your own

Sometimes we must realize that our families will not join us in the recovery process. We may have to recover on our own with the help of a support system we create.

Jean is the oldest of six children, very anxious, and an alcoholic. Her father started sexually abusing her when she was very young. By the time she was 10, they were having intercourse. She consistently made protests to her mother, but her mother only replied, "What can I do?" Jean's mother was jealous of her daughter and her husband. As Jean began to recognize her mother's jealously, she used it against both parents. By age 16, she couldn't stand the situation any longer, ran away, and never returned.

Jean's mother still resents her. She really doesn't try to have a relationship with Jean's father, with Jean, or with Jean's daughter. Jean's father, on the other hand, wants everything to be OK. He wants Jean to forget the past. Jean is working through recovery. Although it would be extremely helpful if her family would also enter recovery, Jean is beginning to realize that her dysfunctional mother and father are unwilling to do so at this time. She is accepting the fact that she must continue in recovery on her own. She can no longer look for them to change so that she will feel better.

✎ **If your family chooses not to pursue recovery from dysfunctional behavior, in the margin describe how this decision might affect your recovery.**

If your family has chosen not to pursue recovery—and many make that choice—you will need to find ways to seek support and strength from significant other people. You may need to establish emotional, psychological, and maybe even physical boundaries to protect yourself if your family is abusive.

The decision will—
_____
_____
_____
_____
_____
_____

Assignment for the lesson

✎ **Repeat three times Isaiah 54:4, your Scripture memory verse.**

☞ **Say aloud these affirmations five times.**
I accept God's love and kindness toward me.
The truth will set me free!
I am worthy to have God lead me and comfort me.
I am clean.

☞ **Pray for yourself and for each member of your _Shelter from the Storm_ group.**

LESSON
5

"Be quiet now, my sister; he is your brother. Don't take this thing to heart." And Tamar lived in her brother Absalom's house, a desolate woman.
–2 Samuel 13:20

A Biblical Example

God speaks the truth even when it is ugly. The Bible records examples of sexual abuse and family dysfunction. Amnon, one of King David's sons, sexually abused his half-sister Tamar. He pretended to be ill to lure Tamar into his room: "He took hold of her and said to her, 'Come, lie with me, my sister.' But she answered him, 'Don't, my brother, Don't force me. Such a thing should not be done in Israel! Don't do this wicked thing.' ...But he refused to listen to her, and since he was stronger than she, he raped her" (2 Samuel 13:11-12,14).

Tamar reported the incident to one of her other brothers, Absalom. In the margin read what Absalom said to his sister Tamar.

It seems that the pattern was no different for a dysfunctional family in biblical times than for a family in the present. The problem for victims is also the same—when they remain silent, they become desolate. Discussing your abuse does not mean getting up in church or another public place and announcing to everyone that you have been sexually abused. It does mean that you need to tell your story in a safe, supportive environment.

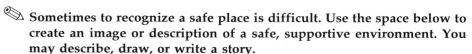 **Sometimes to recognize a safe place is difficult. Use the space below to create an image or description of a safe, supportive environment. You may describe, draw, or write a story.**

Carol described a safe place as, "Where I can cry and never run out of tissues. The room would be light blue with lots of pillows." We hope that your support group can be like that—a place where you can find rest and peace and relationships to cushion the harsh reality of abuse.

Abuse often leaves the victim without deep friendships and without hope.

When Samuel said Tamar remained in her brother's house and was desolate, he was saying she was forlorn and lonely, without friends or hope. Abuse often leaves the victim without deep friendships and without hope. Often the victim is forced into isolation, feeling friendless and in great despair.

✎ **Do you identify with Tamar? If you have felt isolated and in despair, below describe your feelings.**

_____

_____

_____

_____

One of the greatest needs of survivors of sexual abuse is to break through this isolation and to develop relationships. You need to experience "not feeling alone." Breaking out of isolation is difficult because it involves trust and openness. Discuss with your group what it feels like to you to think of developing relationships with others in the group.

✎ **Use this space to describe your feelings about developing relationships with others in the group. Describe both your positive and negative feelings.**

_____

_____

_____

_____

_____

Read the entire story of Tamar in 2 Samuel 13:1-20 from the Bible. After you have read the complete story, respond to the following learning activities based on the characters in the story.

Amnon became frustrated to the point of illness on account of his sister Tamar, for she was a virgin, and it seemed impossible for him to do anything to her.
–2 Samuel 13:2

✎ **What kind of attitude about himself and about human sexuality do you see reflected in Amnon's frustration over the situation with Tamar? Check all the responses that apply.**

❑ 1. He was self-centered, only interested in what he could do to her.
❑ 2. He considered Tamar as an object, not as a person.
❑ 3. He was angry because he was used to getting his way.
❑ 4. His idea of sexuality had nothing to do with emotional intimacy or genuine love.
❑ 5. Other _____

You could have chosen any or all of the responses about Amnon. Next Amnon followed the evil advice of his friend Jonadab. Amnon planned and prepared to rape Tamar. He pretended to be ill and asked David, who was his father and his half-sister Tamar's father, to send Tamar to care for him.

So Amnon lay down and pretended to be ill. When the king came to see him, Amnon said to him, "I would like my sister Tamar to come and make some special bread in my sight, so I may eat from her hand." David sent word to Tamar at the palace: "Go to the house of your brother Amnon and prepare some food for him."

–2 Samuel 13:6-7

✎ **Read the verses that appear in the margin. Not only did Amnon plan to rape Tamar, her father unknowingly but directly contributed to the rape. Check the response you think might best describe Tamar's feeling toward her father.**

❑ 1. Betrayed, "he set me up for this."
❑ 2. Angry, "this is his fault!"
❑ 3. Frightened, "I don't dare tell my father what happened."
❑ 4. Bewildered, "what can I do?"
❑ 5. Other _____

Describe your feelings about David in the story.

_____

_____

Remember that Tamar was not objectively reading these words on paper. She was experiencing the hurt and shame of sexual abuse. Whether or not David understood the consequences of his actions, the fact is that he contributed to her sexual abuse, and he did nothing to correct the situation after the rape. Tamar certainly could have felt all the feelings above and more.

Then [after the rape] Amnon hated her with intense hatred. In fact, he hated her more than he had loved her. Amnon said to her, "Get up and get out!" ... He called his personal servant and said, "Get this woman out of here and bolt the door after her."

–2 Samuel 13:15,17

Next notice in verse 15 that after the rape Amnon hated Tamar. He increased the violation by blaming her and sending her away. Still worse he called a servant—thereby assuring that others would blame her—and he had Tamar thrown out of the house.

✎ **Remember that you are not responsible for any part of the behavior of a person who abused you. Do not use this activity to excuse or to blame but simply to understand. Describe why you think Amnon suddenly hated Tamar.**

_____

_____

We cannot know another person's thoughts or motivations but one explanation seems probable. Amnon knew that what he had done was wrong. Rather than accept responsibility for himself, he shifted the blame to Tamar.

✎ **Have you experienced someone treating you like Amnon treated Tamar—first sexually abusing you and then blaming you for the abuse?** ❑ Yes ❑ No

If you responded yes, describe how it felt to be blamed.

_____

_____

"Be quiet now, my sister; he is your brother. Don't take this thing to heart."
–2 Samuel 13:20

The next injury for Tamar resulted after the rape. She went to her brother Absalom. Absalom's response was typical of many family members of sexual abuse victims. Absalom said: "Keep the secret." "Don't let anybody know about the family trouble." "Don't shame the family by talking about this."

✎ **Below write what you would like to say to Tamar instead of the dysfunctional messages she received from her family.**

_____

_____

We would like to make a number of statements to Tamar. We would like to tell her that she was not to blame and that she needed to talk about her feelings with some safe people. Tamar did not have the resources and opportunities that we have today.

⇨ **Spend a few minutes in prayer. If you can, thank God for providing you a safe group with which to share. Thank Him for recording the story of Tamar in Scripture so that you would know that you are not alone in the betrayal of sexual abuse. Honestly share your feelings with God. He will not respond as many people do. He will not say, "Don't take it to heart." God will listen and will patiently walk with you toward healing.**

God intends for you to walk in joy and peace, free from guilt and condemnation.

Working through these family issues is painful and will probably continue to be so for a while. If you feel desolate, betrayed, and alone, reach out to someone who can help you. Attend your *Shelter from the Storm* group regularly, even when it seems more difficult to go than to stay away. You need the support, and God wants you to overcome this tragedy in your life. God intends for you to walk in joy and peace, free from guilt and condemnation.

Unit Review

✎ **Look back over this unit. What statement or activity was most meaningful for you?**

_____

_____

✎ **Can you remember any statements or activities with which you were uncomfortable? Write those below.**

_____

_____

✎ **Write a prayer asking God to help you in your areas of struggle.**

_____

_____

UNIT 6

Letting Go of Shame and Guilt

This Unit's Affirmation:
I am wonderfully made.

Focal Passage

There is now no condemnation for those who are in Christ Jesus.

–Romans 8:1

"I FEEL GUILTY FOR JUST EXISTING."

Cathy described in a counseling session how ashamed she feels about her body. "It feels dirty. It is dirty. As soon as my Dad would get through with me, I would immediately take a shower, but I could still smell him, and I knew I had done something wrong. I felt bad. I felt guilty, as if someone were watching. I felt evil.

"Believe it or not, my pastor knew something wasn't right with me and my Dad. He turned us in. I mean, turned him in. The abuse stopped, but now it's ten years later and I still feel so much shame. I think I'll be OK and I'll get dressed up and ready to go out. Then suddenly a picture will flash in my mind of his sweaty body on top of mine, and I'll lose it. I'm totally devastated. I feel dirty and evil all over again. Sometimes I think that if I wouldn't have these flashbacks, I wouldn't feel so guilty. The truth is sometimes I feel ashamed for no reason. I feel guilty for just existing."

Growth goal

This week's goal

You will let go of feelings of shame and guilt related to the sexual abuse.

The Painful Emotion of Shame	A Further Look at Shame	The Weight of Guilt	The Damage of Secrecy	The Potter's Hand
Lesson 1	Lesson 2	Lesson 3	Lesson 4	Lesson 5

Memory verse

This week's passage of Scripture to memorize

There is now no condemnation for those who are in Christ Jesus.

–Romans 8:1

LESSON 1

The Painful Emotion of Shame

Every victim of sexual abuse needs to recover from the shame and the guilt that result from the experience. Shame is the feeling of humiliating disgrace of having been violated. Shame tells you that you are bad. Guilt is the feeling that you did something wrong. You may carry a false sense of guilt caused by the burden of knowing some great offense was committed and the belief that you must be responsible. In the process of recovery, victims must let go of the shame and recognize that both the responsibility and the guilt belong to the person who committed the offense.

Cathy described in a counseling session how ashamed she felt about her body. "It feels dirty. It *is* dirty. As soon as my Dad would get through with me, I would immediately take a shower, but I could still smell him, and I knew I had done something wrong. I felt bad. I felt guilty, as if someone were watching. I felt evil.

"Believe it or not, my pastor knew something wasn't right with me and my Dad. He turned us in. I mean, turned my Dad in. It stopped, but now it's ten years later and I still feel so much shame. I think I'll be OK and I'll get dressed up and ready to go out. Then suddenly a picture will flash in my mind of his sweaty body on top of mine, and I'll lose it. I'm totally devastated. I feel dirty and evil all over again. Sometimes I think that if I wouldn't have these flashbacks, I wouldn't feel so guilty. The truth is sometimes I feel ashamed for no reason. I feel guilty for just existing."

✎ **Describe the difference between guilt and shame.**

_____

_____

_____

Shame is about personhood. It is related to lie #2 in unit 3—*I must be a terrible person for him/her to do this to me!* Guilt is about behavior. It is related to lie #1 in unit 3—*It's my fault!* Remember John 8:32, "You will know the truth and the truth will set you free." You are not a terrible person and the abuse was not your fault.

Shame invades both the mind and the body

First let's look at shame as it appears in the lives of victims. This very painful emotion invades both the mind and body of the victim. It is planted in guilt, nourished by memories, and watered by secrecy. "I know you tell me," Cathy continues, "that now that I no longer keep everything inside, I will get better. But it's been a secret so long I am afraid to tell! Listen to me! (She was starting to whisper.) I'll try to tell you everything I can remember, I promise… but not today." Later Cathy does go on to tell her story, again and then again. First she discloses it in individual sessions and then in a sexual abuse group. For Cathy, and for every victim of sexual abuse, telling the story is one of the most important and necessary events in achieving recovery.

Shame is planted in the soil of guilt, nourished by memories, and watered by secrecy!

Just like Cathy, you may begin to talk in a whisper as you speak about your experience of abuse. Choosing to tell someone about your abuse is perhaps the most difficult challenge of the entire recovery process. Many of you have been threatened emotionally and physically that you are never to tell a word about what has happened.

Many victims have been shamed into believing that if they tell, terrible things would happen to them or to someone close to them, perhaps their mother or sister. They had to hear such things as, "Everyone will know this is your fault," "Everyone will be mad at you," or "Mother will leave if she finds out." The threatening statements that some of survivors have been led to believe go on and on.

✎ **Compare your feelings about talking about your abuse with Cathy's feelings. Complete the sentence: "When I talk about it, I...**

- ❑ whisper
- ❑ talk faster
- ❑ hug a pillow
- ❑ close my eyes
- ❑ curl up in a ball
- ❑ other _____

What were you told would happen if you shared your story? If you don't remember, describe how you feel about not remembering. What did you think would happen?

_____

_____

_____

Talking about the abuse is difficult for all survivors. It may be more difficult for some than others in your group. Each survivor remembers as much as he or she needs to at each point along the recovery journey. Let God put each memory in its place and in its proper time. Remember to let yourself be "where you are." Seek to accept yourself as a person in process. You are growing and changing. Give yourself time. Comparing yourself in a negative way with others will hinder your recovery.

Assignment for the lesson

There is now no condemnation for those who are in Christ Jesus.
                                    –Romans 8:1

✎ **Write your own paraphrase of Romans 8:1, this unit's Scripture memory verse.**

_____

_____

↪ **Say aloud these affirmations five times.**

I accept God's love and kindness toward me.
The truth will set me free!

I am worthy to have God lead me and comfort me.
I am clean.
I am wonderfully made.

➥ **Ask God to strengthen and guide you in this phase of your recovery.**

LESSON 2

A Further Look at Shame

Webster's dictionary defines shame as "a painful emotion excited by a consciousness of guilt, shortcoming, or impropriety; disgrace, dishonor." The Hebrew concept of disgrace includes the idea of being uncovered physically, particularly the genital area; it can also refer to having one's plans and expectations frustrated or disappointed. Both definitions apply to the effects of sexual abuse.

Any form of sexual molestation, rape, or abuse transfers to the victim the disgrace of the abuser. Sexual abuse creates shame in the victim. Often when victims tell about their abuse, their listeners add to the feeling of shame because the listeners have distorted ideas about abuse. They say things like: "Why didn't you do something?" "I knew someone had you before we got married!" "You coulda done something!" "It went on so long, you must have gotten something out of it." You need to protect yourself as much as possible from such responses. You may need to review Unit 1 which contains material to help you educate your listeners.

Shame is a natural response to feeling uncovered or exposed.

Shame is a natural response to feeling uncovered or exposed. During the abuse your body was probably uncovered, but there was also the uncovering of your mind. Your sense of innocence was destroyed and trust was lost. Innocence and trust must be restored. Survivors of abuse are left with frustrated hopes and plans. Dreams for having a healthy relationship with a father, a mate, a mother, a brother, or a child have been demolished. The abuse leaves victims believing that they are insignificant, of no account, no good. As you become aware of and overcome shame messages, these messages will have less power over you.

✎ **Below write the following statements three times.**

I am significant.

_____

_____

_____

I do count.

_____

_____

_____

I am worthwhile.

_____

_____

_____

This exercise may feel uncomfortable at first but eventually you will be able to feel significant, that you do count, and that you are worthwhile.

The shame message of sexual abuse springs from three major areas: 1. the actions of the abuser, 2. the response from your own body, and 3. verbal and nonverbal messages from others.

The Message of the Abuser

The deliverer of the first of these messages is the person who abused you who says, "What I want goes, and what is best for you is of no concern to me." These and all other messages that convey worthlessness are shame messages. You must begin the difficult work of identifying the shame messages from the persons who abused you and the persons who aided them by ignoring or covering up their actions.

An adult female victim tells her story of abuse. "I was eight years old when the abuse stopped. I'm not sure when it started. It stopped because my mom and stepdad got a divorce. I never fought, I never did anything when he would hold me close to him. I never did anything when he touched me except freeze and hope it would be over soon. I just felt bad. From the way people looked at me, I was sure everyone knew, and it made me feel guilty and useless. It happened again later with my stepmother, when I was a teenager. She said she was putting medicine on me. I would look away, down at the floor, sighing in hopes that she would stop touching me.

"I didn't know how to stop it. I couldn't tell anyone about my stepmother; it was just too bad. I told a pastor about my stepdad. What a joke that pastor was. He said, 'Don't you understand that your stepfather felt lonely and sad during the divorce and all he wanted was some affection?' Well, of course, I agreed. But after that, I felt even more shame than before. I never told anyone else, that is, until now. But I am 48 now, and there are a lot of wasted years. I wish I would have known to tell and to keep telling until I found someone who would listen and believe me."

The wisdom of God can remove the shame imposed by the abuse message. You can learn to speak God's Word about yourself, not the damaging words of the person who abused you.

🖉 **In the margin read what the apostle Paul wrote about God's message. Below check the purpose God has intended for us according to the passage. God intends His secret wisdom—**

❏ to shame us
❏ to make us feel inadequate
❏ for our good

"We do, however, speak a message of wisdom among the mature, but not the wisdom of this age or of the rulers of this age, who are coming to nothing. No, we speak of God's secret wisdom, a wisdom that has been hidden and that God destined for our glory before time began."
–1 Corinthians 2:6-7

Learn to believe and give thanks to God. He wants us to experience His goodness, not to expose our shame.

✎ **Read Psalm 139:14 appearing in the margin. How did the psalmist say you were made?**

_____

_____

The psalmist says that you were fearfully and wonderfully made. Do not allow us or anyone else to tell you how you feel, but you can learn to challenge your own thinking and thus to change your own feelings.

✎ **As your own decision to change your thoughts about yourself, please write three times below _I am fearfully and wonderfully made._**

_____

_____

_____

God does not intend for you to feel shame!

✎ **Below write any shame messages that the person or persons who abused you said to you.**

_____

_____

_____

_____

_____

For each shame message write a response that declares that these messages are not true!

_____

_____

_____

_____

Suzanne, a victim of date rape, was told by her date that he could tell by the way she dressed that "she wanted it." He said, "You knew I thought that red dress was sexy." Suzanne had heard others say that he really liked her red dress. She did want to look nice for their date, but she did not wear it to

I praise you because I am fearfully and wonderfully made; your works are wonderful, I know that full well.

–Psalm 139:14

seduce him. Red went well with Suzanne's dark hair. When Allen turned down a dark side street she told him she wanted to go home. She was in an unfamiliar neighborhood, and when he stopped, she was afraid to get out of the car and afraid to stay.

The Message from Your Own Body

A second area of shame has to do with feelings about your body or body parts. Many victims see themselves as fat and ugly. Some purposely get fat or take little care of themselves in order to ward off further abuse. Some focus on a particular body part that they hate. Some are consumed with self-hatred.

✎ **Below describe your feelings about your body. Do you particularly feel repulsed by or ashamed of part(s) of your body?**

_____

_____

_____

_____

Twelve-year-old Kimberly tells her mother that she hates her body, all except her breasts. She likes starting to develop, but she feels bad about it for some reason. When Kimberly was raped, her breasts had not yet developed so her abuser did not touch that part of her. Because of this, Kimberly does not feel shame toward her breasts, but she still feels confused. In many victims, sexual abuse develops a self-hate toward their body parts. Some victims hate to have certain or all parts of their bodies stimulated—even by their mates.

Verbal Messages from Others

A third area of shame can occur even without physical sexual abuse having taken place. Children—and adults, too—can be shamed by statements like "You can't do anything right," "You're stupid," or "You can't be my child." Being neglected also brings about shame. For example, if no one was ever home for you or cooked a meal for you, or acted as though they didn't want you around, you probably felt insignificant and worthless.

Do not conform any longer to the pattern of this world, but be transformed by the renewing of your mind [do not believe the message of shame, but rather God's wisdom]. Then you will be able to test and approve what God's will is—his good, pleasing and perfect will.
 –Romans 12:2

Jesus can transform this hate toward the body or toward the mind, as Paul points out in Romans 12:2. The verse helps us begin to understand that as Christ works healing, the abuse will no longer continue to haunt us.

✎ **Write a prayer, asking God to remove feelings of hatred toward your body and to replace them with realistic true feelings about yourself.**

_____

_____

_____

One woman wrote the following prayer, "Dear God, I am 40 pounds overweight. I accept that and know I need to change that. I will not feel shame about it anymore. I will stop putting myself down by saying I am fat."

If the message from any of these areas produces shame and condemnation, it is a false message. God plans to restore you to the truth. Each memory, each thought, each negative message touched by God's restorative power overcomes the marring effects of sexual abuse. When you allow God to restore your soul from the effects of shame and guilt concerning your abuse, you can begin to embrace what God has already said: you are acceptabl. (see Hebrews 10:14).

Assignment for the lesson

✎ **Write on a card Romans 8:1, the memory verse for this unit. Carry the card with you and regularly review the verses.**

↪ **Say aloud these affirmations five times.**

I accept God's love and kindness toward me.
The truth will set me free!
I am worthy to have God lead me and comfort me.
I am clean.
I am wonderfully made.

↪ **Pray for each member of your group.**

There is now no condemnation for those who are in Christ Jesus.
–Romans 8:1

LESSON
3

The Heaviness of Guilt

Sexual abuse produces strong feelings of guilt and inadequacy. Whether you are a victim of child sexual abuse or a victim of rape, you may have received messages like, "You are not worth as much as I am. My needs are more important than yours." At the time of the abuse, you the victim, are helpless. You cannot do anything to stop what is happening to you. Even though you cannot stop the abuse, you feel responsible because it is happening to you, not to someone else. The experience powerfully reinforces any feelings of inadequacy you already have fixed in your mind.

Gloria, a beautiful young woman, describes how she uses guilt to help her get things done with two small children and an ambitious husband. Clearly the cost of this kind of motivation is destructively high.

"I have a lot to do without much help at home. So whenever I get behind on things and feel depressed, I deliberately think about my abuse. I begin to feel sick and useless about myself. Then when I really need a boost of guilt, I begin to remember all the guys I slept with, and I start to cry and feel really bad. But it works, and I get everything done. It's like I punish myself and the penalty is to work real hard. I know, though, that the reason I am here and the reason I come to this group is that I hope it will help my children. Also, my husband makes me feel guilty about everything.

"I know now that this is because I am so good at feeling guilty. In fact, I'm better than anybody at doing that. I realize that while using this guilt on myself makes me get things done, it also makes me feel really sad. The reason I beat myself over the head is because most of the time I just lie around and do nothing. I just don't have any energy. I guess I am depressed."

The Joy of Objectivity

Guilt often produces anger turned inward, which can lead to depression, as it did for Gloria. This is only one of guilt's devastating effects on victims. To combat those effects, we urge you to begin by examining the areas of life where you feel guilty. To effectively examine our areas of guilt is often difficult because sexual abuse robs us of our objectivity and leaves us feeling guilty about almost everything, even though there is no basis for doing so.

✎ **List several things that you frequently feel guilty about.**

_____

_____

_____

Review your list. Place a checkmark beside those items that represent attitudes and behaviors that were your responsibility. Draw a line through those that are feelings of false guilt—items that are someone else's responsibility. Place a question mark beside those that you are unsure about.

Remember that you were the victim of a crime. Many adult victims and most child victims never make a sound while they are being subjected to abuse. They are frozen and unable emotionally to deal with the victimization. People are victims when they are unable to stop what is being done to them.

The Danger of Denial

Beware of the universal reaction of denial. Don was a bicyclist whose ambition was to ride a "double century." A "double century" ride is 200 miles in 24 hours. Don entered a ride that consisted of four 50-mile courses. He rode the first hundred miles and was near exhaustion. He was only able to complete the third 50-mile loop about midnight by pushing his bike the last few miles. Don did not attempt to ride the final 50 miles. Instead he drove home, fell into bed, and was unable to walk the next day. That experience was 20 years ago, and Don still blames himself for not completing the 200 miles. He continues to blame and condemn himself with statements like, *I had eight hours left and I only had 50 more miles to go, why did I quit? I could have finished the ride. I'm a wimp and a failure.*

✎ **Compare Don's story with the millions of times when a child or an adult is sexually victimized by someone who is older, stronger, or more intimidating and then the victim thinks, *Why didn't I _____* (you fill in the blank: *make them stop, run away, scream, tell someone ...*). In the margin describe what is wrong with both Don's thinking and with the sexual abuse victim's thinking.**

The trouble with denial-based thinking...
_____
_____
_____
_____
_____

You may have explained the problem in one of many ways. The problem is denial. Don exhibits irrational thinking over something as simple as a goal he could not reach. In the same way those of us who have suffered sexual abuse continue to blame ourselves and to think we should have done something differently. The feelings of guilt spread to every area of our lives. These feelings grow from our unrealistic expectations of ourselves. To feel guilty is easier than to accept the fact that we were powerless. Don did not have the power to ride one more mile. We did not have the power to stop the abuse.

✎ **How have you practiced denial by blaming and punishing yourself?**

_____

_____

_____

_____

One victim is now able to laugh at herself as she describes her feelings of guilt. "First I feel that I am not doing enough for God; then I feel guilty about my husband. Next I overwhelm myself with guilt feelings about my children. Then come my parents. Finally I get to my dog and feel guilty because I don't spend enough time with her. After that I watch some talk shows and end up looking in the mirror and trying to forgive myself for not taking care of me."

We need to be objective about our guilt feelings.

As humorous as this story might seem, it illustrates how we need to be objective about our guilt feelings if we are to make progress. Examining our thoughts helps us to see if God is convicting us to change areas in our lives. Healthy guilt points out the areas where we need to make a change. This kind of guilt leads to a change of heart which the Bible calls repentance. In Romans 2:4 Paul says that the goodness of God leads us to repentance. If we allow God to overcome our thoughts of guilt, both real and false, the path of freedom more than rewards us for the effort.

↪ **Read your list of guilt feelings again. Spend some time praying about the feelings on your list. Ask God to help you to let go of false guilt and to accept forgiveness for any behaviors and attitudes that are harmful to you and others.**

Assignment for the lesson

✎ **Below write the unit's Scripture verse from memory. To check your work refer to page 92.**

↪ **Say aloud these affirmations five times.**

I accept God's love and kindness toward me.
The truth will set me free!
I am worthy to have God lead me and comfort me.
I am clean.
I am wonderfully made.

↪ **Pray for yourself and each member of your group.**

LESSON 4

The Damage of Secrecy

Secrecy gives shame and guilt the power to torment you. Secrecy isolates you within your own mind. It can cause you to believe that you are the only one experiencing such devastating trauma. We spoke earlier of shame being like a plant whose existence depends on water. People, like plants, must have water to survive. A human can live for many days without food, but only three days without water. To use that metaphor in another way, secrecy is the water that the memories of the abuse depend on for their life.

✎ **Describe your life of secrecy during the victimization and/or your life of secrecy after the victimization. How does it feel to have a secret life?**

_____

_____

_____

Destroying the Strength of Harmful Memories

As you tell your story—in a safe environment with a pastor, counselor, or support group—you will dilute and destroy the strength of the memories of the abuse. By telling the story you destroy the power of shame and guilt. By telling the story you gain power and control over the memories. In our analogy, the memories are the nourishment of the guilt. The kind of toxic guilt and shame experienced in sexual abuse leads to feelings of condemnation.

There is now no condemnation for those who are in Christ Jesus.
–Romans 8:1

You are working to memorize Romans 8:1. Reciting this Scripture is not enough. Begin to move its wisdom from your head to your heart. Do this by quoting the Scripture, then writing a note to yourself every time a shame memory flashes across your mind. Determine in your heart to tell this memory to someone. As you apply the Scripture and break the silence, you will create an environment to neutralize the tendency for flashbacks. You may remember a new circumstance or incident. God will remove the obstacles blocking your memories and allow you to remember as necessary so that you can experience healing. When your memories cause you to feel shame, quote Romans 8:1 to remind yourself that there is no condemnation, no shame, or worthlessness. The memories can be just memories, without shame and guilt.

If you have not already done so, we would encourage you to begin writing your story when you are with a supportive person in a safe place. You need time alone to do your recovery work, but beware of isolating yourself. You need the presence and encouragement of others.

First review your affirmations:

> I accept God's love and kindness toward me.
> The truth will set me free!
> I am worthy to have God lead me and comfort me.
> I am clean.
> I am wonderfully made.

Quote your memory verse for this unit and any other Scriptures that have been meaningful to you.

✎ **Write down as many details as you can about one incident of sexual abuse. Write as though you were a reporter, answering the questions— who, what, when, where. Use additional pages as needed or write in a separate journal. For the sake of confidentiality you may want to write in a separate journal, following this format.**

Who

_____

_____

What

_____

_____

_____

_____

_____

_____

When

_____

_____

_____

_____

Where

_____

_____

_____

_____

Thank God for walking with you through this process.

If you could only write one sentence, celebrate your ability to do that. Go for a walk, take a bubble bath, or listen to your favorite tape. It will get easier! For now read your affirmations again and thank God for walking with you through this process. You will make it!

Assignment for the lesson

 In the margin write the Scripture verse for this unit from memory.

 Say aloud these affirmations five times.

> I accept God's love and kindness toward me.
> The truth will set me free!
> I am worthy to have God lead me and comfort me.
> I am clean.
> I am wonderfully made.

Pray for each member of your *Shelter from the Storm* group.

The Potter's Hand

The Book of Jeremiah records an important story that applies to sexual abuse. God sent Jeremiah to observe a potter at work. The potter was making a pot, but he discovered a flaw. Possibly the potter allowed his hand to slip, knocking the pot off center on the wheel. At any rate, the pot was damaged. So the potter remade the pot into another vessel. Read Jeremiah 18:4 that appears in the margin.

Just as a pot can be damaged by the action of the potter, sexual abuse victims have been marred by the actions of abusers. The abuser shapes a vessel that is full of shame, guilt, fear, and despair.

Then God spoke to Jeremiah and gave the second half of the picture. He said,

> "O house of Israel, can I not do with you as this potter does?" declares the Lord. "Like clay in the hand of the potter, so are you in My hand, O house of Israel."
>
> –Jeremiah 18:6

When a pot has been damaged, the potter does not throw away the clay. The potter reuses and reshapes the clay into a new vessel. God said that just as the potter can use the damaged clay, He can make something beautiful from the ruins of our lives. Contrast Jeremiah 18:4 and a passage that you have read previously. Psalm 139:14 states, "I praise you because I am fearfully and wonderfully made; your works are wonderful, I know that full well."

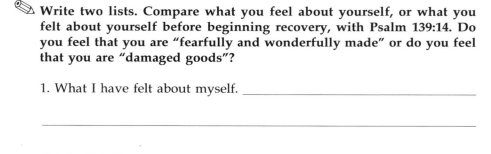 Write two lists. Compare what you feel about yourself, or what you felt about yourself before beginning recovery, with Psalm 139:14. Do you feel that you are "fearfully and wonderfully made" or do you feel that you are "damaged goods"?

1. What I have felt about myself. _____

_____

_____

LESSON 5

But the pot he was shaping from the clay was marred in his hands; so the potter formed it into another pot, shaping it as seemed best to him.

–Jeremiah 18:4

2. What the Scripture says about me. _____

_____

_____

People injure us when they abuse us, but God is the true Potter who takes the damaged clay and makes it into a beautiful vase. Let God make you aware that you were created to be a vase full of life, full of value, full of worth. You can recover as you allow God to remake you according to His plan.

Leave Your Burden with the Perpetrator

Shame and guilt are both tremendously destructive. To restore your life, you may need to forgive yourself for your own sinful choices. Please do it. Be cautious, however, to leave the shame and responsibility of sexual abuse with the person who abused you. Most of us felt the need to seek God's forgiveness for our abuse as well as from choices that we had made based on our faulty thinking. For us to ask for and accept God's forgiveness for our wrong choices is appropriate. For us to seek forgiveness for what others have done to us is fruitless. You need not seek forgiveness for someone else's actions.

✎ **In the paragraph above you read about two kinds of forgiveness most of us feel a need to seek. From your life experience name at least one example of each.**

1. An example of my abuse (for which I do not need to be forgiven is)

_____

_____

2. An example of a bad choice I made based on my wrong thinking is

_____

_____

Many of us are accomplished self-guilt artists. For the first response you may have listed any of the actions of your abuser or of those people who aggravated the abuse by their actions or their inaction. For the second response many of us have made wrong choices in dating or other relationships. We sometimes have been vindictive, or critical, or defensive. We need forgiveness for our choices. Read the words of the psalmist that appear in the margin.

For you, Oh Lord, are good and ready to forgive [our trespasses–sending them away, letting them go completely and forever], and you are abundant in mercy and lovely riches to all those who call upon you.

–Psalm 86:5, Amplified

✎ **Below, as an act of faith, please write, "I thank You, Lord Jesus for your willingness to forgive my sins by sending them away, letting them go completely and forever."**

_____

_____

_____

You are the victim of another person's sin. If you had been shot by a bank robber and you had been paralyzed for life you would be a victim of that person's crime and sin. There would be no reason for shame or guilt on your part.

Many times we feel false guilt because we think our actions caused the abuse. Sometimes the fact that we have made bad choices adds to the problem. In the case of the bank robbery, suppose you had slipped away from the office during working hours, against company policy, to cash a check. You would be guilty of violating company rules but not of wanting to be shot!

✎ If some negligence or action on your part contributed to your sexual abuse, describe that negligence or action.

_____

_____

_____

Did you, by that action or inaction, desire to be sexually abused?
❑ Yes ❑ No

Did you commit the crime by sexually abusing yourself or did someone else commit the abuse? (Yes, the question seems ridiculous.)

❑ I did it.
❑ The perpetrator did it.

God forgives lavishly and freely.

If you committed some indiscretion—whether great or small in your eyes—confess that action or negligence. God forgives lavishly and freely. But just as in the example of the person who was shot during the bank robbery, leave the perpetrator's guilt with the perpetrator, and leave any guilt that belongs to the enablers or co-perpetrators with them.

Exercises for forgiveness

Because we so frequently carry a load of guilt, some of it appropriate but most of it false, we usually need to work through our guilt issues. The following exercises will help you to sort out the appropriate and the inappropriate guilt surrounding your abuse.

✎ **Describe anything surrounding your abuse about which you need to feel forgiven.**

_____

_____

Carolyn was only five years old when her parents left her alone and told her not to leave the house. She was afraid, so she walked down the street to her uncle's home. Her uncle sexually abused Carolyn. For the next 40 years Carolyn blamed herself for the abuse. She believed that, because she disobeyed her parents, she was to blame for the abuse.

Perhaps you have been carrying a weight of guilt and anger toward yourself for being drunk, disobeying your parents, or just using poor judgment about where to be. None of these mean you were responsible for the abuse. However, you may need to ask God to forgive you and you may need to forgive yourself for your poor judgment before you can continue to recover.

 Describe any choices that you have made based on faulty thinking as a result of the abuse.

_____

_____

_____

_____

You may have described your difficulty relating to authority figures because of an abusive parent, or the consequences in your life caused by maintaining the secret. You may have made poor choices as a result of poor boundaries. Many survivors become sexually promiscuous as a result of the abuse. One woman in recovery reported that she just recently had her first date ever that did not end in bed. She said she simply did not know she had the right to say no to sexual advances. Blaming ourselves for our poor choices will not help, but we do need to ask and accept forgiveness so we can move forward with our lives.

They sinned against Me: I will change their glory into shame.

–Hosea 4:7

In the Old Testament we find that people suffered the consequences of the sins of others as we do today. God, however, responds with a plan to redeem the victim of abuse. In the margin read what God said in Hosea 4:7 about the priests who were abusing their office and the people. They were haughty and proud, but God promised to place the shame where it belonged—with the abuser rather than the victims. The sexual abuser sins not only against the victim, but also against God. The shame belongs to the person who committed the abuse.

 In Isaiah 54:4, God speaks to His people using the imagery of a barren woman. What He says speaks to the victim of sexual abuse as well. Circle any word or phrase that gives you hope.

"Fear not, for you will not be put to shame;
Neither feel humiliated, for you will not be disgraced;
But you will forget the shame of your youth,
And the reproach of your widowhood you will remember no more.

"For your husband is your Maker,
Whose name is the Lord of hosts;
And your Redeemer is the Holy One of Israel,
Who is called the God of all the earth.
"For the Lord has called you…" (Isaiah 54:4-6, NASB).

Give yourself and God the time to complete the good work He has started in you. This is a very difficult and painful part of your recovery. It may take a long time. But please try to remember that even in the valley, God is with you. He will redeem the time. You can draw strength from God's promises in

Isaiah 54:4, "fear not for you will not be put to shame ... humiliated ... [or] disgraced ... you will forget the shame of your youth."

✎ Complete the following sentences, keeping in mind that God sees you from a different perspective than you see yourself right now. Let God redefine how you see yourself. If necessary, review this unit and your work thus far in *Shelter*. We have completed the first sentence as an example.

For the Lord has called me *to be His beloved child.*

In the Lord's eyes I am _____

_____

For the Lord has called me _____

_____

In the Lord's eyes I am _____

_____

For the Lord has called me _____

_____

In the Lord's eyes I am _____

_____

We pray that you were able to include words like *beautifully and wonderfully made, His daughter/son, clean, worthy of love, to be healed, to be free from shame and guilt.*

Unit Review   ✎ **Review this unit. What statement or activity was most meaningful for you?**

_____

_____

✎ **Can you remember any statements or activities with which you were uncomfortable? Write those below.**

_____

_____

✎ **Write a prayer asking God to help you in your areas of struggle.**

_____

_____

_____

UNIT 7

Feeling the Anger and Hurt

This Unit's Affirmation:
I have permission to feel my anger and hurt.

Focal Passage
Be angry and yet do not sin.

–Ephesians 4:26, NASB

ANGRY AT MYSELF

A young woman who had been a child victim of sexual abuse described how rejected and humiliated she felt as a young girl when the police came to her house. She said, "I had been walking home from school when a man approached who said he would give me candy. I never got candy, even though I went to the woods with him. He raped me. I was so sore, and blood was all over me. He tore my dress. A woman had seen me go with him, but it was over so quickly. My mother got real mad at me and kept saying, 'How could you be so stupid as to go anywhere with a stranger?' With that statement, my mother gave me a good weapon to punish myself. I was so confused. I didn't think anything could feel worse than what he did to me, but this was worse. I thought, *She's right, my mom's right. Why did I go into the woods? I was stupid. I hate myself.*"

In this unit you will examine anger and hurt in the life of survivors.

Growth goal

This week's goal
You will acknowledge your anger and begin to learn methods for expressing your anger in appropriate and non-destructive ways.

Healthy Expressions of Anger	A Healthy Expression of Anger, Part Two	The Danger in Denial	But I'm Angry at God	The Message of a Nail Print
Lesson 1	Lesson 2	Lesson 3	Lesson 4	Lesson 5

Memory verse

This week's passage of Scripture to memorize
Be angry, and yet do not sin.

–Ephesians 4:26, NASB

LESSON 1

Healthy Expressions of Anger

Sara, a 25-year-old woman, was expressing her feelings in a sexual abuse group. "I am angry at my brothers! I am angry at anyone who looks like my brothers! I am just angry!" For eight years Sara had been tormented by her brothers. She had been held down, tied up, and forced to imitate pornographic material. She described many humiliating and vicious acts perpetrated against her. Sara had begged her parents for help, but they ignored her pleas. She is very angry about what happened to her as a child.

Almost everyone would acknowledge the right of the victim to be angry about being abused. Yet many people feel uncomfortable allowing survivors the right to express their anger. All victims have anger and need to learn to express it appropriately—whether or not the person who committed the abuse, those who enabled the abuse, the church, or the world might be offended by the victim's anger.

As a general rule, expressing anger appropriately does not mean blowing up or throwing things. It never involves using any form of violence. In fact, these methods do not work and can become addictive behaviors leading to more emotional pain.

Most of the time expressing your anger appropriately means acknowledging, accepting, and expressing your anger in a mature and controlled manner. Sometimes recovery from abuse requires more intense expressions of anger and rage than would, in most situations, seem appropriate. You will learn some ways of channeling these intense feelings in your *Shelter* group. You can also ask your therapist to help you express and release these intense feelings.

✎ **In the list below circle words or phrases that describe how you typically express your anger. In the margin write any additional ways you express anger.**

❑ Throw things   ❑ Run
❑ Yell   ❑ Curse
❑ Stuff it inside   ❑ Control people
❑ Write   ❑ Control circumstances
❑ Talk it out   ❑ Be a perfectionist
❑ Slam doors   ❑ Be nice

Writing and talking out anger will help you to clarify your feelings.

Some of the responses above are more helpful than others. Writing and talking out anger will help you to clarify your feelings. Sometimes yelling, throwing things, and slamming doors does release some built-up tension. However, others may be in your path so be careful to determine whether your anger is being destructive to yourself or to others. You may not even realize when you are using behaviors such as controlling and perfectionism.

A Preliminary Word of Caution

Before you proceed with the main focus of this unit, consider this caution: If you cannot use restraint in expressing your anger and you may harm others or yourself, immediately seek the help of a professional. A qualified Christian counselor can help you to explore the factors that make it difficult for you to deal with anger constructively. Lack of proper rest, physical problems, improper diet, depression, or being overwhelmed by memories of abuse can all impair your ability to cope with anger.

If you are prone to outbursts, you may find it helpful to meditate on Galatians 5 and the Book of Proverbs. Try to recognize any behavior patterns in yourself that you learned from being around angry people. For example, if you had an explosive parent, you may be imitating his or her uncontrollable temper. If you get "too angry," you can delay your response to the source of your anger and remove yourself from the circumstances until you have received professional counseling.

✎ **Below write a description of your behavior the last time you were very angry.**

_____

_____

_____

_____

Be honest with yourself about your anger. If you need to seek help to control your anger see your group leader or your counselor.

✎ **Do you need professional help to deal with your anger? Why or why not?**

_____

_____

_____

Jane realized that she was taking out her anger on her husband and her children. She felt sad as she realized that she was building a wall between herself and her family. She determined to focus her anger where it belonged. She began a feelings journal and started talking about her anger with her support group.

Give Yourself Permission to Be Angry

Anger always will be expressed in some way. Either you express it appropriately or it seeps out in ways that damage you and others. Let's look at the need to give yourself permission to be angry. Some of you may laugh at this idea because you consider yourself an angry person, or others consider you an angry person. You may say, "I don't have any trouble being angry." The challenge lies in allowing yourself to give appropriate outward expression to the inner anger you feel toward those who abused you and those who made it possible for them to abuse you. Taking out your anger on yourself or on others who are not involved is not appropriate. Some of you shut down your anger a long time ago, and you wonder what it's like to feel angry.

Taking out your anger on yourself or on others who are not involved is not appropriate.

At the end of this section you have the chance to make a list of everyone with whom you are angry. This list should include everyone from the actual people who abused you to all the people who allowed the abuse. People who enabled the abuse—sometimes called co-perpetrators—include everyone who, by what they did, or what they didn't do, allowed the abuse to happen or to continue. Those who enable abuse can include parents, siblings, teachers, pastors, and protective services. You may also need to consider your anger toward the legal system and even toward God.

The role of the legal system is particularly important if you were molested as a child. For example, many states require children as young as five years old to testify in front of their abusers. Victims who have experienced these types of circumstances have a great deal of anger about the way the legal system re-victimized them.

A 36-year-old woman described the experience of reporting her second rape by the same man. She had not reported the first assault because she thought it would be better if no one knew, including her husband and family. But when she was raped a second time, she chose to tell her family and the police. Instead of help, however, she incurred accusations from them and eventually was encouraged by them to drop the charges.

Virtually every victim feels great anger toward God.

Because of the deep hurt and anger involved, do not leave out any person, system, or organization when you make your list of abusers and enablers. Don't be afraid to include God in your list. Virtually every victim feels great anger toward God. Later in this unit you will explore the issue of anger toward God. Cindy was so angry with God that she left the church for a few years and made a decision to be an atheist. Last, but certainly not least, make sure you include yourself. You probably have been beating yourself over the head for years anyway, so put yourself on the list. Take plenty of time and allow God to reveal everyone toward whom you feel anger. Don't misdirect that anger toward those not involved or toward yourself alone.

✎ **Make a list of every person who abused you, every person who enabled the abuse, and every organization or system that you feel has hurt you, let you down, or toward which you feel anger. You may choose to use coded responses rather than names, or to complete the exercise on separate paper.**

Abusers	Enablers	Organizations
_____	_____	_____
_____	_____	_____
_____	_____	_____
_____	_____	_____
_____	_____	_____

✎ **In the margin list the people toward whom you feel angry because they didn't understand your pain or support you when they learned about the abuse.**

Your list needs to include your abuser or abusers and others who enabled the abuse. You may have also included friends, relatives, and others who knew you at the time of the abuse. Most people also experience anger at God. Review your list and add any people or organizations necessary.

Assignment for the lesson

✎ **Write your own paraphrase of Ephesians 4:26, this unit's Scripture memory verse.**

_____

_____

☛ **Say aloud your affirmations. You may wish to repeat those you have been using only once. Repeat the new affirmation five times.**

I accept God's love and kindness toward me.
The truth will set me free!
I am worthy to have God lead me and comfort me.
I am clean.
I am wonderfully made.
I have permission to feel my anger and hurt.

☛ **Pray for yourself and for each member of your _Shelter from the Storm_ group.**

Be angry, and yet do not sin.
–Ephesians 4:26, NASB

LESSON 2

Healthy Anger, Part 2

Anger is a part of God's nature. The New Testament records that Jesus expressed anger on several occasions. We can conclude that anger in itself is not bad, but unresolved anger becomes destructive. Unresolved anger inevitably causes us inner turmoil. The Bible says in Ephesians 4:26, "Be angry, and yet do not sin" (NASB). Most of us know how to be angry, but what we need to learn is how to be angry without sinning.

✎ **Fill in the blank of the following statement.**

Anger is a part of _____ nature.

How do you feel about that statement? What effect does the fact that anger is a part of God's nature have on your recovery?

_____

_____

Anger is a signal that God has given us.

Anger is a signal that God has given us, just as pain is a signal. Anger tells us that we are being hurt, that something is wrong, or perhaps that someone is demanding too much. Sometimes our anger becomes generalized and we

To remove the anger,
you need to acknowledge it.

use it as a defense. When you understand the simple dynamics of anger, you see that, as a survivor of abuse, you have been deeply hurt. Anger would be a natural response. To remove that anger, you need to acknowledge it. Hurt may be a residual emotion that you feel even after you have dealt with the anger. You may express your anger in sudden outbursts, or you may reveal it in passive ways such as isolation or depression. If you have displayed your anger in unproductive ways, you will probably retain that anger until you can learn how to release it positively, and use it to find out more about yourself instead of lashing out against yourself and others.

Anger is a surface emotion. Underneath the anger you will usually find other feelings that also need expression.

✎ **Circle the feeling word below that creates the greatest emotional response.**

- Hurt
- Rejection
- Shame
- Used
- Humiliation
- Alone
- Unimportant

You may be using your anger to protect yourself from feeling humiliated, used, or hurt. To feel anger is less painful than to feel the underlying emotion.

When you have been rejected, humiliated, used, or when you have been hurt mentally, physically, or emotionally, the normal response is to become angry. A young woman who had been a child victim of sexual abuse described how rejected and humiliated she felt as a young girl when the police came to her house. She said, "I had been walking home from school when a man approached who said he would give me candy. I never got candy, even though I went to the woods with him. He raped me. I was so sore, and blood was all over me. He tore my dress. A woman had seen me go with him, but it was over so quickly. My mother got real mad at me and kept saying, 'How could you be so stupid as to go anywhere with a stranger?' With that statement, my mother gave me a good weapon to punish myself. I was so confused. I didn't think anything could feel worse than what he did to me, but this was worse. I thought, *She's right, my mom's right. Why did I go into the woods? I was stupid. I hate myself.*"

✎ **Because we have trained ourselves not to feel our emotions, sometimes we can more easily feel angry about the abuse that happened to someone else. Describe your feelings about what happened to the little girl you just read about.**

_____

_____

_____

✎ **Describe your feelings about the fact that the victim was blamed for the abuse.**

_____

_____

✎ **Is your story similar to the story of the little girl? Explain.**

_____

_____

_____

When Bill read the story it reminded him of how his father had shamed him because of the abuse he suffered from an aunt. He was finally able to be angry at his father for not listening to him and understanding.

✎ **How is your story different?**

_____

_____

_____

Survivor's Song

JESUS LOVES THE LITTLE
  CHILDREN,
ALL THE CHILDREN OF THE
  WORLD
RED AND YELLOW, BLACK
  AND WHITE
God, keep me safe from him tonight.
JESUS LOVES THE *other*
  CHILDREN IN THE WORLD.

JESUS LOVES ME, THIS I
  KNOW
But when I sleep, where does He go?
Other kids TO HIM BELONG
THEY *are right, but I am wrong.*
YES, JESUS LOVES ME
I hope He LOVES ME.
YES, JESUS LOVES ME
THE BIBLE TELLS ME SO.

DEEP AND WIDE, DEEP AND
  WIDE,
Why do I feel so bad inside?
DEEP AND WIDE, DEEP AND
  WIDE,
My only safety is to hide.[2]

double bind–adj. a circumstance in which you lose or you are punished, no matter which choice you make

You need to allow yourself to feel your anger about your abuse and about the way others reacted to your abuse.

✎ **Check all of the following methods you have been using to deal with your anger.**

- ❑ I suppress it.
- ❑ I have sudden outbursts.
- ❑ I become depressed.
- ❑ I turn it inward through self-hate.
- ❑ I act in passive-aggressive ways.
- ❑ I am self-destructive.
- ❑ Other _____

None of the methods listed above are healthy expressions of anger. Acknowledging that you are angry, validating your own significance, and focusing your anger on the abuse are healthy ways to deal with your anger.

✎ **Describe your feelings about how others have reacted to your abuse.**

_____

_____

Jim had panic attacks when he thought someone needed something from him. He discovered the source of those attacks. He had never allowed himself to be angry at the soccer coach who sexually abused him. Jim hated what the coach did to him in the locker room but craved the coach's praise on the field. Jim was also angry at himself for wanting the praise. Sexual abuse often puts the victim in a double-bind situation.

Remember your memory verse. Your anger is not a sin. To feel angry when others take advantage of you is healthy and normal. As you feel your anger you can deal with it in appropriate ways. Then you will use less of the destructive ways mentioned above.

Assignment for the lesson

Be angry, and yet do not sin.
–Ephesians 4:26, NASB

✎ **On a card write Ephesians 4:26, this unit's Scripture memory verse. Carry the card with you. Whenever you do some routine task like getting a drink of water, review your memory verse.**

☞ **Say aloud your affirmations. You may wish to repeat those you have been using only once. Repeat the new affirmation five times.**

> I accept God's love and kindness toward me.
> The truth will set me free!
> I am worthy to have God lead me and comfort me.
> I am clean.
> I am wonderfully made.
> I have permission to feel my anger and hurt.

☞ **Pray for yourself and for each member of your group.**

LESSON 3

The Danger of Denial

Some victims deny that they feel any anger. "No, I'm not angry at my mom; she just didn't know it was happening, that's all!" Others say, "Well, it was so long ago, it doesn't matter any more," while still others claim, "I forgave the person and just put it in the past." Certainly God is full of miracles, but most people need to process the trauma of this experience and not push it under the rug—not even a spiritual rug. Anger that is not dealt with will come out through inappropriate depression, psychosomatic ailments, relentless shame, and guilt.

Depression: Anger Turned Inward

We are tempted to allow anger to become bitterness. Genesis 4:5-6 relates that "Cain was very angry and his face was downcast. Then the Lord said to Cain, 'Why are you angry? Why is your face downcast?'" This kind of anger turned inward becomes depression. We can make one of three choices with anger. Either of the first two choices will eventually lead to emotional destruction.
1. We can turn it outside where we blame others for all the bad things that have happened to us.
2. We can turn it inside and blame ourselves.
3. We can learn to express our anger with God-given biblical principles.

✎ **Paraphrase the three choices that you have concerning your anger.**

1. We can turn it _____

_____

2. We can turn it _____

_____

3. We can learn to _____

_____

How I dealt with anger...
Turning it outward _____
_____
_____
_____
Turning it inward _____
_____
_____
_____
Expressing it to God _____
_____
_____
_____

Clearly the third choice is best for our emotional and spiritual health. During this time of recovery you can learn to express your anger appropriately. You no longer need to hold it inside in order to survive.

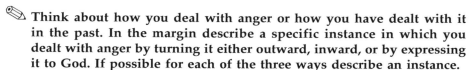 **Think about how you deal with anger or how you have dealt with it in the past. In the margin describe a specific instance in which you dealt with anger by turning it either outward, inward, or by expressing it to God. If possible for each of the three ways describe an instance.**

A young man was asked, "How can you keep the schedule you do?" He replied that he had so much hate and anger inside from having been abused as a child that it gave him the energy to get up every day at 5 a.m. and go until midnight. He did, however, complain about headaches, stomach problems, and an occasional rash. He insisted that he needed his anger, that it was a friendly companion. The young man was partly correct. Anger may seem like a friend, but it is destructive when it controls you.

The effects of child sexual abuse can lead to chronic anxiety, eating disorders, dissociative disorders, depression, promiscuity, alcoholism, and a host of other problems. If you had not been abused, your life would have been different. You might have been more confident, less angry, and more stable in your personal behavior. But the reality with which you must deal is that you were deeply hurt, and you do have a great deal of anger. You may need to express appropriately your anger again and again until you have been released from the rage within. Allow yourself to feel the loss that you have experienced due to your abuse.

Describe how your life might have been different had your abuse not happened.

_____

_____

_____

Describe how you feel about the losses you just described.

_____

_____

_____

The summer after Brenda graduated from high school she was abused by her employer who was a friend of the family. She did not tell anyone because she did not want the man's wife to be hurt. Brenda had graduated from high school with honors but found that she could not concentrate at college. She also could not sleep because of nightmares. She was placed on academic probation after she failed three classes. At age 30, after several crisis-filled years, Brenda has now returned to school.

Dealing with Hurt

As we learned in the previous lesson, our anger is often only the surface emotion protecting us from the painful feelings of humiliation, rejection, and hurt. In order for us to deal with anger, we must also deal with the hurt that is at its root. In sexual abuse, the hurt—the wound or injury—takes the form of mental, physical, and emotional pain. The hurt you experienced was the harm, the evil, and the damage done to you as well as the betrayal and loss of innocence you suffered.

 Review the definition of hurt that appears in the margin. Circle the words that describe your experience.

hurt–v. to cause harm, physical injury, or damage; to impair the value, usefulness, beauty, or pleasure of something; to wound the feelings of someone or to distress (Webster's)

To experience recovery you must acknowledge your hurts. By no longer denying, discounting, or minimizing the effects your abuse has had upon you, you can learn to make anger and hurt a valuable ally. As you find the roots of your anger and hurt, you can find more appropriate and constructive ways to express your anger. The Scriptures, wise counseling, and the support of those who have preceded you in your journey out of the storm will help you. You can experience growth in your relationship with others and with God. Even though you may become discouraged and not want to go on, you can push on with Christ. You can survive a day at a time until you overcome.

 Describe how anger can be constructive.

_____

_____

_____

_____

As Gayle acknowledged the reality of her abuse, she became very angry at her uncle. She determined to do all that she needed to recover. Her anger at the uncle caused her to resolve that he would take no more of her life from her. Gayle used her anger as the energy and courage she needed to inform the family and therefore stop him from abusing other nieces and nephews.

Passive Abuse

Another very real form of abuse that victims suffer is passive abuse—neglect. That kind of abuse occurred when no one was there to put them to bed, to say "I love you," or to hold them when they hurt. It was there in all the times the wrong words were said and in all the times of silence when no words were spoken.

Read the words of Ezekiel that appear in the margin at the top of the next page. Ezekiel was speaking of the nation of Israel, but certainly many survivors of abuse identify with his words.

No eye looked on you with pity or had compassion enough to do any of these things for you. Rather, you were thrown out into the open field, for on the day you were born you were despised.

–Ezekiel 16:5

I will gather you from all the countries and bring you back into your own land. I will sprinkle clean water on you, and you will be clean; I will cleanse you from all your impurities and from all your idols. I will give you a new heart and put a new spirit in you."

–Ezekiel 36:24-26

✍ **Have you ever felt abandoned in the way the Scripture verse describes?** ❏ **Yes** ❏ **No** **If so, describe your feelings.**

_____

_____

You can acknowledge the evil, the loss, the damage that was done to you, not in self-pity, but in God's pity. You can have the courage to remember the pain so that you will no longer need anger as your protector. Read God's compassionate words from Ezekiel 36:24-26 that appear in the margin. In the passage, God is speaking to a nation, but today He uses the same compassion with us as individuals. In the following activities apply each of God's promises to yourself as a sexual abuse survivor.

✍ **God promised the Israelites that He would gather them from all the countries and bring them back to their own land. What "territory" has sexual abuse taken from you that you want to reclaim?**

_____

_____

God said, "I will sprinkle clean water on you, and you will be clean." In what ways do you desire God's cleansing in your life?

_____

_____

God also said He would give a new heart and put a new spirit in you. Describe what changes in your heart and spirit you would like to see.

_____

_____

☞ **Look again at the list of desires you have just written. Take a prayer break and ask God to fulfill His promise in you. He desires to give you the territory that abuse has taken away. God desires to cleanse you of everything that is harmful in your life, and He desires to give you a heart and spirit that is alive and able to experience joy and wonder.**

✍ **Describe passive abuse you have experienced.**

_____

_____

What successful strategies have you used to deal with both active and passive abuse?

_____

_____

Remember, don't stuff your feelings to protect others. "You will know the truth and the truth will set you free" (John 8:32).

Assignment for the lesson

 Below write Ephesians 4:26, this unit's Scripture memory verse. Continue to work to memorize the verse.

_____

_____

➥ Repeat your affirmations. Work to memorize any that you do not know by heart.

> I accept God's love and kindness toward me.
> The truth will set me free!
> I am worthy to have God lead me and comfort me.
> I am clean.
> I am wonderfully made.
> I have permission to feel my anger and hurt.

➥ Pray for yourself and for each member of your *Shelter from the Storm* group.

LESSON 4

But I'm Angry at God

Many survivors wonder where God was when they were being abused. As we've said before, no easy answer exists, but God gives us wisdom on all questions. Some struggle with the question "Why does evil exist?" Others have cried out to God from the time of the abuse to the present. Some speak of seeing Jesus or of some miracle that seemed to have taken place during their abuse, while others simply have had a hope of something good about life. It seems that many were unable to let go of this hope, no matter what was done to them or what they did themselves. They never stopped hoping for something good to happen to them.

God was at work in this belief, hope, and desire. Even though we may not have been aware of it, God was there. He was there when you were being abused. God was there in your loneliness. He was there in your pain. God was the One who gave you this hope.

 Describe your feelings about God as you read the previous paragraphs. Can you identify with the feeling of the presence of God and of hope? Maybe those feelings are not there for you yet but you wish they were. Write your response.

_____

_____

Surely our griefs He Himself bore, and our sorrows He carried... He was pierced through for our transgressions, He was crushed for our iniquities;

–Isaiah 53:4-5, NASB

Letter to God

Dear God,
The Bible says that Father
  Is a comfort word...
Please don't be offended
  But I think that's absurd!

You gave us earthly fathers
  To help us find our way—
I'm here to tell—it didn't work!
  'Cuz mine led me astray!

So many times I've wondered...
  How?...Could he do these
things!!!
Did he know about the hate
  And misery incest brings?!

I tried to tell my pastor—
  But he had this to say:
That I should read more Bible
  And take more time to pray . . .

I only felt condemned
  When I tried what he said . . .
I felt I was unworthy—
  My spirit felt like lead.

In many ways, dear God
  The church has let me down—
Confrontation made them scared...
  They blindly stepped around.

Your church is different now, today
  And more open with the truth—
I know you can...and want to
  Heal the deep hurt of my youth.

The Bible tells me God—
  That you can take my pain—
You'll take out the ugly—
  And turn it into gain.

As I learn to trust—
  My hand held tight in yours—
Let me help some others
  To open their closed doors.[1]

Isaiah 53 describes Jesus as a man who was despised and forsaken. The New Testament tells of Jesus being spat upon, beaten, and mocked. All sin was poured on Him when He was on the cross. Jesus has borne all pain for us, even the pain of sexual abuse. Give Jesus your heart one memory at a time, one hurt at a time. No one hurts for your loss more than Jesus does.

After you acknowledge your hurt, take the list you made in lesson one of this unit and write each of those persons, organizations, or systems a letter that you will not mail. Take these letters and read them to your group, a trusted individual, or to an empty chair. Then write God a letter expressing your anger. In the past you may have thought, *I can't express anger toward God,* even though you would whisper thoughts in your mind. He, of course, knows exactly what you are thinking and feeling, whether those thoughts are angry or happy.

You may have to write some of your letters two or three times. You will probably find that as you process anger in one area, God may bring additional issues to mind. Remember recovery takes place one day at a time, and if need be, one letter at a time. You may need to write a person who has died, which is quite appropriate. Writing these letters is a way to deal with your anger and hurt. Because writing these letters is a major step in recovery from anger, you can be completely candid about your feelings. You may have been carrying some of these feelings since you were very young. Do not leave out anything, and do not express your anger just about the sexual abuse. Express it also about any other types of active or passive abuse. Accept the challenge. Express yourself honestly and process your anger instead of stuffing or ignoring it.

Reading the Psalms may help you to accomplish this important step in your recovery. Pick out the ones that cry out, "Come quickly," "How long, O God, will you turn from me?" and so on (for example see Psalm 6:3; 13:1-2; 79:5). You may want to express to God: "Oh, God, where were You? Why didn't You help me? You were all I had to believe in. You failed me. You betrayed me. Surely You could have done something. Why didn't You?"

One survivor says: "I wept for a long time. Nothing seemed to happen. I didn't hear angels singing or trumpets blowing. I just felt better. I got up, and after a time, I realized I was better. And I wasn't so angry. Finally, I wrote a letter to myself containing all the false and real accusations against me. I wrote about all the times I should have known better than to act as I did and all the times I believed that what had happened was ultimately my fault. I recounted all the mistakes I had made as an adult, whether or not they were a result of the abuse. I finally began genuinely to believe in Romans 8:1: 'There is now no condemnation to those who are in Christ Jesus.' I began to accept myself."

Begin writing your letters. People abuse others for many different reasons, and victims blame themselves for many different reasons, too. Don't get stuck trying to understand every reason. Your job right now is to recognize that you suffered. You need to give yourself permission to feel your hurt, anger, grief, and loneliness.

➦ **You may want to use space in your journal to write your letters. Share all or part of at least one of your letters with your support group.**

✎ Begin by choosing one person or organization on your anger list. Write a letter expressing your anger. Be sure to include other feelings such as hurt and humiliation. You might begin like this:

When you _____ I felt angry because _____

_____

_____

Assignment for the lesson

✎ Below write from memory this unit's Scripture verse. You may check your work on page 109.

_____

_____

☞ Say aloud your affirmations.

I accept God's love and kindness toward me.
The truth will set me free!
I am worthy to have God lead me and comfort me.
I am clean.
I am wonderfully made.
I have permission to feel my anger and hurt.

☞ Pray for yourself and for each member of your *Shelter from the Storm* group.

LESSON 5

The Message of a Nail Print

Hopefully this unit has helped you to identify and begin to work through some of the anger and hurt you have felt about your abuse. Jesus came to provide healing for your emotional pain.

✎ Read Isaiah 49:15-16 that appears in the margin. Below describe how much God loves us according to the passage.

_____

_____

_____

Can a mother forget the baby at her breast and have no compassion on the child she has borne? Though she may forget, I will not forget you! See, I have engraved you on the palms of my hands.
–Isaiah 49:15-16

Isaiah quotes God as saying that He loves us more than any human mother could love her baby. Then, in words that lead us to think of Jesus' death on the cross, God says His love can be seen by the nail prints in the hands of the Savior.

Rosaline, a bright 35-year-old nurse, described her anguish about her hurt. "If Jesus had really felt my hurt, surely He would have helped me. The pain of the abuse was overwhelming. The complications of my life were overwhelming. I was full of anger and frustration. I couldn't sleep. I have felt this way most of my life. One night I woke up at about 3 a.m. I felt troubled; my stomach was tied in a knot; I was worried. I went for a walk and just started crying. I said, 'God, I am trying to believe You love me…. I want to believe… help me to believe in You.' Then the thought entered my mind that Jesus was holding my hand, and I could feel the nail print in His hand. In one moment, I knew He felt my hurt. In fact, God felt my pain so deeply that He took the pain on Himself.

"I could feel the nail print in His hand."

"I looked at my hand and clasped His in mine. I knew God loved me—the nail print said just how greatly He loved me. I began crying at the joy of knowing and feeling His love. I felt God was saying to me, 'Yes, see how I love you.' I felt so loved and so encouraged that I knew everything would be OK."

Imagine holding the nail-pierced hand of Jesus. That hand was pierced for you.

✎ **In the space below or in your journal write a letter to Jesus. Tell Him about all the hurt and pain of your abuse. Express your willingness to allow Him to use your hurt and pain to help you to grow.**

_____

_____

_____

_____

_____

_____

_____

_____

_____

_____

If anyone is in Christ, he [or she] is a new creature, the old things passed away; behold the new things have come.
–2 Corinthians 5:17, NASB

Rosaline concluded her story, "I used to think that I needed God magically to take away all my emotional pain. Sometimes I still wish that could be true, but what I really need to know is that God doesn't see me as damaged goods. God hears me when I cry and shares my anger about the unfairness and injustice over what happened to me. God loved me before the abuse happened, during the abuse, and will love me forever."

✎ **Write a brief statement telling God about your anger at your abuse and thanking God for being angry too. Thank God for loving you before, during, and after the abuse.**

_____

_____

_____

_____

_____

God has not abandoned you

You might have expressed your anger over the unfairness of your abuse. You may feel jealous of others who have not had to struggle with the aftereffects of sexual abuse. Like Rosaline you may have told God how you realize that He really does love you and has been with you all the time. You were abused because people violate God's plans and laws. Abuse happens in a lost world. We can thank God for redeeming us. God has not abandoned you.

Unit Review

✎ **Look back over this unit. What statement or activity was most meaningful for you?**

_____

_____

✎ **Can you remember any statements or activities with which you were uncomfortable? Write those below.**

_____

_____

✎ **Write a prayer asking God to help you in your areas of struggle.**

_____

_____

_____

_____

Notes
[1]Shannon L. Spradlin, *Does God Know About This?* (Henderson, Nevada, 1993), 35.
[2]Ibid., 43.

UNIT 8

Healing Loneliness and Fear

Focal Passage

You did not receive a spirit that makes you a slave again to fear.

–Romans 8:15

This Unit's Affirmation
In Christ
I am never alone

I FEEL SO SCARED

"How can he have sex with me at night and act normal the next morning? How can he do that? I keep looking at him just to see if he will give me a sign. No, he just acts normal. Just like nothing happened last night. This scares me. I must be crazy, because I don't feel normal. How can he act normal? Why doesn't he even ask how I am? I told him it hurt. He told me to shut up. Maybe he will ask me in a minute how I am.

"I know what he said to me is true—that anyone I told about it would say it's my fault. Just the same, I think I'm going to tell my teacher today. She likes me. I think my grandmother knows. Why does she think he is so great? Oh, I guess I won't tell my teacher today after all. Daddy said I would be in bad trouble, real bad, if I tell anyone anything. He slapped me across the face and it left a mark. No one even noticed. I guess I won't tell today, but maybe tomorrow. I feel so scared!"

In this unit you will examine the loneliness and fear that plagues survivors.

Growth goal

This week's goal

You will evaluate your own feelings of fear and loneliness and take steps to meet your need for love, acceptance, and companionship.

Alone and Afraid	The Fear of Abandonment	The Fear of the Unknown	Compensating for Fear and Loneliness	The Comfort of Restoration
Lesson 1	Lesson 2	Lesson 3	Lesson 4	Lesson 5

Memory verse

This week's passage of Scripture to memorize

Even though I walk through the valley of the shadow of death, I will fear no evil, for you are with me; your rod and staff, they comfort me.

–Psalm 23:4

Alone and Afraid

How can anyone describe the loneliness of abuse? How can you describe the terror, the despair, the desolation of the nights and the days? How can anyone touch the feeling of abandonment felt by a victim? One child said to herself: "There is no one to turn to . . . no one. You must obey your father. He says you must be a good little girl. What is wrong with you? Your daddy comes just to see you. You be nice to him. You take care of Daddy."

A person in this situation experiences much confusion, fear, and loneliness. She despairingly asks, "How can he have sex with me at night and act normal the next morning? How can he do that? I keep looking at him just to see if he will give me a sign. No, he just acts normal. Just like nothing happened last night. This scares me. I must be crazy, because I don't feel normal. How can he act normal? Why doesn't he even ask how I am? I told him it hurt. He told me to shut up. Maybe he will ask me in a minute how I am. I know what he said to me is true—that anyone I told about it would say it's my fault. Just the same, I think I'm going to tell my teacher today. She likes me. I think my grandmother knows. Why does she think he is so great? Oh, I guess I won't tell my teacher today after all. Daddy said I would be in bad trouble, real bad, if I tell anyone anything. He slapped me across the face and it left a mark. No one even noticed. I guess I won't tell today, but maybe tomorrow. I feel so scared!"

An adult who has been sexually abused experiences some of these same feelings. If you were abused as an adult you may also feel confusion, fear, and loneliness. The person who abuses typically continues with life as it was before, especially if the victim is in a situation without legal recourse. This is one of the reasons why talking about the abuse is important for your recovery. Talking validates your experience and helps you to feel less lonely. You have the opportunity to talk about the confusion, to confront your fears, and to experience care and concern.

Shut down.
  Don't feel.
    For the pain inflicted
Is more than a child knows how to
  handle.
And for comfort
  You'll be handed nothing.
And if you cry
  You'll cry alone.

You are not alone. As we have talked with many survivors we have heard about thousands of lonely and desperate days. We hear many stories from many lives, with different details, but all repeating the same theme of fear and abandonment.

A teenager struggles to tell her story: "I can't go to school. I don't know why; I'm just afraid. Sometimes when I turn the corner at school, I think I see his face. Then I look again and it's someone else's. He doesn't even go to my school. It only happened once, two years ago. Why can't I just forget it? It was in the summer. He was my brother's friend. He raped me. I just can't stand the thought. When I even think of it, I want to run, to just get out of here. I can't even breathe. I'm not going to school. I'll tell my mother I'm sick. I can't spend the night with anyone anymore. I just want to be at home. I just want to stay in my room.

"I have an emptiness all inside me. It's like a big hole, as if you'd look at me and you couldn't see my middle. He took my middle that night. I didn't say a word. I just let him. It's like I was motionless. I think I was in shock. Maybe that's why I didn't move. I pretended I was asleep. I sure can't tell anyone now. It's been too long. When I see him anywhere, he just smiles this sickening smile. My brother isn't his friend any more, but it's like this creep knows how afraid I am. I can hear him saying, *Don't look at me; you liked it! You just took it and never said a word.* I can't go to school. I can't go anywhere!"

One male victim told of being left with foster parents when he was in the sixth grade. At the time, he hated them, but later, in recovery, he realized they were just simple, nice people. During his stay with this family his sixth-grade teacher molested him. He told me that no one seemed to notice or to care much when the teacher would take him places. "It felt good, but I felt dirty," he said. "I hated kissing him. Afterward all I thought about was sex. I started masturbating several times a day, and I would try to touch every girl I saw.

"But then I met Jesus Christ and something inside me was different."

"I finally left the foster home and went to live with my dad. I graduated from high school and a couple years later, I got married. It was easy to get sex in high school and college. There was always plenty of sex. Even after I married, I slept with everyone I could. I felt driven to prove my masculinity, I guess. I needed to be known as a man who got the women. But then I met Jesus Christ and something inside me was different. I actually began to love my wife. I began to see the tragedy of my life. I saw the fears—fear of being alone, of homosexuality, of life. It took a long time for God to work with me, but finally I was able to receive His help. I don't have perverted thoughts or do unspeakable things any more. Now I'm not afraid to face life. I don't have to be macho or even prove I'm OK."

✎ **Write down something that you have felt afraid or confused about that you have not discussed with one of your supportive people.**

_____

_____

Have you avoided talking about the issue you identified? If so, are you aware of the reason for your avoidance? ❑ **Yes** ❑ **No Describe the reason.**

_____

_____

_____

We sometimes avoid talking about issues when they stir strong feelings in us. If you are experiencing one of these feelings circle it.

- embarrassed
- hurt
- confusion
- shame
- fear
- anger

Many survivors of sexual abuse feel confused about some of their sexual desires and urges. Like the man mentioned above, you may have been focused excessively on sexual experiences. Sometimes survivors have a difficult time knowing what is healthy sexual behavior, and they are afraid to ask. Even though we live in a highly sexualized culture, we seem to have difficulty talking about sex. Sometimes we are just timid. Some people feel shame. Our culture also seems to tell us that we need to deal with our own problems without needing anyone else, so we are embarrassed when we do not feel strong and secure. Avoidance is a response to fear, but it results in loneliness.

 Have you allowed Jesus to speak to you when you are hurting? When you are alone or afraid? Write a letter telling Jesus about your feelings right now.

 Now imagine Jesus sitting in a chair across from you. Read your letter to Him.

How do you think He responds to you? Remember Jesus wants to listen to all your feelings! You are not alone!

Jacque says, "When I tell Jesus about feeling ashamed or embarrassed, I can imagine Him saying, 'You are my child and I am pleased with you. I understand when you make a mistake or when you feel confused or afraid. I love you all the way through your struggles and beyond them.'"

Fear of the Perpetrator

Many victims are crippled with fear of the person who abused them. Consider the following story.

A 25-year-old woman with a sweet southern accent tells of being attacked by an older family member. "He had already tried six times, but I always fought so hard that I got away. Then one night he came in my bedroom and grabbed me and put a rag over my mouth. It had a terrible smell. I began to feel sick at my stomach, and my head was spinning. I'm not really sure what happened, but when I woke up later, I could still smell my vomit even though it had all been cleaned up.

"It never happened again, but almost every night for a long time afterward I would wake up terrified. I would think that someone was holding me down and putting chloroform over my nose. I would feel so helpless, so alone and afraid. I'd lie there silently, hoping my breathing wasn't making a noise, and I wouldn't move because I knew if I did, even the tiniest bit, something bad would happen."

Overcoming the fear of the person who abused you may require a long recovery process

Overcoming the fear of the person who abused you may require a long recovery process, depending on the victim, the abuse, and the perpetrator. For Belinda, an eleven-year-old girl abused by two men, it has taken more than three years to overcome her fear of men. The men anally, orally, and vaginally raped her. They tied her up, threatened her with violence, and taunted her about getting her pregnant. When asked to draw pictures of her abusers, she showed them as dark figures with mean faces. She drew all men in this same fashion, whether or not they were the ones who abused her. After long-term counseling and a change in family structure (new stepfather and baby brother), her drawing of the family portrait changed slightly. The non-perpetrator stepfather and the baby brother were still shown as dark figures, but in the midst of the picture, the infant was wearing bright green clothes. The difference in the drawing was slight, but it signified a major step in her recovery. At the writing of this book, Belinda has asked to go with this loving stepfather on a couple of short errands.

Another reaction caused by her abuse was that, during her mother's pregnancy, Belinda became quite concerned that she too might be pregnant. Even though at least three years had gone by since her abuse, her mother's pregnancy triggered this deeply embedded fear.

✎ **As you read the previous stories you may have become aware of some specific fears you have now or have had in the past as a result of your abuse. List those fears in the space below and if possible any effects or limitations the fears have caused. We have given you an example.**

Fears	effects of the fears
fear of the dark	I cannot drive or go out at night

Everyone develops methods to protect themselves or make up for their fears. For example, you could have learned to avoid working in situations that cause you to interact with men if you were abused by a male. You may have learned to overachieve to avoid your fear of failure or to overcome feeling ashamed. These methods of compensating helped you survive the abuse and live with the fact that it occurred. However they may or may not be healthy for you today. You need to evaluate how you are reacting to your fears. You can begin to decide what you want to do with those reactions.

You need to evaluate how you are reacting to your fears.

✎ **Review the list you made above and choose one or two fears. Below describe ways you have compensated for those fears.**

Every survivor's story contains the issue of fear. Some of these fears are very rational; others are not. Obviously, God wants us to have wisdom and general respect for the reality of life's circumstances. For example, being wary of jogging alone at 10 o'clock at night in a city could hardly be considered an irrational fear. But if you are afraid to take a desirable job in a reputable area across town, you need to discover whether it is simply because the job is inconveniently far from home, or whether you have deeper fears that you need to overcome. You can accomplish this through telling your story and sharing your feelings with a counselor, a recovery group, or a meaningful friend, and by all means, claiming God's redeeming, healing promises.

Even though I walk through the valley of the shadow of death, I will fear no evil, for you are with me; your rod and staff, they comfort me.

–Psalm 23:4

Assignment for the lesson

✎ **Write your own paraphrase of Psalm 23:4, this unit's Scripture memory verse.**

_____

_____

➥ **Say aloud your affirmations. You may wish to repeat only once those you have been using. Repeat the new affirmations five times.**

I can find hope and healing.
I accept God's love and kindness toward me.
The truth will set me free!
I am worthy to have God lead me and comfort me.
I am clean.
I am wonderfully made.
I have permission to feel my anger and hurt.
In Christ I am never alone.

➥ **Pray for yourself and for each member of your _Shelter from the Storm_ group.**

The Fear of Abandonment

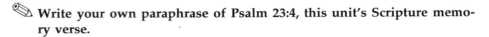

One root fear that most victims process is the fear of abandonment. Once in a group for teenagers in crisis, a beautiful 16-year-old girl entered the circle. She was tense, and we were stunned by the relentless, distant stare of longing in her eyes. She soon related that she was pregnant with her father's child. She had run away from home to keep the baby, but she said she hated this yet-to-be-born life. She moved and talked like the rest of us, but never before had we seen such hopelessness in a person's eyes. How could anyone help her make sense out of her life? At this time, all we could do was help get her through the pregnancy and delivery. In her view, no mother, father, husband, or God existed. She couldn't kill a life, but she really didn't know why because life, to her, wasn't worth living. In her opinion, if God existed, He was on another planet. She felt abandoned by the world.

The sexual abuse victim's fear of abandonment is like that of someone left in a forest alone, confused, and in pain. It is dark and the forest contains many dangers. Fear grips you and you can turn to no one for help. If you walk straight ahead, you're afraid of the danger that faces you, yet turning back may be just as risky. You know you must go on, but a part of you, or maybe even all of you, is overwhelmed with fear and just wants to sit there and die. But even that thought frightens you.

In recovery you have found the way, although it may seem that you are still in the forest. Identifying your fear of abandonment and feelings of loneliness, then facing these realities, is the path out of the forest, even though the journey may be a long one.

LESSON 2

DEEP AND WIDE,
 DEEP AND WIDE,
Why do I feel so bad inside?
DEEP AND WIDE,
 DEEP AND WIDE,
My only safety is to hide.

✎ **In the margin read the definition of the word *abandoned*. Below write your own definition of the word.**

_____

abandon-v. to withdraw protection, support, or help (Webster's)

Describe what being abandoned means to you.

_____

_____

_____

_____

List the people that you feel abandoned you and describe how they abandoned you.

Who	How

✎ **Spend some time writing in your journal about your feelings of abandonment. You might want to write a poem or a song. You may want to write a letter (that you will not mail) telling the person how you felt. You may want to draw a picture that describes how you feel. If you can, share your experience of this work with your support group.**

The Fear of Harm

One way we abandon others is to fail to protect them when they need our protection. Many victims speak of fears for their safety. A young child says she knows that Daddy can't see her for one year because the law said so. But she explains that when she goes to bed at night, she's afraid just the same. She thinks that Daddy will come across town, climb over the fence, crawl across the backyard, and then come in her window and get her.

Another child, six years old, forced to testify against the person who abused her, explains that she knows the judge will be there and the jury will be there. One, two, three . . . twelve of them. The police will be there. But her abuser will be there too, and when no one else is looking, he will fall down on the floor and crawl past the jurors and the judge and come behind the witness stand and get her.

Fear often doesn't make sense.

Such fears are very real to these children, although they may seem groundless to an adult. Fear often doesn't make sense. Adult victims sometimes continue to fear their perpetrators even after the people who abused them are

Reconnecting the feelings to the cause moves the survivor toward recovery.

imprisoned. Some adult survivors do not make the connection between their sexual abuse and their fears. Their fears often are indirect, not very specific, and unexpected. In these cases, their feelings have become separated from the cause of those feelings. Reconnecting the feelings to the cause moves the survivor toward recovery.

✎ **Describe a past situation when you felt unsafe or unprotected.**

_____

_____

_____

_____

Jacque remembers a time when a brush fire was burning near her house. "I was about four years old. I woke up from my nap, looked out the window, and saw the fire. I screamed and cried but no one came. I was terrified. I felt alone and abandoned. I didn't know my family was outside fighting the fire."

Do you ever feel unsafe now? Describe how and when.

_____

_____

_____

_____

What are some things you can do to feel safe?

_____

_____

_____

_____

We can help ourselves to feel safe many ways. We can list the names of supportive people. We can make wise decisions about where we go and who we go with. We can develop assertive behaviors that establish healthy boundaries without creating walls between us and others.

Assignment for the lesson

✎ **Below write Psalm 23:4, this unit's Scripture memory verse. Continue to work to memorize the verse.**

_____

_____

➡ **Say aloud your affirmations. You may wish to repeat only once those you have been using. Repeat the new affirmations five times.**

I can find hope and healing.
I accept God's love and kindness toward me.
The truth will set me free!
I am worthy to have God lead me and comfort me.
I am clean.
I am wonderfully made.
I have permission to feel my anger and hurt.
In Christ I am never alone.

➡ **Pray for yourself and for each member of your** *Shelter from the Storm* **group.**

LESSON 3

"I know it doesn't make sense, but I can't stand it."

Fear of the Unknown

Many adult survivors continue to experience tension or anxiety of unknown origin. They may feel uneasiness or be afraid to do things. One adult survivor describes walking into an airport and becoming so anxious that she found herself running to the seating area and collapsing into an empty place in the corner. She doesn't know why; she was just so afraid. Others speak of being afraid of large crowds or of being alone; of fear of spiders, snakes, people, authority figures, and a host of other things. Many survivors have problems sleeping, often because of terrible nightmares.

One survivor told how she frequently dreams of spiders and of dead people. She's not sure if she is dead in the dreams, but there is no one to help her. Another victim describes shadows as black spots. She tries to see into them, but there isn't anything there. At first she thinks she's seeing bugs, but when she looks again, she sees nothing. Some people tell of waking up at night feeling terribly afraid. One victim says it's as if there are 20 Boston stranglers outside the door who are about to come in and get her. Another has a terrible fear of thunderstorms. "I know it doesn't make sense, but I can't stand it. I have tried to figure it out, but I am afraid." Still another victim describes her fear of being closed in. She can't be on elevators. She will walk up 10 flights of stairs if she has to, rather than get on an elevator, where she fears she can't breathe.

✎ **Do you ever experience a fear of the unknown or an irrational fear?**
❑ **Yes** ❑ **No**

Below describe your fears. Don't be timid. Remember, a fear doesn't have to make sense.

_____

_____

_____

✎ **What helps you when you are afraid?**

_____

_____

_____

You may have listed things like calling a trusted friend, praying, or using positive self-talk. You can evaluate the fearful situation according to known truths.

The Bondage of Fear

To the degree that fear controls our lives, we are in bondage. To run away from fear, to ignore it, or try to compensate for it does no good. Perhaps right now you are in too much pain or fear to do anything about your situation. Sometimes reading Scripture helps in those times. You may find it helpful to memorize one or more of the Scriptures suggested here. They offer help in many situations. For example, read Jesus' loving words in Matthew 11:28: "Come to me, all you who are weary and burdened, and I will give you rest." Second Samuel 22:2 assures us that the Lord is our rock and our fortress and our deliverer. When you pray the words of Matthew 6:13, "but deliver us from evil," you can apply this request to any fears you have. You may also want to pray the Lord's Prayer every day (Matthew 6:9-13).

Cindy's Story

"The truth is I was afraid of people."

"At one point my own life was so full of fears that I isolated myself from practically everybody. In my freshman year at college, I would eat my lunch in the third-story bathroom of the library. Not many people ventured there, so I was alone and I felt safe. The truth is I was afraid of people. It's been years since I had those fears, but I can sympathize with you. Wherever you are, you can begin the process of overcoming your fears."

✎ **In the following list of words, circle the actions you use to run away from your fears. Underline those actions you use to face your fears.**

Read	Work	Eat
Spend money	Draw	Isolate
Pray	Ignore them	Spend time with
Use alcohol	Use drugs	friends
Talk to others	Stay busy	
Write in journal	Write letters	Other _____

✎ **Add any other items to your lists that are a part of your experience.**

✎ **What would you like to change about your lists?**

_____

_____

_____

Jana discovered that she ate every time she was afraid. For years she had struggled with her weight. When she understood that her eating was a way to relieve her fears, she began to face her fears instead of feeding them.

⇨ **Pray about those changes and ask God to give you the courage to begin today to set small goals for yourself in at least one area.**

Assignment for the lesson

✎ **Below write Psalm 23:4, this unit's Scripture memory verse. Continue to work to memorize the verse.**

_____

_____

⇨ **Say aloud your affirmations. You may wish to repeat only once those you have been using. Repeat the new affirmations five times.**

> I can find hope and healing.
> I accept God's love and kindness toward me.
> The truth will set me free!
> I am worthy to have God lead me and comfort me.
> I am clean.
> I am wonderfully made.
> I have permission to feel my anger and hurt.
> In Christ I am never alone.

⇨ **Pray for yourself and for each member of your group.**

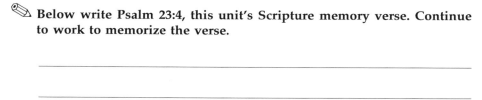

LESSON 4

Compensating for Fear

We try many ways to compensate for our fear and loneliness. Some of those ways are healthy; however, many are not healthy and only keep us in bondage to our fear. You may have listed some of those at the end of the last lesson.

✎ **Below we have listed some additional methods people use to compensate for fear and loneliness. Check those methods that you sometimes use.**
- ❑ Minimize your problems
- ❑ Deny that you have any problems
- ❑ Fix other's problems so that they will appreciate you
- ❑ Ttry to be perfect, to have a perfect home, perfect children, and a perfect spouse
- ❑ Use anger as a shield to protect yourself from experiencing the reality of your fears
- ❑ Try to control circumstances and people
- ❑ Become a daredevil, taking up skydiving, motorcycling, and other risky activities

Other ways to compensate include eating or drinking everything in sight or endlessly shopping for bargains; withdrawing and isolating ourselves; or by contrast, giving total devotion to church or volunteer work, serving day and night in every conceivable role.

✎ **On the list you just completed, review the ways you have attempted to compensate for fear and loneliness. Below describe how those ways have or have not been helpful.**

_____

_____

_____

Below write some methods for dealing with fear and loneliness that might work better for you. Share your ideas with your support group.

_____

_____

_____

But no matter how many things we try to use to compensate for our fear and loneliness, we are destined to discover that only those plans that fit with God's plan for us will work. God is the Deliverer and Restorer. One of the best ways to face our fear and loneliness is by telling our story to appropriate others and releasing those burdens to God.

Restoration from Loneliness and Fear

Let's deal first with loneliness. For God to enable us to overcome loneliness, we can acknowledge each lonely feeling, one by one, and hand it to God. We can do the same with the ways we've compensated for those lonely feelings and the ways we've survived one more day. We can pray again Psalm 51:6, asking God to leave no stone unturned in revealing the truth of our loneliness.

Surely you desire truth in the inner parts; you teach me wisdom in the inmost place.

–Psalm 51:6

The process of uncovering the truth will probably be painful. Many share that they have never hurt so much as they did during the early stages of the recovery process. Many survivors shut down at first in order to survive the terror of the moment. Later they realized that no matter how much it hurt to remember, they would have to try. Remembering hurts, and sometimes it hurts for a long time. But one day you will wake up and realize that the pain isn't quite as intense as it was. Then the next week, the pain may be less. The next month, other memories no longer hurt, and so on, until one day you will feel whole.

The psalmist assures us: "Because you will not abandon me to the grave, nor will you let your Holy One see decay. You have made known to me the path of life; you will fill me with joy in your presence, with eternal pleasures at your right hand" (Psalm 16:10-11). Loneliness and abandonment describe the condition of a person who is shut down emotionally. Be assured that God is

He restores my soul.

–Psalm 23:3

willing to show you the true and joyous path of life. As you begin to pray specifically for your restoration from loneliness, allow God to touch that emptiness and fill your life with His love. You may want to pray Psalm 23:3, asking Him to restore your soul.

✎ **Below write a list of your thought statements that cause you to feel lonely. Beside each statement describe the feeling it brings. These thoughts usually are false beliefs that keep us in bondage to the loneliness. We have given you two examples.**

Nobody really wants me around.

They didn't even notice I was in the room.

_____

_____

_____

_____

_____

_____

✎ **Now take each thought and rewrite it with an opposite statement that is more realistic. We have given you two examples. Notice that these statements give you greater responsibility and control over your life.**

Somebody wants me around. I'll just have to find them.

I can speak to people and then they will know I am here.

_____

_____

_____

_____

_____

The next important step is to become aware of the circumstances and people which provoke your fear. You can deal with irrational fears by submitting them to God, one at a time, and receiving His restoration from abusive situations. This process takes time, of course. And it also takes seeking and accepting accurate information. For example, Belinda, the young teenager we described earlier, eventually realized that her fear of being pregnant for three years was irrational.

✏ **Review your list of fears from lesson 3. Do your fears protect or serve you in any way?** ❏ **Yes** ❏ **No If so, explain.**

_____

_____

_____

_____

One person wrote: "I was angry when my counselor gave me this exercise because it forced me to realize that I no longer needed to fear the past, but I was afraid to let it go! My fears became manageable as I began to write and talk about them and to share them with my support group."

Some fears are legitimate. We need to protect ourselves from violent, abusive, or manipulative people.

✏ **Below write a paragraph describing actions you can take to protect yourself from dangerous people or situations.**

_____

_____

_____

_____

The assignment may have been difficult for you. If you are facing a situation in which your personal safety or another person's personal safety is in danger, consider talking to your group facilitator, pastor, or a counselor.

For God hath not given us a spirit of fear; but of power and of love and of a sound mind.
                        –2 Timothy 1:7, KJV

Another realm of fear with which the victim must deal is the spiritual. In the margin read the apostle Paul's words to Timothy. Remember Romans 8:15, "For you did not receive a spirit that makes you a slave again to fear, but you received the Spirit of sonship. And by him we cry, "*Abba,* Father.""

Assignment for the lesson

✏ **Below write from memory this unit's Scripture verse. You may check your work on page 125.**

_____

_____

☞ **Say aloud your affirmations. You may wish to repeat only once those you have been using. Repeat the new affirmations five times.**

I can find hope and healing.
I accept God's love and kindness toward me.
The truth will set me free!
I am worthy to have God lead me and comfort me.

I am clean.
I am wonderfully made.
I have permission to feel my anger and hurt.
In Christ I am never alone.

➥ **Pray for yourself and for each member of your group.**

The Comfort of Restoration

LESSON 5

As you allow God to know your fears, His love can make up to you for all the days of anxiety you have endured. If you have a heart full of holes and marked with bruises, He can take that heart and make it whole. You may still be wondering, "How will God restore me?" The answer is easy to say but difficult to do. He will restore you as you allow Him to do so. You cooperate with God as you—

- write
- talk
- read
- pray
- draw
- sing
- reflect
- remember

Recovery happens one day at a time as long as you keep doing these things. When you shut down, recovery shuts down too. Some days obviously are more focused on recovery than others. Just be careful when you begin to start feeling like hiding and avoiding. Like the following examples, one day you will be able to say that you too have experienced the joys of recovery.

One victim who couldn't see anything good about her childhood marveled after recovery at how God could draw forth memories of good things—memories so buried in sorrow she had lost them. Another victim in a sexual abuse group laughed one day, "I must be getting better—I can remember funny things about my childhood."

You can begin to live out your life as a person created in the image of God.

Past loneliness and abandonment are realities, but in the recovery process God can redeem our pain and loss. Below you will find a most beautiful and comforting Scripture, 1 Corinthians 13:4-8. First read the passage as it is, then we will give you some instructions that will help you begin to see the personality of God and how you can begin to live out your life as a person created in the image of God.

> *Love is patient, love is kind, and is not jealous; love does not brag and is not arrogant, does not act unbecomingly; it does not seek its own, is not provoked, does not take into account a wrong suffered, does not rejoice in unrighteousness, but rejoices with the truth; bears all things, believes all things, hopes all things, endures all things. Love never fails.*
> —1 Corinthians 13:4-8, NASB

➥ **Now go back and read the passage a second time, replacing the word** *love* **with the word** *God.*

Does this fit with your image of God? Do you know God as a God of love, who is patient and kind, who seeks to believe in you and endure with you?

A God who never fails? First John 4:18 says that "perfect love drives out fear." God is perfect love!

✎ Below describe what you are feeling and experiencing right now. If you feel the need to use more paper to draw your feelings or write a letter or poem, do so. One person responded to this exercise by making a collage. She found pictures in magazines that described her experience with the God who is love!

_____

_____

_____

_____

_____

God said in Genesis 1:27 that you were created in His image. That means that God placed within you some characteristics like Himself.

God never fails.

While you are in your recovery process, remind yourself regularly that God is love. God never fails. His love never fails. God will never abandon you. Remember not to abandon yourself. Sometimes we become discouraged in recovery, and we forget to be patient and kind to ourselves. We can recognize that our fears and our tendencies to feel alone will not go away over night but with prayer, time, and talking about the abuse, these feelings will change.

Unit Review

✎ Look back over this unit. What statement or activity was most meaningful for you?

_____

_____

✎ Can you remember any statements or activities with which you were uncomfortable? Write those below.

_____

_____

✎ Write a prayer asking God to help you in your areas of struggle.

_____

_____

_____

_____

UNIT 9

Beginning to Trust Again

This Unit's Affirmation
I can trust myself and others.

Focal Passage
For he has not despised or disdained the suffering of the afflicted one; he has not hidden his face from him but had listened to his cry for help.

–Psalm 22:24

"I COULDN'T TRUST ANYONE"

Jeanie said, "Growing up, I knew I couldn't trust anyone. My mother was off doing her own thing, and who knows where my father was? I could trust my stepdads, uncles, and brothers for one thing—they were going to take what they wanted. The only good thing was that I knew one day I would grow up. What I didn't know, though, was that for close relationships I would pick every lousy person that was out there. No one was there for me growing up and no one was there for me afterwards. I've married three times. They were all bums. One even molested my daughter. I really wanted my life to be different, to be better. I don't even worry anymore about whether or not I can trust them; I know I can't trust my own head, so I just don't get involved."

In this unit you will examine ways to develop appropriate trust.

Growth goal

This week's goal
You will define trust and determine individuals in your life that you can trust. You will recognize how you have used control to feel safe and secure. You will compare nonproductive attempts at control with productive ones. You will learn how to pray for the serenity to accept the things you cannot change, the courage to change the things you can, and the wisdom to know the difference.

Why Is Trust So Difficult?	Learning to Trust	The Problem of Control	Steps to Trust and Discernment	Peace in the Midst of the Storm
Lesson 1	Lesson 2	Lesson 3	Lesson 4	Lesson 5

Memory verse

This week's passage of Scripture to memorize
May the God of hope fill you with all joy and peace as you trust in him, so that you may overflow with hope by the power of the Holy Spirit.

–Romans 15:13

LESSON 1

Why Is Trust So Difficult?

A survivor tells a story that demonstrates how deeply suspicion is embedded in the minds of victims. "Late one night, as I was sitting in a restaurant, I ordered decaffeinated tea because caffeine keeps me awake. When the tea came, I checked the tea bag to make certain that the tea was decaffeinated. There was no label. Immediately I became suspicious and called the waitress to the table. I asked her to confirm that I was truly drinking decaffeinated tea. She quickly answered in the affirmative. I pointed out to her that there was no label stating that the tea was decaffeinated. We exchanged a few more words of doubts and assurances. She left the table. As I drank the entire pot of tea, I kept wondering if this was decaffeinated tea."

The fact that you were abused when you should have been safe has damaged your ability to trust. God intended that every person would have parents and other significant people who would firmly establish trust in their minds and hearts. As a survivor of abuse, especially if you are a victim of childhood incest, you had the very core of trust taken from you. You have a very difficult road ahead to regain the God-given ability to trust that should have been your birthright. If you were abused by a non-family member and have a healthy, nurturing family you may be able to respond somewhat more quickly to the right intervention. If you came from an unstable and unreliable family, you face a greater challenge in developing the ability and faith to trust.

The word *trust* has at least seven possible meanings, each in direct opposition to the action that takes place in sexual abuse. One of the Hebrew words for trust means "to support, to stay, and to be faithful."

✎ **Place an X on the following scale to represent your ability to trust**

1	2	3	4	5	6	7	8	9	10
I Never Trust			Sometimes I Can Trust				I Trust too Easily		

trust–n. assured reliance on the character, ability strength, or truth of someone or something, dependence on something future, hope (Webster's)

✎ **Read the definition of *trust* that appears in the margin. Below write your own definition of the word.**

_____

_____

_____

Ask a couple of friends to tell you what trust means to them. Write their response in the space below.

_____

_____

_____

Survivors of sexual abuse experience the exact opposite of these meanings of trust. The person who abuses them instills the message *don't trust, don't trust, DON'T TRUST ANYBODY.*

I would play, 'Something Bad Is Going to Happen.'

A young woman described her childhood situation this way, "In one way it was always the same with my father—we never knew what was going to happen. Dad could be four different people in one night. I can remember, when I was three or four years old, sitting in a corner after he blew up, wondering what I had done. I couldn't figure it out. It seemed to me that every time this happened, it was because I didn't do something that I was supposed to do. However, as I got older, I knew it was because he was drunk! At any rate, all during those early years I would play a game in my head called 'Something Bad Is Going to Happen.' It made me feel better to remember that. That way I wouldn't hurt so bad when the inevitable happened. I would just tell myself, 'Stupid, what did you expect? You knew it was going to happen.'"

Every victim develops a system to help them to survive the lack of support and the betrayal of confidence, whether this be physical, mental, or spiritual. We readjust in order to survive the chaos in which we live. We have already noted that trust is a God-given ability, to be learned by humans from humans through parental nurturing and stability. A dysfunctional family system destroys that ability. Sexual abuse, especially from within the family, destroys the ability to trust.

✎ **Describe what trust means to you.**

_____

_____

_____

What feelings do you experience when you think of trusting someone?

_____

_____

_____

_____

Test for safety before you make yourself vulnerable.

Many survivors cannot remember ever trusting anyone. Some remember only situations in which they feel their trust has been violated. Give yourself the time and space necessary to struggle with the issue of trust. It takes time to learn to trust again. It also takes experiencing safety in relationships. Trust is about allowing someone inside your boundaries. Survivors tend to have boundaries that are too open or too closed. Test a situation for safety before you make yourself vulnerable. This will allow you to develop trust.

Trust as Hope and Expectation

One of the most precious definitions of trust listed in our dictionaries is "to place hope in someone or something; to expect confidently." Victims learn only too well not to have confident expectations. They learn to survive, usually alone. Many victims believe that people in general are cruel and must be avoided at all costs. The problem, of course, is that God created us not to be alone but to be in communion with other humans and with Him. Without the ability to trust, the ability to risk—to allow oneself to be vulnerable—is lost. Many victims can't even trust themselves.

✎ **What about you? Describe what affect the ability to trust or not trust has had on your life.**

_____

_____

To live a life without security and to be in constant fear is a terrible tragedy. Once a survivor grows to adulthood, the danger is that the fear and the insecurities evoked by the abuse will remain. The survivor may or may not deal with these issues daily. The adult victim often feels a lack of security, of hope, and of confidence. Living in fear destroys trust.

Assignment for the lesson

✎ **Write your own paraphrase of Romans 15:13, this unit's Scripture memory verse.**

_____

_____

⮕ **Say aloud your affirmations. You may wish to repeat only once those you have been using. Repeat the new affirmation five times.**

> I accept God's love and kindness toward me.
> The truth will set me free!
> I am worthy to have God lead me and comfort me.
> I am clean.
> I am wonderfully made.
> I have permission to feel my anger and hurt.
> In Christ I am never alone.
> I can trust myself and others.

⮕ **Pray for yourself and for each member of your _Shelter from the Storm_ group.**

Learning to Trust

LESSON

2

In the first lesson you began to study the issue of trust. In this lesson you will begin to identify the characteristics of a trustworthy person.

✎ **In the following story underline all the people who have violated Jeanie's trust.**

Jeanie said: "Growing up, I knew I couldn't trust anyone. My mother was off doing her own thing, and who knows where my father was? I could trust my

---

May the God of hope fill you with all joy and peace as you trust in him, so that you may overflow with hope by the power of the Holy Spirit.

–Romans 15:13

I really wanted my life to be different, to be better.

stepdads, uncles, and brothers for one thing—they were going to take what they wanted. The only good thing was that I knew one day I would grow up. What I didn't know, though, was that for close relationships I would pick every lousy person that was out there. No one was there for me growing up and no one was there for me afterwards. I've married three times. They were all bums. One even molested my daughter. I really wanted my life to be different, to be better. I know there are good people out there. I've seen them at church, though sometimes I even wonder about them. But there must be someone that is good. I know I haven't been perfect, and I have a lot wrong with me, but I really can't believe all this evil. I don't know why I keep getting with the wrong guys. It's like I have a great big sign on my head that says, 'Hey! Come abuse me!' I don't even worry anymore about whether or not I can trust them; I know I can't trust my own head, so I just don't get involved. I have learned to trust one thing—money. All I think about now is putting money in the bank. I do put some away every week, but it doesn't seem to add up too fast."

✎ **List the people in the story who violated Jeanie's trust.**

_____

_____

Jeanie realized that her ability to make wise decisions about relationships had been damaged.

One person underlined *mother, stepdad, uncles, brothers, ex-husbands.* Then she realized that she needed to underline Jeanie's name also. Like other survivors, Jeanie realized that her ability to make wise decisions about relationships had been damaged. She did not know how to make wise decisions about people. She could not recognize a person who would abuse her. Jeanie needed guidelines to help her rebuild her own ability to tell safe people from abusive people.

✎ **Think of a person that you perceive as being a safe, healthy person. Below describe that person.**

_____

_____

List the characteristics that cause you to believe this person is trustworthy.

_____

_____

_____

Make a list of guidelines to help you determine if someone is trustworthy. Share your list with your group members.

_____

_____

_____

Trustworthy people do not take advantage of others. They do not ridicule or criticize. Trustworthy people seek the good of others.

✎ **What are your hopes and expectations in relationships? Consider issues such as level of openness, time, and energy.**

_____

_____

_____

_____

A pattern at work

Jill recognized a pattern in her relationships that caused her to be hurt repeatedly. She would make a friend and immediately begin to call several times a day, dropping by without an invitation. She was invading the other person's life. When the friend would begin to establish boundaries to gain some control over her life, Jill would feel hurt and rejected. As Jill learned to establish healthier patterns, her hurt diminished.

✎ **When do you feel hurt in relationships? Describe repeated patterns you experience in relationships.**

_____

_____

_____

_____

Share these with your group members. Ask them to help you evaluate your hopes and expectations. You can help each other to identify the expectations that are realistic and those that are unrealistic.

Trusting Trustworthy People

Sometimes we try to control everyone and everything around us.

As victims of abuse, we tend to have problems with trusting others. We trust too little or too much. Sometimes we withdraw passively into an emotional shell to protect ourselves from being hurt again, and we do not even trust people who are safe and trustworthy. Sometimes our lack of trust compels us to try to control everyone and everything around us. We are not passive then; we are demanding, intimidating, and dominating. Sometimes we trust others blindly. We believe those who have proved over and over again that they are not to be trusted. When we trust blindly, we use trust as a bargaining chip to earn acceptance, to please people, and to avoid conflict.

The Book of Proverbs has much to say about the wise and the foolish. To trust only those who have proved that they are faithful, honest, and kind is wise. To trust those who are undependable or dangerous is foolish. Learning to trust involves the process of controlling risks. We trust a person with a small thing, and if that proves to be a positive experience, we then can choose to trust the person with a little more. When this incremental escalation of trust is blocked, we do not go back to the bottom. Instead, we go back to the last safe place of trust. We communicate clearly and calmly, and we continue to move forward in building the relationship.

We can take the incremental steps to learn to trust wisely.

In sexual abuse, the perpetrator, every enabler, and every passive co-perpetrator has violated our trust. In the safety of the support group, we can take the incremental steps to learn to trust wisely—not too much or too little. During the recovery process, we become stronger. We no longer withdraw passively to keep from being hurt again. We no longer pretend people care about us just because we are too afraid to admit that they do not. In the process, we learn that God is the only one who is completely and absolutely trustworthy—and even then we do not understand Him all the time.

✎ **Below describe how you have experienced the extremes of trusting too much, trusting too little, or both.**

_____

_____

_____

✎ **Below check the description that best describes your response to God at this time in your recovery.**

❑ I shut myself off from God.
❑ I recognize God's presence.
❑ I doubt that God exists.
❑ I am disappointed by my inability to trust God.
❑ I am waiting for God to give me an unmistakable sign.
❑ Other _____

✎ **Explain your response. Share your response with your group.**

_____

_____

_____

Libby says she cried every day of her childhood that she can remember, and every day she asked God to let her die. She begged Him to help, to rescue her from her horror. She even prayed that her daddy would die. She prayed every kind of prayer she could think of for God's help. "So why then," she asked, "should I believe God cares when I pray now?"

Many of you are asking these same questions. We can't give you an overwhelming answer that will light up the sky with fireworks. We can only tell you that God does care. He does hear your prayers. Keep praying. The ultimate failure is when you give up and stop talking to God.

God was and is there with you in your pain.

No matter how it looked to you as you were suffering from the deceptions of abuse, God was and is there with you in your pain. He also is present for your recovery. The issue of trust is one that not only affects you personally, but also every person you encounter. Trust affects every relationship—relationship with God, relationship with spouse and family, even casual relationships. The need to be able to trust is at the very core of your existence. You were created as a being who has the choice as to whom or what you believe and whom or what you trust.

✎ **Make a list of the people you trust.**

_____

_____

_____

_____

Write a letter to each of these people telling about how you feel. You may include how, why, and even when you realized that you could trust them. These are letters you probably will not give to them. Remember the letters are for your recovery. You may want to share them with your group.

Assignment for the lesson

May the God of hope fill you with all joy and peace as you trust in him, so that you may overflow with hope by the power of the Holy Spirit.
–Romans 15:13

✎ **On a card write Romans 15:13, this unit's Scripture memory verse. Carry the card with you. Whenever you do some routine task like getting a drink of water, review your memory verse.**

⇨ **Say aloud your affirmations. You may wish to repeat only once those you have been using. Repeat the new affirmation five times.**

I accept God's love and kindness toward me.
The truth will set me free!
I am worthy to have God lead me and comfort me.
I am clean.
I am wonderfully made.
I have permission to feel my anger and hurt.
In Christ I am never alone.
I can trust myself and others.

⇨ **Pray for yourself and for each member of your _Shelter from the Storm_ group.**

**LESSON
3**

The Problem of Control

Sexual abuse distorts our understanding. As we try to compensate for an inability to trust and to feel secure without fear, we tend to isolate, rationalize, avoid, and run away. We attempt to check out everything. We tend to suspect all others. Mainly, we decide we can—and must—maintain control over our own lives. We must not experience the terror of losing control.

Even when we fail in our attempts to control, we continue trying. We set conditions and expectations for all relationships, including our relationship with

Hiding our vulnerability

God, so we do not have to risk trusting. The problem is that we are miserable. We are not in control, but we are in fear. Sometimes we believe that if we let down even for a moment someone will find out that we can be hurt easily. Any sign of weakness or vulnerability is unthinkable. If others discover we are weak, they will have power over us and this knowledge will be used against us. We need a haven to which we can go and learn again to trust. Christ-centered support groups, Christian counseling, and a loving church family provide just such a place—a safe environment where individuals can be loved for who they are. In our work with groups we hear survivors say again and again that the only place they feel safe is when they come to the group. And eventually, as the Lord continues to work in their lives, they begin to feel safe in other places and with other people.

✎ **Reread the paragraph above and underline the ways that survivors use control to attempt to compensate for the difficulty they experience in trusting others.**

If you are a victim of abuse, you have endured one storm after another. It is never too late to get out of the storm and into an atmosphere of regeneration. You can learn to trust.

Martha began to allow herself to cry, to forgive, to love again.

Martha couldn't hug anyone when she first came to group. She kept her distance by pushing her chair to the outside of the circle and only sharing occasionally. To see how much she hurt was easy. We hoped that she would talk to us about her pain. After several sessions she began to talk about the trauma of abuse by her brother, the guilt of three abortions, and the misery of living with an abusive husband. Letting go of her emotions, she began to allow herself the freedom to cry, to forgive, to love again. As she gave the control to God and took steps to trust in Him, she cried very deeply and for a very long time. Now she hugs a little and smiles a lot more, and she believes in herself. She always trusted God for her salvation, but now she trusts Him for her refuge. When she stopped trying to control everyone and everything in her life, she realized that for the first time she was no longer being controlled. She was free—free to make choices she had always wanted to make, free to love, free enough to trust someone to really love her.

✎ **Describe how you have used control to provide safety and security in each of the following areas of your life—**

your relationships

_____

_____

Maybe you always need to be in charge. You find it frightening to allow others to make decisions. At other times you may be passive and depend on others to make decisions.

your body

_____

_____

_____

We sometimes have a difficult time responding sexually because we cannot relinquish control over our bodies. We attempt to control our weight, our appearance, and the perceptions of others about us.

your circumstances

_____

_____

A rigid set of rules

Survivors sometimes have a difficult time with change. They live life according to a rigid set of rules. Sometimes they resist rules because of the need to avoid being controlled by others.

your environment

_____

_____

Some survivors only feel safe when their environment is stable and unchanging. Moving to a new house, town, or job can be extremely stressful. New situations can make a person feel out of control.

✎ **Do you have a tendency to—**

1. isolate yourself?   ❏ Yes   ❏ No
2. dominate?   ❏ Yes   ❏ No
3. be suspicious?   ❏ Yes   ❏ No
4. avoid conflict?   ❏ Yes   ❏ No
5. run away?   ❏ Yes   ❏ No
6. place conditions and expectations on other people?   ❏ Yes   ❏ No

Learning True Control

Every victim of abuse, to one degree or another, must deal with the issue of control. Because you had absolutely no control in your life over sexual abuse, you are tempted to feel that if you are in control now, you will no longer be abused. Almost certainly, the more you attempt to control your circumstances, the more your circumstances will control you. You need to realize that as long as you attempt to control, you will never really attempt to trust. In other words, if you can control circumstances, then you really have eliminated the need to trust.

The more you attempt to control your circumstances, the more your circumstances will control you.

Of course, as you already know, you can't control your circumstances; consequently, you end up confused and broken. Controlling is a way of "playing God." Some people, for a period of time, are successful at controlling their environment, but eventually this fails because it is impossible to sustain. To manipulate and control your environment takes a great deal of energy. To deny the pain of abuse takes still more energy. These exhausting painful and negative emotions, pushed down, will eventually emerge as physical problems (psychosomatic illness), emotional problems (depression or anxiety), or behavioral problems (withdrawing, fixing, cursing).

You may have attempted many ways of readjusting to deal with your fears and insecurities, but learning to trust wisely is the road to recovery. One group member said it this way, "When I learned to trust God, no matter what the circumstances were, I knew that I was a long way down the road in my own recovery. At first, I attempted to trust God in small areas and at the same time, to learn to trust myself. I don't know exactly when it happened, but finally one day when the circumstances were very difficult, I somehow still knew that He would get me through this ordeal.

"Until this point in my life, I thought I was in control; I thought I had trusted God completely and that I was a great woman of faith. Suddenly I realized that control blocks faith. Now I try to trust God completely—even when I see things happening that I don't like. I've learned and am continuing to learn to trust people. I have learned that some people can be trusted only for certain things and others can be trusted more completely. I don't need to control them. I don't need to keep people at a distance. I know that I need people, and that is good. In fact, God made us all to need each other."

✎ **In the paragraphs above find the three sentences that appear in the margin box, and fill in the blanks.**

✎ **Below describe your feelings about the three statements you just completed.**

_____

_____

_____

_____

All of us need people. One of the consequences of abuse is that our ability to trust other people and ourselves is damaged. Control blocks our faith in God. Control is an illusion of power. Learning to trust wisely truly is the road to recovery.

Scott, a good-looking man in his 40s, describes giving up his control. "Being in control was easy for me, since I was a man and I was supposed to be in control. I controlled my wife and my son and daughter. My wife was an abuse victim, so it was easy to dominate her. My daughter ran away and got pregnant, but I never let up. I couldn't let go. They said I didn't know how to delegate.

"Finally I lost it—my control over myself. I cried and cried. I was an abuse victim too, and I hated my abuser and I hated myself for living the lies that I had lived all my life. I told my wife first. For years we'd had sex problems—she had heavy guilt feelings over her own abuse, so I had just been letting that be the issue. But at this point, we were in separate bedrooms and I didn't have any desire for sex.

"Over the years, I tried it all, every form of sex, but for a long time now I haven't wanted any sex at all. I never had any desire for my daughter, but sometimes I'd want my son. Thank God I never did anything to him, but I did control my family in every other way. I determined when we ate, what

---

Complete the sentence

_____ blocks faith.

I need _____.

_____
is the road to recovery!

we ate, where we went, and what we did. I'm exhausted and so is my family. I know the abuse is not the only issue in my life, but it is a deep seed within me, and I really want to be free from the torment."

Nonproductive Attempts to Control

Survivors typically attempt to control their circumstances in every way they can. We've already looked at several examples such as isolation, money, and people. Many more exist, and we will examine some of them. The challenge, more than itemizing the possibilities, is to discover what areas each of us are trying to dominate in our own lives.

Clues of controlling

To recognize the clues often is difficult, especially if the area of control is an integral part of your personality or job responsibility. For instance, if you are very rigid in your daily life, you may think that you are only neat or timely rather than that you are controlling others by forcing them to do everything a certain way at a certain time. You may even feel a real sense of power or of relief because everything went the way it was supposed to. The feeling of power may give you a rush.

✎ **Have you discovered an area of your life that you try to dominate in order to feel safe?** ❑ Yes ❑ No

✎ **If so, what would happen if you began to surrender control over this area of your life?**

_____

_____

_____

As we surrender control we often discover that our control was really only an illusion. We replace control with spontaneity and a new zest for life.

Claire describes Christmas. "The abuse was always worse at Christmas. My dad was home more, and he got drunker. Anyway, I was sure when I grew up that I was going to make things right. Christmas would be special and perfect, no matter what.

I yelled too much at my kids because they didn't want to do things my way.

"When I had my own home, I saw to it that we had all the decorations and everything else ready way ahead of time, even a train under the tree. But I always overspent. I definitely yelled too much at my kids because they didn't want to do things just my way. If anyone was late on Christmas Day, I totally blew up. I was awful. I feel better now that I don't feel compelled to have this perfect Christmas, but I still feel sort of empty."

In Claire's journey of recovery, she finally is learning to let go. She is typical of many victims who try to control their circumstances. They try to make everything perfect, but they have certain underlying expectations of which neither they, nor the people in their lives, are aware.

Unfortunately, Claire attempts to demonstrate this control through her anger—also a typical pattern among survivors. Claire explodes in sudden outbursts of anger at any deviation from her rigid standards. In recovery she is learning not to suppress her pain and hurt, the root cause for her need to control, but to express it appropriately. She is learning to deal with her anger.

Claire has announced that this next Christmas she is going to ask people what special thing they want to do for that day. She plans not to overspend and not to worry about everything being perfect. She earnestly prays every day that she no longer will use her anger as a weapon to control her environment.

"I know I am trying to control when I get angry inside because someone didn't do something just the way I wanted."

Claire is doing well and can even laugh about her own rigidity. She says, "I know I am trying to control when I get angry inside because someone didn't do something just the way I wanted."

Jeralyn controls others by making them feel guilty. She does so much for everyone else that they usually do what she wants just because she is so good to them. But, as Jeralyn admits: "The truth is that I am the one who feels guilty all the time. In fact, I see that I really don't control them as much as they control me. The slightest suggestion that I don't love them or don't want to help them sends me on a guilt trip. Then I would do anything to prove my love and my concern, and unfortunately, I usually do. After I over-extend myself to serve them, I get angry. I don't ever really feel in control."

✎ **Can you identify with either Claire or Jeralyn?** ❑ **Yes** ❑ **No**
If so, describe how you identify with them.

_____

_____

_____

Describe the effect your need for control has had on your relationships with others.

_____

_____

_____

_____

Improved relationships

Susan responded to the question by stating that people were angry because of her need for control. She was not able to accept others' feelings without taking responsibility for them. As she learned to let go, her relationships became less tense and more enjoyable.

✎ **Identify one area where you can give up some control. Perhaps it might be choosing to allow your child to set the table the way he wants to or not telling your friends how they are wrong when they disagree with you. Below write that one area.**

_____

_____

Assignment for the lesson

 In the margin write from memory this unit's Scripture verse. You may check your work on page 141.

➯ **Say aloud your affirmations. You may wish to repeat only once those you have been using. Repeat the new affirmation five times.**

> I accept God's love and kindness toward me.
> The truth will set me free!
> I am worthy to have God lead me and comfort me.
> I am clean.
> I am wonderfully made.
> I have permission to feel my anger and hurt.
> In Christ I am never alone.
> I can trust myself and others.

➯ **Pray for yourself and for each member of your group.**

LESSON 4

Steps to Trust and Discernment

So far in this unit, we've tried to show why, as a sexual abuse survivor, you will want to deal with the issue of how you control as well as how others control you. You will also want to know when to trust and when not to trust. Often survivors are all-or-nothing individuals, making it difficult for them to take even small steps in the area of trust.

We need to develop two related skills. We need to learn to identify trustworthy individuals and choose to trust them appropriately. We also need to learn to identify people who are not trustworthy and choose to protect ourselves appropriately. Most of us have met some individuals whom we've immediately trusted, only to find ourselves revictimized in one way or another. At other times we have failed to recognize trustworthy people who would have helped us. We must develop better skills for trusting appropriately.

Trusting God

The best place to start to trust is with God. We learn to trust God by praying, listening for, and recognizing answers to our prayers. We also read and study the Bible and listen to others as they teach and preach the Bible. As a beginning, we can cry out for God and say we believe in Him. We probably will find that we do believe at a certain level. God will be faithful, and our trust and confidence will be rewarded as we are able to give Him the control of our lives.

Mark 9:24, quoted on the next page, contains the plea of a desperate father. His son was tormented and he could do nothing. He appealed to Jesus with what little faith he had, and asked Jesus to help him to overcome his unbelief.

Often we think in the extremes—that we must do certain things perfectly or not at all. We even apply our extremist thinking to our relationship to God—thinking that our faith must be perfect. In fact, we are imperfect people who can only trust imperfectly, but we can trust God who is a perfect Father. To ask our perfect Father to help us to trust Him always is appropriate.

Immediately the boy's father exclaimed, "I do believe; help me overcome my unbelief!"

–Mark 9:24

⮕ **Read the request of a desperate father from Mark 9:24. Pray and ask God to use the trust you do have to overcome the situations in which you have difficulty trusting Him.**

Each of us, victim or not, can learn to trust God at some point in our life's journey. Even individuals from wonderful, nurturing family systems are challenged in their ability to trust God when they experience trouble. Give yourself time. Most of all, give God time. Your trust in yourself will grow as you are better able to trust God, to place your confidence in Him, to have hope in Him, and to live in freedom from fear, protected by His power.

Discernment

Solid food is for the mature, who by constant use have trained themselves to distinguish good from evil.

–Hebrews 5:14

When to trust or distrust is a gift from God called discernment. Hebrews 5:14 culminates in a passage exhorting us to learn and practice the teachings of God so that our senses have been "trained to distinguish good from evil." Clearly it is not God's desire for any one of us to trust the wicked and distrust the faithful.

Since we have suffered clouded vision as a result of abuse, we need to pray for the ability to discern trustworthy people. This form of prayer is for all of us to pray for the rest of our lives. We need to be able to recognize good and evil and to see the results of both. We need to hear the truth and to sense deception. We also need the experience of being in a group or counseling situation where openness and trust is modeled.

✎ **Do you feel comfortable with your ability to recognize good and evil and to see the results of both? ❏ Yes ❏ No**

What effect has your lack of discernment had on your life?

_____

_____

What do you believe will increase your ability to discern?

_____

_____

No one has a perfect ability to discern good and evil. Everyone gets taken advantage of from time to time. We always experience consequences when we make unwise choices. You may tell someone in confidence and discover later that they have shared your concern or need with someone else. To trust becomes more difficult the next time. As we learn to listen for good character qualities in others, we will make wiser decisions. For example, if they share with you secrets others have told them, the chances are they will share your secrets as well. If they are critical of others, they will be critical of you. Learn to trust, but also be wise!

➥ **Spend some time in prayer. Tell God how you feel about what you have been studying and the work you have been doing. Pray for discernment so you can engage in healing and helpful relationships.**

Attempting to control your world will only lead to disaster.

No one can pave a smooth road for you through this maze of tangled emotions and behaviors. Hopefully, however, you have become convinced that readjusting to your abuse by attempting to control your world will only lead to disaster. A life without trust is a life without freedom—a life in bondage to every area you have chosen to control. It is a life without security and full of fear.

Sheryl said: "I was very angry at God in the beginning, but since I could do nothing, that anger gave way to helplessness. I had no choice but to try to trust God; I had used all my other options. I had even tried all the ways that usually kept me in control. Nothing worked. God was all that was left. And He was there, as always, faithful and strong."

Waiting in Trust

This unit would not be complete without one last definition for trust: "to expect confidently; to wait." About trust, Carol said: "It seems I had waited all my life and I hated to realize that I still had to wait. But to trust is to do what God expects of you, and many times He requires waiting. It's been a long road, a well-traveled road, but a powerful road. There will be a day, even when you sin, even when you are betrayed, even when you feel God is too late, that you will be like the psalmist who wrote these words:

> *For he has not despised or disdained the suffering of the afflicted one; he has not hidden his face from him but had listened to his cry for help.*
>
> –Psalm 22:24

✎ **Describe God's response to the writer of this passage.**

_____

_____

The psalmist cast himself upon God and God delivered him. The psalmist knew God loved him. Trust God and let Him deliver you from all your fears, all your needs to control. Let Him set you free. Let God teach you to trust that which is trustworthy.

✎ **Can you describe a way in which God has delivered you?**
❏ **Yes** ❏ **No**
If so, describe how God has delivered.

_____

_____

_____

We have not ceased to pray for you and to ask that you may be filled with knowledge of His will in all spiritual wisdom and understanding, so that you may walk in a manner worthy of the Lord, to please Him in all respects, bearing fruit in every good work and increasing in the knowledge of God; strengthened with all power, according to His glorious might, for the attaining of all steadfastness and patience.

–Colossians 1:9-11, NASB

Read Colossians 1:9-11 appearing in the margin. Take time to pray. Ask God to give you the wisdom and understanding to trust appropriately. Ask Him to give you the strength to put to work in your relationships the understanding that He gives you.

Assignment for the lesson

In the margin write the Scripture verse for this unit from memory.

Say aloud your affirmations. You may wish to repeat only once those you have been using. Repeat the new affirmation five times.

I accept God's love and kindness toward me.
The truth will set me free!
I am worthy to have God lead me and comfort me.
I am clean.
I am wonderfully made.
I have permission to feel my anger and hurt.
In Christ I am never alone.
I can trust myself and others.

Pray for each member of your group.

LESSON 5

Peace in the Midst of the Storm

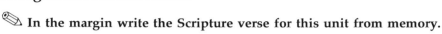

Grief is healthy and necessary for recovery. Sexual abuse survivors normally struggle with the issues of anger, trust, and control. A healthy processing of those issues will bring recovery. You need a way to organize your areas of grief, anger, trust, and control so that you can address each one of them in a manner that leads you through the grief process to resolution and freedom. You need a way to let go of those things in your life that you cannot control or change. By identifying the things in your life that you can control and change, you can set goals and accomplish them.

The "Serenity Prayer" has been a source of strength to many as they have sought peace in the midst of the storm of recovery from sexual abuse. You can use the prayer as an outline to organize your areas of recovery work.

PRAYER FOR SERENITY

God, grant me the serenity to accept the things I cannot change, the courage to change the things I can, and the wisdom to know the difference.
–Reinhold Niebuhr

Healing is virtually impossible without spiritual resources and reflection. In this lesson we would like to show you how to use this prayer in your healing process. Here's how it works. The "Serenity Prayer" is divided into four sections that guide you through the process of recovery.

1. God:

In this section you can reflect on your ideas, beliefs, feelings, struggles, and joys about God.

✎ **Who is God to you?**

_____

_____

_____

_____

When did God become more than just a word to you?

_____

_____

_____

What or who positively affected your concept of God? Explain.

_____

_____

_____

What or who negatively affected your concept of God? Explain.

_____

_____

_____

Our parents are our earliest source of understanding about God.

Our parents are our earliest source of understanding about God. If our father is cold and distant, we tend to view God that way. If our mother was critical and punishing, we also see God as critical and punishing. If our primary caregivers are responsive to our needs, we tend to see God as responsive.

Now, on your own, reflect on the issues that are important to you in your understanding of the character of God.

✎ **What questions would you like to ask about God? What questions would you like to ask Him?**

_____

_____

_____

_____

All of us need to challenge our internalized image of God with who God really is. Sexual abuse causes us to question many of our assumptions about God. You are not alone. Some questions don't seem to have ready answers. We live in a broken world where bad things happen to good people. God does hear your questions.

2. The Serenity to Accept the Things I Cannot Change

The "Serenity Prayer" continues with the request, *"God, grant me the serenity to accept the things I cannot change."* Learning to accept the things you cannot change does not mean passively resigning yourself to circumstances. It does not mean "stuffing" your feelings.

Acceptance is the final stage of the grief process. Acceptance is very active. Accepting your abuse means acknowledging the truth and working through the stages of denial, bargaining, anger, and depression. You will experience these stages of the grief process at various levels and in various combinations. You will then finally accept the fact of your abuse. You eventually will stop saying "if only" and recognize you were not responsible for the abuse. You will get angry at the person who abused you and at the abuse instead of directing your anger at yourself. You will feel the hurt and pain and move beyond it to healing.

✎ **Make a list of "the things" in your past and present life that you cannot change. We have provided you an example.**

I cannot change my father's alcoholism.

_____

_____

_____

_____

_____

_____

_____

_____

You cannot change the things others did or did not do to protect you.

Your list may have included many things you cannot do anything about. You cannot change the fact that you were abused. You cannot change the things others did or did not do to protect you. As you continue your recovery, you will find yourself accepting the reality of the things you cannot change and your powerlessness over those things.

Ask God to grant you serenity or peace about these things as you seek to accept the reality of them and of your powerlessness over them.

3. The Courage to Change the Things I Can

The prayer leads us to ask God to grant, *"the courage to change the things I can."* You cannot change the fact that you were sexually abused but you can begin to change the messages you tell yourself about the abuse. You can begin to change any dysfunctional behaviors you have developed as a way of coping with the abuse.

✎ **Make a list of "the things" you can change. We have given you an example.**

I can change my own negative self talk.

_____

_____

_____

_____

_____

_____

You can change what you do to cope with your fear.

You may not be able to change the fact that you are angry, but you can begin to change the way you choose to express or not express your anger. You may not be able to change the fact that you are fearful, but you can change what you do to cope with your fear. As we begin to change the things we can, God often changes the things that we cannot.

Ask God to show you how to change these things and grant you the courage to share your goals with your group.

4. Grant Me the Wisdom to Know the Difference

Some things in your life may confuse you. You may not know whether to accept them or try to change them. You may wonder if you need to pray for the serenity to accept them and grieve over them or to pray for the courage to change them. The prayer points the way to the solution—ask for wisdom to know the difference.

✎ **List those things you are unsure about—instances where you need the wisdom to know the difference.**

_____

_____

_____

_____

_____

You may be unsure about many things. For example, you cannot change your father's alcoholism, but you can change your response to him. Is that possible? Do you need to have courage and risk some different responses to him?

You can seek God's presence in your journey toward growth and health.

Other survivors have found the parts of The "Serenity Prayer" to be a very helpful method to organize the baffling issues in their lives. The prayer will help you to separate issues and to focus on one at a time as you pray about it. You can seek God's presence in your journey toward growth and health.

Unit Review

✎ **Look back over this unit. What statement or activity was most meaningful for you?**

_____

_____

✎ **Can you remember any statements or activities with which you were uncomfortable? Write those below.**

_____

_____

✎ **Write a prayer asking God to help you in your areas of struggle.**

_____

_____

_____

_____

_____

UNIT 10

The Process of Forgiveness

This Unit's Affirmation:
Because God has forgiven me, I can forgive others.

Focal Passage

But Jesus was saying, "Father, forgive them for they do not know that they are doing." And they cast lots, dividing up his garments among themselves.
–Luke 23:34, NASB

CINDY'S STRUGGLE TO FORGIVE

"I worked to forgive in every area I understood. I forgave the ones who abused me. I forgave the ones who permitted the abuse to happen. I forgave the betrayal of my innocence. I forgave the thieves of my childhood. I forgave the shattering of my identity. I forgave everything I could think of. I began to feel better and less angry, but I still felt empty.

"Then I started forgiving my abuser for each flashback that still tormented my heart and my mind. Every time a memory of abuse burst across my mind, I forgave the person. I asked God to restore His love to me in place of the despair that had come from human sin. Every time I overreacted and became inappropriately angry, I asked God to forgive me for that sin. I asked Him to replace with His love what had been taken from me. It took about 15 months for me to process all my forgiving. Even when I didn't want to forgive, I did it anyway. I was determined to do everything I could to obey God. If He could really restore me, I knew somehow that I could make it through life."

Growth goal

This week's goal
You will confront the issue of forgiveness and determine where you are on your journey toward recovery. You will explore your beliefs about forgiveness and respond to the issue of forgiveness according to your current place on the journey to recovery.

What Is Forgiveness? Part 1	What Is Forgiveness? Part 2	Forgiveness, Not Rationalization	Forgiveness Is for the Survivor	A Decision, Not a Feeling!
Lesson 1	Lesson 2	Lesson 3	Lesson 4	Lesson 5

Memory verse

This week's passage of Scripture
Forgive as the Lord forgave you.
–Colossians 3:13

LESSON

1

What Is Forgiveness? Part 1

Forgiving is not a feeling, and forgiving is not saying that the action was not wrong.

Forgiving is a decision regarding a debt. When I forgive, I decide that I am not going to attempt to collect a debt that you owe me. I am not going to punish you in an attempt to make me feel better.

Until we can forgive, we carry the full weight of the offense.

As we begin each new phase of recovery, our impulse is to say, "this is the most important issue." Each step of recovery is important, but without forgiveness—the focus of this unit—you cannot walk in the wholeness God has for you. We understand that if you are reading through this book very rapidly and have not yet had time to process the difficult pain of your abuse, the very mention of forgiveness may seem unthinkable. But if you ever are to live in freedom, sooner or later you will have to deal with the issue of forgiveness.

Wherever you are in your journey toward recovery, please consider this unit with an open mind. Just because the subject is forgiveness doesn't mean that you must forgive your offender this very instant! You don't have to forgive on schedule. You can forgive when you are ready. A negative reaction only indicates that you need God's further help to heal your pain. Please remember that this unit contains God's principles of forgiveness. You will only be able to forgive with God's help.

The encouragement to forgive may anger you. In the early part of recovery, that response is natural. Forgiveness is a step on the journey toward recovery, but it is not the first step. In this unit you will examine the issue of forgiveness. First, let's consider the reasons why you may not want to forgive.

 Place an asterisk * beside the sentence below that expresses your reaction to the thought of forgiving the person or people who abused you.

I am too angry!
I am afraid to forgive.
As long as I don't forgive I will not be hurt again.
If I forgive, I am saying what happened didn't matter or that it was OK!
It hurts too bad!
Other _____

You may be angry. You still may be too hurt. You may be afraid to forgive. We sometimes choose not to forgive because we have a false belief that not forgiving will protect us from being hurt again. Inevitably the opposite occurs. Until we can forgive, we carry the full weight of the offense. The offense continues to affect us as the pain turns into bitterness. Often by refusing to forgive we cause ourselves greater harm than the original offense. Before we explore what forgiveness *is*, we need to examine some things forgiveness is *not*.

Forgiveness does not mean that the abuse was OK!

Our language patterns sometimes falsely cause us to believe that forgiveness means the offense is now acceptable—that the abuse was not wrong. What do we say when someone apologizes or asks to be forgiven? Typically, we say, "Oh, that's OK!" To forgive an offense does not imply that the offense was any less painful, wrong, or criminal!

In a group, Joyce says over and over, "I will not forgive that rat! He doesn't deserve it. Every time he came near me I said, 'I will never forgive him for this.' Now, if I forgive him, it will be as if he won. He wasn't going to win then, now, or ever. I will not let go. I won't forgive him. It's like saying that what he did was OK."

✎ **Below describe how you might respond to Joyce's statements about refusing to forgive.**

_____

_____

_____

You might say to Joyce: *Your refusing to forgive does nothing to the person who hurt you. Your refusing to forgive only perpetuates the damage of the sexual abuse. Only by forgiving can you ever win over sexual abuse and bitterness. Until you forgive, the person who abused you wins.* We do not forgive primarily for the sake of those who have offended us. We forgive them for two primary reasons. We forgive because it honors Christ, and we forgive because it sets us free from the ongoing damage bitterness causes to us and to those we love.

We forgive for two reasons:
- *because it honors Christ,*
  - *because it sets us free.*

Forgiveness is not permission to hurt you again.

You may fear that forgiving means granting the person permission to hurt you again. Forgiving does not mean the person is free to hurt you. It means that you no longer will be in bondage to the person who hurt you. It means that you will no longer live your life focused on what that person did.

In healthy families, forgiveness is a normal part of life. We learn to forgive even though we will probably be hurt again by the same family members. But with sexual abuse, the crime is so vicious that we grasp for any way, appropriate or not, to deal with the pain. Unforgiveness seems a way to deal with the pain of the abuse. The problem is that refusing to forgive causes an unending cycle of pain and destruction.

✎ **Review the paragraphs you have just read. Below describe what forgiveness does not mean.**

_____

_____

✎ **Complete the sentence, "Forgiveness means..."**

_____

_____

The fact that you were abused will never be any less an offense. You were a victim of sexual abuse. Choosing to forgive will not change that. You have a right as a person created by God to not be abused or taken advantage of. The Ten Commandments and many other passages of Scripture indicate that God wants us to respect one another's property, reputation, and person. God never *excuses* abuse or any other sin, but He does *forgive.*

God never excuses abuse or any other sin, but He does forgive.

✎ Below describe your feelings about the issue of forgiving the person who abused you. Plan to share your feelings with your group.

_____

_____

_____

You might have responded that the idea of forgiving the person who abused you made you angry. You may have just realized that forgiveness is for you, not the person who abused you. You may have just discovered that forgiveness does not mean putting yourself at risk again.

Assignment for the lesson

✎ **Write your own paraphrase of Colossians 3:13, this unit's Scripture memory verse.**

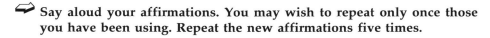

_____

_____

Forgive as the Lord forgave you.
–Colossians 3:13

➯ **Say aloud your affirmations. You may wish to repeat only once those you have been using. Repeat the new affirmations five times.**

I accept God's love and kindness toward me.
The truth will set me free!
I am worthy to have God lead me and comfort me.
I am clean.
I am wonderfully made.
I have permission to feel my anger and hurt.
In Christ I am never alone.
I can trust myself and others.
Because God has forgiven me, I can forgive others.

➯ **Pray for yourself and for each member of your group.**

LESSON 2

What Is Forgiveness? Part 2

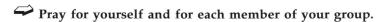

In the first lesson you examined two false concepts of forgiveness. Forgiveness does not mean that the abuse was OK, and forgiving does not give the person the right to hurt you again. For example, to forgive does not change the fact that sexual abuse is a crime. You may forgive people and still expect them to face the full legal responsibilities and consequences for their actions.

Forgiveness does not mean the offense was not great!

In _Search For Significance_ author Robert McGee states several reasons individuals do not forgive. One reason is

You can choose to let go of the bitterness.

because they think the offense was too great. But despite the great offense of sexual abuse, for your own complete recovery you can choose to let go of the bitterness and let go of the offender. Refusing to forgive harms you and adds to the damage caused by the original offense. In fact, the damage you do to yourself by refusing to forgive may be greater than the damage of the original abuse.

Those of us who are survivors can choose to let go of the hurt that results from not forgiving. In the biblical story of Joseph, he had to make the same decision about the abuse he suffered at the hands of his brothers. Joseph boasted about his dreams before his brothers. Then when he went to see his brothers in a pasture far from home, they stripped him of his robe and threw him in a pit. They intended to let him die. Later they changed their minds and sold him to slave traders.

Joseph had to deal with the issue of forgiveness many times in his life. Observe the list of people he had to forgive—

- He needed to forgive his brothers for selling him into slavery, and his father for favoring him above his brothers.
- Perhaps he needed to forgive himself for acting so pridefully about his dreams.
- He needed to forgive Potiphar, his Egyptian master who blamed him falsely and had him imprisoned.
- He needed to forgive his fellow prisoner, the chief cupbearer, who—when he got out of prison—forgot about Joseph (Genesis 40:23).

Joseph had plenty of occasion to refuse to forgive and to become bitter. Joseph must have thought long, hard, and prayerfully over his plight. At some point, he chose to let go of his hurt, anger, fear, and pride. He let go and forgave. The powerful outcome of the story of Joseph came because he forgave his brothers. Joseph's words in Genesis 50:19-20 demonstrate that he had forgiven his brothers.

Joseph said to them, "Don't be afraid. Am I in the place of God? You intended to harm me, but God intended it for good to accomplish what is not being done, the saving of many lives."

–Genesis 50:19-20

✎ **Below explain what you would mean if you made the following statements.**

When I chose to forgive, I chose not to take revenge for the harm that resulted from what others did to me.

_____

_____

I benefit from forgiving even if the person I forgive does not care or want to be forgiven.

_____

_____

Both of these statements indicate a desire to take care of yourself. When you forgive, you appropriately demonstrate that you value yourself and your freedom. Forgiveness validates your survival and grants you the freedom to thrive.

Forgiveness does not depend on the abuser.

Another reason we sometimes find it difficult to forgive is because those who hurt us never said they were sorry. Linda confronted her father, expecting him to say he was sorry. She really wanted to forgive him, all she needed was to hear him ask forgiveness. But he only responded that he didn't remember doing anything to her. The anger burned deep within Linda. She felt as if she had been abused all over again. Finally she grieved and wept because her father would not admit what he had done.

Linda now says that she feels happier than she has in years.

Eventually she forgave her father for the abuse as well as for this denial of the abuse. She now says that she feels happier than she has in years, although a part of her still grieves about a father-daughter relationship that was tainted by his denial.

Linda's forgiveness did not restore a relationship with her father. It did, however, help to restore Linda. She says, "I have a peace, a reality, a maturity about life that I never had before. I don't stay around my dad looking for that word or glance that will tell me how sorry he is. I feel peaceful and joyful about who I am and I have objectivity about who he is. Now, I don't have to look for love from him because what he doesn't give, my Father in Heaven gives me."

We can forgive even if the offense was deliberate or repeated!

Some survivors have difficulty forgiving because the person who committed the abuse did so deliberately and repeatedly. The victim may think that if the abuser had not deliberately planned and committed the offense, forgiveness might seem easier. Yet, if we only forgive accidental sin, we probably will not forgive very much. We also would not want God to only forgive our accidental sin.

✎ **Please review the things that forgiveness does not mean. Complete the following statements.**

Forgiveness does not mean _____

_____

Forgiveness does not _____

_____

We can forgive even if _____

_____

We need to forgive for the sake of our own recovery.

Forgiving is difficult because sexual abuse has such a devastating effect on the life of the victim. The offense is devastating! When confronted, the person who committed the abuse rarely accepts responsibility for his or her behavior. To forgive someone who doesn't deserve that forgiveness seems wrong, but we need to forgive for our own recovery whether or not the abuser benefits. Forgiveness does not mean that the offense was not great. Forgiveness does not depend on the response of the abuser. We need to forgive—for our own good—even if the offense was deliberate and repeated.

You say I must forgive
It's a Biblical Command—
So let's just take a moment
To fully understand…

What forgiveness truly means,
And what it really doesn't
What the truth about it is,
And what it actually isn't

Forgiveness doesn't mean
I'm forced to hide the truth
Of my childlike innocence
Stolen in my youth.

Forgiveness isn't letting go
Because you think I should—
And it's not forgetting…
Because you hoped I would.

Forgiveness doesn't mean
I forget about my pain
So you won't have to look at yours…
And you'll be comfortable again!

Forgiveness doesn't mean
I deny what I feel…
That because you choose denial,
My feelings are not real!

Forgiveness doesn't mean
You've no consequence to pay…
What you did changed my life
In a most dramatic way!

Forgiveness doesn't mean
Your responsibility
Can be ignored by you
And forced to lie with me!

I've got a full-time job
Restoring peace within
From the chaos I've endured
Resulting from your sin.

Forgiveness does not mean
I have to hide what's true
To feed your denial
And keep protecting you.

The process of my healing
Means I see…I feel…I talk—
The freer I become
The stronger I can walk!

✎ **Describe your reasons not to forgive.**

_____

_____

_____

_____

Some of the reasons we use to avoid forgiving include—
- "They don't deserve to be forgiven."
- "The offense cost me too much."
- "What if it happens again?"
- "I should forgive, but I can't."
- "Why doesn't anyone understand? I can't forgive."

✎ **Describe your reasons to forgive.**

_____

_____

_____

_____

Your reasons to forgive may include—
- "It will set me free of this burden."
- "I am tired of carrying the weight of the feelings."
- "Because I want to!"
- "Because Christ forgave me of my sins, and I want to be like Him."

✎ **Describe what forgiveness means to you.**

_____

_____

_____

✎ **What feelings do you experience when you think about forgiving those who have hurt you?**

❑ Anger: They don't deserve to be forgiven!
❑ Sadness: I have lost so much.
❑ Fear: What if it happens again?
❑ Shame: I should forgive, but I can't.
❑ Relief: I can be free of some of this burden.
❑ Lonely: Why doesn't anyone understand?
❑ Joy: I am no longer carrying the burden.
❑ Other _____

You may have discovered that your feelings emerge from your choice to forgive or not to forgive.

✎ **Describe any thoughts you have that make it easier to forgive.**

_____

_____

_____

As you consider the issue of forgiveness, you may think, "I have a long way to go." Or, you may think, "Wow! I can't believe I am considering this." Remember to pray about where you are in the recovery process and then allow God to guide you and to love you right there!

Assignment for the lesson

Forgive as the Lord forgave you.
–Colossians 3:13

✎ **On a card write Colossians 1:13, this unit's Scripture memory verse. Carry the card with you. Whenever you do some routine task like getting a drink of water, review your memory verse.**

➥ **Say aloud your affirmations. You may wish to repeat only once those you have been using. Repeat the new affirmations five times.**

I accept God's love and kindness toward me.
The truth will set me free!
I am worthy to have God lead me and comfort me.
I am clean.
I am wonderfully made.
I have permission to feel my anger and hurt.
In Christ I am never alone.
I can trust myself and others.
Because God has forgiven me, I can forgive others.

➥ **Pray for yourself and for each member of your group.**

LESSON 3

Forgiveness: Not Rationalization

Some do not forgive. They find an excuse for the offense. They rationalize the offender's behavior and excuse him by saying such things as:
- "She couldn't help it."
- "He had such a bad childhood."
- "She won't do it again."
- "God forgave him so I need to just forget it."

The problem with this logic is that rationalization is not forgiveness. We, too, would feel very sorry for someone whose early years had been marred by bad circumstances, but a tragic childhood doesn't give a person permission to rape or commit any other sin. Many thousands of people with painful childhoods choose to find more productive ways to live than sexually abusing someone. Survivors particularly tend to rationalize the role of the person who enabled the abuse. Tammy explains: "I just don't feel I need to forgive my mother. She didn't know what was happening. Yes, she was in the house sometimes, but she was always in the other room. She had so many problems of her own to deal with that truly she just didn't have time. I had five younger brothers and sisters. She had to work part-time. I am surprised that she didn't run away from it all. When she found out, she was brokenhearted. She told me she had been abused as a child herself. It's true that when the abuse happened I wondered why she didn't do something to help me. I sometimes thought that she surely must know what was going on. Sometimes I cried and thought she just didn't care enough about me to see anything."

Tammy finally forgave her mother for passively enabling the abuse. Like Tammy, every victim needs to see that the co-perpetrator also needs to be forgiven. That old fragment in the memory of the victim needs to be released with the freedom of forgiveness.

Tammy's mother sat in a session crying. "I knew something wasn't right. I felt uncomfortable. It was as if God was telling me that something was wrong, but I said to myself, 'Don't be foolish.' I just ignored it."

Rationalizing lets us hide from the truth by making excuses for those who have hurt us. Have you been rationalizing rather than forgiving?

🖉 **List rationalizing statements you have made about the person who abused you. We have given you an example.**

He was also an abuse victim.
_____
_____
_____
_____

🖉 **List rationalizing statements you have made about those who enabled the abuse or who by their reaction aggravated the abuse. We have given you an example.**

She didn't know what was happening.
_____
_____
_____
_____

You can only forgive as deeply as you have acknowledged the offense.

Rationalization is not forgiveness. Rationalization attempts to rescue another from the offense. When we acknowledge the offense, forgiveness becomes possible. You can only forgive as deeply as you have acknowledged the offense. God does not rationalize our sin. He never minimizes it. He recognizes the complete extent of our sin—then He forgives us.

Codependency: a symptom of rationalization and denial

The term *codependency* describes a lack of objectivity and a distorted sense of responsibility. Sexual abuse damages our sense of self and our boundaries so that we often believe that we are responsible for the abuse others inflicted on us.

Codependents take responsibility for the actions of others.

Codependents lose themselves in others. They take responsibility for the actions of others. They emotionally exchange places with another person and lose their identities. Tammy felt responsible for her abuse. Because of her lack of objectivity and her inappropriate feelings of responsibility, Tammy did not accurately perceive the abuse, therefore she did not see anything to forgive. Since she did not recognize the offense, she could not forgive. She could not forgive until she clearly perceived—saw and understood—the abuse.

One counselor explained the dynamics of codependency in this way, "Codependent victims may not feel free to forgive because of a type of role reversal, in which they have emotionally exchanged places with the people who committed or enabled the abuse. They do not see themselves as victims. They see themselves as abusers or as co-perpetrators. Additionally, these same codependent victims may think it unnecessary to forgive because of being partly responsible—in the exchanged role—for the abuse."

✎ **Review the discussion of codependency and the counselor's explanation above. Then below check all the responses that reflect how codependency affects forgiveness.**

❑ 1. Codependents don't think they need to forgive because they don't recognize the offense.
❑ 2. Codependents may identify so strongly with those who abused them that they lose their own identity.
❑ 3. Codependents minimize the need to forgive others because they take the blame upon themselves.
❑ 4. Codependents want to please others so much that they lose their identities in the process.
❑ 5. Codependents refuse to see faults in certain other people.
❑ 6. Codependents minimize, rationalize, and internalize.

Codependency blocks forgiveness in many ways. You could have checked all six of the answers to the activity. They all reflect how codependency affects forgiveness.

✎ **Describe ways you continue to feel responsible for the abuse. Are you protecting a person who by inaction played a part in the abuse? Describe your feelings about the codependency material you just read.**

_____

_____

_____

_____

_____

When You Forgive All Those Who Contributed

You may expect that, at some point in your journey toward recovery, God will make you aware that you need to forgive all those who hurt you. In the biblical story of Joseph (Genesis chapters 37—47), he forgave many people who had actively or passively injured him. He did that, and we saw earlier that God restored him to the position of second in command to the Pharaoh in Egypt. We also noted that Joseph and the wife given to him by the Pharaoh had a child whose name, Manasseh, translates into English as "causing to forget." The Bible does not tell us how Joseph processed his hurt and anger or how he came to forgive, but his actions demonstrate that he did the work of forgiving.

Forgiveness means we choose to let go of our need to carry the offense.

Forgiveness does not mean that the offense was OK or any less devastating. Forgiveness means that we choose to let go of our need to carry the offense with us. We choose to let go of our need to stay connected to the offense to declare it as a wrong. Forgiveness is impossible as long as you deny the abuse.

Sexual abuse is epidemic in our culture. Anger is a normal response to that abuse. Allow yourself to have a healthy anger that people are used and abused; however, do not allow your anger to consume you. Let your awareness direct you to work to support and encourage other survivors. Find ways to educate others about the devastating consequences of sexual abuse. As you assign appropriate responsibility to the abuser, you will be able to declare that the abuse was wrong. Because bitterness does not control you, you will be able to be objective.

✎ **List some ways you can continue to express your concern about sexual abuse in our culture without becoming bitter and hostile.**

_____

_____

_____

You will no longer feel helpless and hopeless.

As you assign appropriate responsibility for the abuse, you will no longer feel helpless and hopeless. You will be able to acknowledge the depth of the offense. As you hold the offender accountable, you then can choose to forgive. You can share with others the devastating effects of sexual abuse without being hostile and bitter.

✎ **What would you like to say to God about the presence of sexual abuse in the world?**

_____

_____

_____

God would—and does—call the sexual abuse in our world an abomination! He expresses properly directed anger toward the sin while expressing loving support to all who are damaged by sin. He is both loving and objective.

Assignment for the lesson

 Say this unit's Scripture memory verse aloud three times. Continue to work to memorize the verse.

 Say aloud your affirmations. You may wish to repeat only once those you have been using. Repeat the new affirmations five times.

> I accept God's love and kindness toward me.
> The truth will set me free!
> I am worthy to have God lead me and comfort me.
> I am clean.
> I am wonderfully made.
> I have permission to feel my anger and hurt.
> In Christ I am never alone.
> I can trust myself and others.
> Because God has forgiven me, I can forgive others.

Pray for yourself and for each member of your *Shelter from the Storm* group.

LESSON 4

Forgiveness Is for the Survivor

As victims, many of us mistakenly believe that unforgiveness will somehow hurt those who have hurt us. By refusing to offer forgiveness, we hope to "get even" with them. But the opposite is true. Abusers, unforgiven, go right on doing what they want to do. They never considered us in the first place, and our unforgiveness has absolutely no affect on their behavior. However, unforgiveness does have a tremendous negative impact on our lives.

Both the Greek and the Hebrew verbs for *forgive* may also be translated "to send away." For the victim it could mean to send away the hurt, the anger, the bitterness, the sadness, and, most importantly, the abuse. Jesus, not you or I, is the One Who died on the cross for the forgiveness of sin, even if we do feel as if we have been crucified. At some point, we must recognize that the forgiveness we grant benefits us.

Check the items that forgiveness allows God to remove from our lives.

- ❑ the feelings of responsibility for the abuse
- ❑ the anger
- ❑ the bitterness
- ❑ the fact that the abuse occurred
- ❑ the hurt
- ❑ the sadness
- ❑ that the abuse was wrong

Forgiveness is not denying that the abuse occurred or that it was wrong.

Forgiveness is choosing to resolve the hurt, the anger, the bitterness, the sadness, and, most importantly, the abuse. Forgiveness is not denying that the abuse occurred or that it was wrong. Forgiveness is not absolving the person of the responsibility for the abuse. It is recognizing that the person must answer to God and possibly to the legal system but not to you.

Our unforgiveness holds us in bondage to the pain of the abuse.

Our unforgiveness holds us in bondage to the pain of the abuse. Certainly our forgiving the people who hurt us affects our responses and relationship to them, but an abuser is not fully forgiven unless he or she goes before God and seeks God's forgiveness. God is the one who takes the away sin of the world. God is the one who atoned for sin. Most important, God is the one, and the only one, who pardons the sin of sexual abuse.

In the Old Testament, the Hebrew word for *pardon* is only used in connection with God and implies forgiveness by God when God is offended. Certainly humans sin against humans, but sin is primarily against God. Sexual abuse is a sin against God and must be pardoned by God as all other sin must be pardoned by Him.

✎ **Describe your feelings when you think about forgiving the person(s) who abused you.**

_____

_____

_____

_____

"I want him to be punished for what he did to me."

Angie expressed her feelings by saying: "I don't want my abuser to be forgiven. If I forgive him, it will be like he escapes responsibility. Like he gets off scot-free. I hate that! All he has to do is say, 'I'm sorry,' and I'm supposed to forgive him. Baloney! I just hate the whole idea. It makes me sick even to think about it. I want him to be punished for what he did to me. I've been punished for 47 years."

As Angie demonstrates so well, forgiveness confronts us with a difficult challenge, but unforgiveness will create a multitude of problems. Refusing to forgive forces you to bear again and again the offenses of the sexual abuse. George, who refuses to forgive his uncle, constantly relives in his mind the torment of the sexual abuse. We need to understand that when we don't forgive, we risk walking in bitterness and despair as we feel the force of unforgiveness through stress, turmoil, and horrible memories.

✎ **List the consequences Angie and George experienced as they chose not to forgive.**

_____

_____

_____

Angie feels responsible to punish her abuser by not forgiving. She loses vital energy for life. George continues to relive the memories. In their attempt to hold their abusers to the offense, they are trapping themselves. The abusers are unaffected. Forgiveness will give them control over their lives again.

✎ Do you identify in any way with Angie or George? ❏ Yes ❏ No
If so, what consequences are you experiencing as a result of your choice not to forgive?

_____

_____

_____

_____

Assignment for the lesson

✎ Below write from memory this unit's Scripture verse. You may check your work on page 162.

_____

_____

☞ Say aloud your affirmations. You may wish to repeat only once those you have been using. Repeat the new affirmations five times.

I accept God's love and kindness toward me.
The truth will set me free!
I am worthy to have God lead me and comfort me.
I am clean.
I am wonderfully made.
I have permission to feel my anger and hurt.
In Christ I am never alone.
I can trust myself and others.
Because God has forgiven me, I can forgive others.

☞ Pray for yourself and for each member of your group.

A Decision, Not a Feeling!

LESSON 5

Every survivor decides to forgive or not to forgive. Most of us are not so overwhelmed with love nor have we become so spiritual that we just find ourselves automatically forgiving everyone. Forgiveness is a decision.

Cindy's Decision to Forgive

Cindy tells how she made the decision to forgive. "I prayed for restoration, and eventually God allowed me to grieve the pain that I experienced. The process was not a one-time event, even though I believe that the first time I forgave met all the scriptural requirements. Typically, the process requires a long period of time."

As you continue to read Cindy's story, circle the statements that give you hope. Write in the margin any actions you identify that you need to take in your recovery journey.

"I was aware of the obvious effects my abuse had upon me, and I worked to forgive in every area I understood. I forgave the ones who abused me. I forgave the ones who permitted the abuse to take place. I forgave the betrayal of my innocence. I forgave the thieves of my childhood. I forgave the shattering of my identity. I forgave everything I could think of. I began to feel better and less angry, but I still felt empty.

"Every time I overreacted and became inappropriately angry, I asked God to forgive me."

"Then I started forgiving my abuser for each flashback that still tormented my heart and my mind. Every time a memory of abuse burst across my mind, I forgave the person. I asked God to restore His love to me in place of the despair that had come from human sin. Every time I overreacted and became inappropriately angry, I asked God to forgive me for that sin. I asked Him to replace with His love what had been taken from me. It took about 15 months for me to process all my forgiving. Even when I didn't want to forgive, I did it anyway. I was determined to do everything I could to obey God. If He could really restore me, I knew somehow that I could make it through life.

"Eventually people began to notice an inner change. One friend said to me, 'Cindy, what happened to you? You're not as angry.' I couldn't explain to her at that time. I just smiled and said, 'God has happened to me.' I could intellectually remember the abuse, but God had caused me to forget the pain of it. I didn't feel dirty, used, or anything negative. I felt full of life and hope. Of course, my worth, my confidence, my identity were not instantly restored, and I wasn't sure who I was or who I was supposed to be, but I was on the right road. Sometimes I meditated and pondered things in my heart. I still felt anxious, but not as anxious. I still had self-doubt, but not as often. I realized God had given His love to me and caused the pain to leave, but it seemed clear that He still had more for me to learn. He wanted me to find my significance in Him. God wanted me to find a new joy in relating to others. He wanted me to have abundant life—not merely survival.

If you're not ready to forgive, God will help you to get there.

"Recovery is between us and God. Yet God does not offer us the option of unforgiveness. In the Lord's Prayer, we are taught to pray to God to 'forgive us our debts as we forgive our debtors.' Each day, I still pray for forgiveness and restoration. If someone sins against me or if I sin, something has been lost to me. Sin takes but God gives. God gives restoration as a by-product of forgiveness. Don't be dismayed at this point. If you're not ready to forgive, God will help you to get there. If you can make a decision to forgive and if you can trust what God says even just a little, He will restore you.

"A woman in my group yelled at me, 'Cindy, if you are lying to me I am going to want to kill you.' I assured her I was not lying to her, not because of what I said, but rather because of what God has said. God will restore all the love that has been stolen. Forgive. Send away all the hurt, the bitterness, the pain, the anger, and the abuse. Allow God to replace the despair, the loneliness, and the betrayal with His love, His joy, and His blessings."

You may or may not be ready to begin the process of forgiveness. That is a decision only you can make. Cindy has given you an example of how she chose to forgive.

✎ Make a list of all the effects of the abuse on your life. For example, you may include abandonment, fears, and loss of your sense of innocence.

_____

_____

_____

_____

_____

_____

_____

_____

☞ Now take each item on your list and, if you are willing, choose to forgive the offender and anyone else that contributed to that loss. Ask God to help you to let go of the need to carry the offense. If you are not willing to forgive some of the people on your list, ask God to help you to grieve and become willing to forgive. You may need to spend days, weeks, or months working through your list.

✎ As you pray, on the list above mark through each offense as you choose to forgive.

✎ Make a list of the behaviors that you have developed in order to compensate for the effects of the abuse (overreacting, control, perfectionism, etc.)

_____

_____

_____

_____

_____

_____

_____

☞ Now take each item and ask God to restore your awareness of His love to you in place of the feelings of hurt and despair. Ask Him to help you forgive yourself for these behaviors and the consequences they produce in relationships. Ask God to replace your losses with His love.

Unit Review

✎ Look back over this unit. What statement or activity was most meaningful for you?

_____

_____

_____

✎ Can you remember any statements or activities with which you were uncomfortable? Write those below.

_____

_____

_____

✎ Write a prayer asking God to help you in your areas of struggle.

_____

_____

_____

_____

_____

_____

_____

_____

_____

UNIT 11

Confronting the Perpetrator

Focal Passage

I will be glad and rejoice in your love, for you saw my affliction and knew the anguish of my soul. You have not handed me over to the enemy but have set my feet in a spacious place.

–Psalm 31:7-8

This Unit's Affirmation:
I can speak the truth.
I can be free!

WELL PREPARED

Jim decided to seek help from a professional counselor before he confronted his mother. He needed to explore his feelings, needs, and expectations. Jim also wanted to determine how to make the confrontation safe for himself and to prepare himself for the reaction of his family. He was concerned about several nieces and nephews.

Jim really wants his mother to seek help. He wants the family to be safe. He is afraid. Jim knows he is not prepared to respond to denial from his mother or rejection from the family. He has images of his mother apologizing to him. Jim wants the counselor to help him evaluate his expectations and define a successful confrontation.

In this unit you will define the issues involved in a successful confrontation.

Growth goal

This week's goal

In this unit you will become aware of the characteristics of perpetrators. You will learn how to confront the perpetrator in a healthy way. You will evaluate your own need about whether or not to confront your perpetrator based on your personal safety and expectations.

Mixed Feelings About the Abuser	Understanding Abusers	The Anatomy of Confrontation	Reconciliation: Unity and Peace	The Decision to Confront
Lesson 1	Lesson 2	Lesson 3	Lesson 4	Lesson 5

Memory verse

This week's passage of Scripture to memorize

When I kept silent, my bones wasted away through my groaning all day long.

–Psalm 32:3

LESSON 1

Mixed Feelings About the Abuser

Victims of sexual abuse often feel helpless in dealing with the person who abused them. This unit will provide you with some facts about abusers and address the value of confronting the person who abused you. You may have been overwhelmed with fear at the very thought of such a confrontation. This fear is understandable.

Fear can make you feel helpless. As you grow in recovery, God's wisdom will replace paralyzing fear.

Please understand as we discuss the characteristics of the person who commits sexual abuse that we do not intend to minimize or discount the effects of your abuse, nor to vindicate the abuser. Be reminded that discussing these things in no way indicates any taking the side of the aggressor or ignoring the devastating results of the sexual abuse in your life. No one can justify the vicious crime of sexual abuse.

The authors of this text are not suggesting that you need at this time to confront the person who abused you. To confront prematurely would be a mistake. The purpose of this unit is to help you to address the issue of confrontation in a safe, supportive environment. You can decide the time, place, and planning for confrontation when you are ready.

If you feel unable to work in this unit, please put it aside. Remember this book is intended to help you in your recovery, and sections of it should be read or studied when you are ready for each new challenge.

 Circle the words that describe how you feel about the person who abused you. If the words listed are not appropriate for your feelings, use the spaces provided to list your own words.

Feelings toward the abuser

anger	terror	pity
fear	sadness	pain
love	grief	sorrow
confusion	loss	
empty	sick	_____
rage	helpless	
numb	hate	_____

Review the words you circled. In your own words describe what you are feeling.

_____

_____

_____

_____

_____

Mixed Feelings

You probably have confused feelings toward those who abused you. Survivors often experience mixed feelings. This is especially true in situations where the person who committed the abuse is a family member or is a highly valued person, such as a pastor, coach, or an inspiring teacher. For example, if the abuser is a father, the survivor may have many conflicting emotions from loathing to loving, particularly if the father had been relatively nurturing and supporting for a number of years before the abuse began. You can sort through these contradictory emotions and feelings.

 As you read the next five paragraphs about the problem of confused and confusing feelings toward the person who abused you, underline the words or phrases that describe your experience.

Your relationship with the person who committed the abuse affects the feelings you may experience about the person. If you are a survivor of rape by a stranger, mixed feelings are not as likely; however, you should still be mindful of feelings and emotions and not sweep any of them under the spiritual rug. As Christians, we sometimes think we have taken care of all our feelings because we want the offender to be with Christ, or because we spend time praying for the offender. To view offenders with a Christlike concern is good, but we need to respect all the emotions God has given us and process all of our damaging emotions.

Missing Childhood

Many years ago
There was a little girl
With bright blue eyes
And long blonde curls.

She came into this world
On a cold winter day—
And little did she know
She'd live her life that way.

While other little girls
Were playing with their toys
She was being taught
Girls were not the same as boys.[1]

You may have been a child victim. If so, you wanted the attention and affection of your parents and other significant adults. After all, that is what God intended. You may have a very strong attachment to the person who abused you. You may want to protect that person from the consequences of his abusive behavior. You wanted the abuse to stop, but you didn't want the relationship to end. What you really wanted—and have always wanted—was a healthy, caring relationship.

You may have carried a heavy burden of inner turmoil about your mixed feelings of love and hate. The emotions you have experienced are normal. Those feelings may include helplessness, pity, sorrow, anger, guilt, and rage. You can work through these feelings and develop a healthy attitude toward the person who committed the abuse.

We can identify our feelings and examine them. Those feelings may be as unhealthy as the hate that never leads to forgiveness or the fear that paralyzes us. To become thrivers we need to do more than say that we assign responsibility to the person who committed the abuse. Even to behave in a way that assigns responsibility to that person is not the final goal. We need to—and with time and growth we can—emotionally assign the responsibility to the abuser as well. Part of recovery is learning to fire ourselves from the job of being the abuser's caretaker. We need to allow abusers to be responsible for their own choices.

In many families the victim experienced both pleasure and pain. Despite the abuse, to experience some pleasant memories and feelings about a family member or friend is natural. These positive feelings, however, should not keep us from holding the abuser accountable. You do not have to lose the positive times in order to say no to the abusive ones. Ask God to help you let go of any shame you feel for caring about a person who abused you.

✎ **If you remember a pleasant time with the person who abused you, take time right now to describe that pleasant memory.**

_____

_____

_____

_____

Rebecca remembered how much fun it was to go to work with her dad. He drove a city bus for years and she rode the bus with him. It felt good when he bragged on her to his customers. He was warm and caring and paid special attention to Rebecca. She was his little girl on those days, and she wasn't afraid of him on the bus. This was the daddy she loved. "Why can't he be like this all the time? Why did he have to get drunk? Why did he have to get so mad? That's what hurts. He didn't have to say those things to me or touch me like that. He replaced my good memories with memories of horror."

A Common Reaction

Anger is a common reaction to the subject of confrontation. "How dare you ask me even to think about confronting! I am too hurt, too betrayed!" You may even have felt angry at just reading the word *abuser*. This, of course, is all right. If, as you read through this chapter, you will make notes when you feel especially angry, they will help in your eventual confrontation. If your anger is consuming you, go back to unit seven, which deals with feeling and overcoming anger. Then at a later time try again to work in this present unit. If you are feeling afraid, remember you are in control of what you choose to do and you have the right and responsibility to yourself to choose safe ways of getting your needs met.

Normal Feelings

If your feelings toward the person who abused you are a mixture of extremes—including love and hate, attraction and revulsion—we encourage you not to deny, bury, or stuff those feelings. You can work through the emotions and, like a miner who separates the gold from the worthless sand, you can keep those feelings and memories that are of value to you. You can process and dispose of the fragments that are painful or worthless. You may have enjoyed much of your relationship with the person who abused you. To have enjoyed the healthy part of the relationship is perfectly alright.

Allow God to supply the love, nurture, and affection that you did not receive in your childhood.

You need to deal with all your feelings about your abuser. You will reach a point in your recovery when you will begin to grieve the relationships you missed. For example, you may begin to feel a longing for a daddy, and you may wish for his love. You may have a need to feel special. God created these feelings. He intended every child to have a nurturing and loving family. Don't condemn yourself for wanting what God intended. Allow God to supply in the present the love, nurture, and affection that you did not receive in your childhood. God meets these needs through your time with Him and through relationships with healthy people such as those in your group.

Words of Comfort

But God, who comforts the depressed comforted us...
–2 Corinthians. 7:6, NASB

Do not take these feelings of longing for a loving family and suppress them. Instead, take them to the cross and grieve for the loss of your childhood. Read in the margin how the apostle Paul speaks of the comfort God sent Paul in the coming of his friend Titus. God will comfort you also, and He can restore the lost love of your broken heart.

Allow yourself to grieve over the fact that the relationship was not what you wanted it to be. Don't deny the pain of the loss. Recognize that when you are bargaining you are trying to find a way to make happen what you wanted to happen. Bargaining means you are continuing to take responsibility for the behavior. Let it go. Let yourself feel the anger of the loss of the relationship and the depression and sadness about what was not yours that should have been had the person been healthy and well.

✎ **Describe your feelings concerning the material you have read in this lesson.**

_____

_____

_____

_____

Mike had never realized how much he needed to grieve over the loss of a special friend. As a youngster he had looked up to Stan, the youth minister at his church. He could hardly wait to turn 13 so he could be in the youth group. Stan loved basketball and taught Mike all kinds of new moves and plays. Stan was usually there when Mike needed a friend—till that afternoon when the sexual abuse began. As Mike read this material he couldn't hold back the tears. Stan had betrayed his trust. Under Mike's anger was a genuine love for Stan. He hated Stan for disappointing him. Mike felt used and he felt that Stan had taken advantage of him.

If you are a victim of rape or if the person who abused you was not a family member or friend, you may not identify with or understand the needs described in this lesson. Go back to the activity above and write what you feel in relationship to your situation.

If you are a survivor of rape you may feel exposed, invaded, vulnerable, and angry. You may fear confronting your abuser and want to avoid the whole issue.

Assignment for the Lesson

When I kept silent, my bones wasted away through my groaning all day long.
–Psalm 32:3

⇨ **Below write your own paraphrase of the Scripture memory verse for this unit.**

_____

_____

➥ **Say aloud your affirmations. You may wish to repeat only once those you have been using. Repeat the new affirmations five times.**

I accept God's love and kindness toward me.
The truth will set me free!
I am worthy to have God lead me and comfort me.
I am clean.
I am wonderfully made.
I have permission to feel my anger and hurt.
In Christ I am never alone.
I can trust myself and others.
Because God has forgiven me, I can forgive others.
I can speak the truth. I can be free!

➥ **Pray for each member of your support group.**

LESSON 2

Understanding Abusers

As you read the following material, keep a pen or pencil in hand and underline the characteristics of abusers that are similar to the person(s) who abused you. Let this list remind you that you are not responsible for the abuse. Only the person who abused you can be responsible. In this lesson you will seek to understand some factors in his or her life that may have contributed to the development of the criminal and immoral behavior.

Sexual abusers usually are "me first" individuals who think of their own pleasure. Some have dominant personalities and may exercise tyrannical control of their homes. Often they are unable to have meaningful relationships with persons in their own age group. They usually are emotionally dependent upon others and unable to express their emotional needs appropriately.

Just as with victims, abusers can be male or female, adolescents or adults, rich or poor. They can be fathers, mothers, brothers, sisters, baby-sitters, uncles, aunts, neighbors, or strangers. Abusers can be doctors, pastors, lawyers, teachers, as well as vagrants. They can come from any place within the family and from any place within society. Personality characteristics frequently found in people who commit abuse include poor impulse control and low self-esteem. Often offenders are involved with some type of substance abuse and are full of self-pity. They often use pornography, both for their own stimulation and for attracting possible victims. They may have been emotionally deprived in childhood and may also have been victims themselves. Possibly they have had a great deal of responsibility in their families of origin.

Those who commit sexual abuse may come from family systems that did not set appropriate boundaries. Often their home situations may be (or may have been) chaotic, with no family members having had their needs met appropriately. Some perpetrators' families may have attempted to isolate their children from the community; some offenders have been extremely overprotected. Their families may sometimes exhibit rigid and extreme religious and moralistic attitudes.

Confrontation and Perpetrators of Ritualistic Abuse

Victims of ritualistic abuse sometimes cannot confront their abusers. Often the aggressors are unknown to the victim. Perhaps the victim was drugged during the abuse. Perhaps the abuse occurred in a ritual child-dedication ceremony and is lost in the victim's memory. Many possible reasons could be listed. Possibly even if these perpetrators could actually be found and confronted, they would attempt to abuse again. In such cases, we rely on a simulated confrontation. In a simulated confrontation you can express your anger, hurt, and fear in safe surroundings.

Other Dangerous Perpetrators

For the wrath of God is revealed from heaven against all ungodliness and unrighteousness of men, who suppress the truth in unrighteousness.
–Romans 1:18, NASB

For this reason God gave them over to a depraved mind, to do those things which are not proper.
–Romans 1:28, NASB

Romans 1:18-32 describes the progressive degeneration that sin causes. The passage begins with our sin-driven desire to reject and suppress the truth. In stages the passage describes how people reject God's plan and He gradually gives them over to an increasingly depraved mind—a mind morally corrupted by evil.

The description in Romans does not apply just to satanic ritualistic abuse, but may also fit others who commit abuse. Rapists may have many of the characteristics listed in that Scripture. If you have been a victim of a person displaying such characteristics, for a variety of reasons, including your safety, you may need to use a simulated confrontation.

Great caution is required in face-to-face encounters with people who are unstable. A teenager describes the abuse she endured from her cousin. "He was evil and wicked. He watched pornographic movies to get new ideas to abuse me. He never showed mercy when I cried and begged him to stop. I couldn't trust him. He invented his own evil. He had no understanding and no love within him, yet every Sunday there he was in church. He was full of deceit in every way."

Tanya, a 15-year-old girl, describes the terror of being raped by her criminally insane perpetrator. He broke into her home in broad daylight. Because of her abuse, she had to process overwhelming dread and recurrent feelings of panic. She worked many months to get past the damaging fear that resulted from her powerlessness to stop the rape. Finally she was able to write a letter of confrontation giving him the responsibility for the rape. After a period of time she was able to read the letter to an empty chair during a simulated confrontation. After a further period of time she was able to express her anger and describe what she deeply felt about the rape.

✎ **Review the lesson. List those characteristics that you underlined.**

_____

_____

_____

_____

_____

Individuals who sexually abuse can have any of the following characteristics: low self-esteem, self-centeredness, poor impulse control, substance abuse, or emotional dependence. They frequently use pornography. They have difficulty expressing their emotions. Sometimes they exhibit rigid and extreme religious and moralistic attitudes.

✎ **Do these characteristics indicate anything to you? If so, what?**

_____

_____

_____

_____

These characteristics indicate that the abuser is emotionally, psychologically, and spiritually ill. The fact that the abuser was sick does not excuse the behavior, but it does help us to understand the abuser's actions. Abusers are needy people who choose to use sexual abuse as a way to meet personal needs.

Survivors often begin to feel pity or sorrow for their abusers when they begin to understand what contributes to a person who chooses to abuse. Notice the word *chooses!*

Being a victim of abuse does not justify becoming a perpetrator.

Being a victim of abuse does not justify becoming a perpetrator. After all, thousands of victims grow to adulthood and do not molest a child or rape an adult. When abusers understand their own background, it can help in guiding their recovery process. There is hope for the person who commits the crime of sexual abuse, but the long process of recovery that is required cannot be taken lightly. The abuser's having said "I'm sorry" is simply not enough basis for believing that restoration has occurred. Remember, the abuser chose to abuse! It didn't just happen!

Sexual offense usually is only one aspect of the offender's dysfunctional behavior. If the offense is compounded by evidence of serious psychopathology such as psychosis, substance abuse, or indiscriminate sexual activity manifested in exposing, peeping, or displaying chronic attraction to children, an extensive recovery program is required. Many medical professionals and resource persons in the sexual abuse field find that certain individuals never recover. For example, aggressors who begin pursuing their negative behavior in adolescence and continue into adulthood may simply prefer such a lifestyle and find it too satisfying and pleasurable to give up.

The sexual offender who never takes responsibility but blames the offense on the victim or on the influence of substance abuse is unlikely to benefit from a recovery program. A perpetrator who will not admit the impact the abuse has had on the victim, or a perpetrator who points to the "pleasure" the victim derived from the act, is in complete denial about the crime. These offenders can still receive help in an effective sexual offenders' program, but unless their attitudes are actually changed, they will not recover from their dysfunctional behavior.

✎ **Beside each of the following statements write _T_ for true or _F_ for false.**

___ 1. If a perpetrator says he is sorry and won't do it again, that means he is in recovery.

___ 2. A perpetrator that points to the "pleasure" of the victim is in complete denial of the crime.

___ 3. The perpetrator that says "But it happened so long ago and only three times. How could it really matter?" is in recovery.

___ 4. A person who makes the following statement is not in denial but is just taking up for himself. "It wasn't my fault. Everyone knows that when a girl goes parking she is saying she wants it. How was I to know she didn't?"

Unless the perpetrator acknowledges the full impact of the abuse and takes full responsibility for it, he or she is in denial of the abuse. The perpetrator must fully acknowledge the abuse to recover. The answers are, 1. F, 2. T, 3. F, 4. F.

When Others Support and Defend the Perpetrator

A realistic problem for many victims is that everybody seems to rally around the person who committed the abuse. Many of our clients have stated angrily in sessions, "All he has to do is say he is sorry, and everybody wants to treat him great!" Unfortunately this is all too common. In fact, many family systems invite the abuser to the family activities but exclude the victim. Whether intended or not, revictimization of the victim is inevitable in this situation. Often the attitude is that the victim needs to hurry up and forgive and get the family together again. This is a grave mistake that can increase recovery time by causing the victim to feel abandoned again. Recovery takes time. Many people need a minimum of two years to process the wound of sexual abuse.

"All he has to do is say he is sorry, and everybody wants to treat him great!"

✎ **Are your parents and siblings aware of the abuse? ❑ Yes ❑ No If they are, how have they responded to you? If not, how does that affect your relationship with them?**

_____

_____

_____

_____

The Perpetrator in Recovery

You are not responsible for taking care of your perpetrator. Confrontation always makes waves in the family. You are not responsible to fix the family situation. Family members may respond with anger, denial, fear, and confusion. Do not excuse or protect them. You may need extra support as you stand in the midst of your family's reaction to the truth of sexual abuse.

The perpetrator who is in recovery may seek your forgiveness. Do not feel that you are forced to extend it. When you are ready, God will show you His grace and aid you in the process of forgiving. Be honest about your feelings.

If you, O Lord, kept a record of sins, O Lord, who could stand? But with you there is forgiveness; therefore you are feared.

–Psalm 130:3-4

The psalmist in Psalm 130:4-5 reminds us that God is a God of forgiveness. Otherwise who could stand? The word translated *fear* in the English text is *yare'* in the Hebrew and can also be translated *reverence*. God's holiness allows Him to be both forgiving and just. Some survivors react very negatively to hearing that God will forgive those who abused them. It doesn't seem fair or right. These emotions just indicate that God has not yet completed restoring you. You have not yet processed the grief and loss. God's love will restore you in time. But, for now, please remember that we have a loving God who does not desire that any should perish. The perpetrator cannot give back to you what he or she took, but God can restore you. Even though the perpetrator is responsible for the aggression, God gives him or her the opportunity to choose to ask for forgiveness. Forgiveness depends on true repentance.

The genuine repentance that results in healing is not just the type of sorrow Judas felt about the sin of betraying Jesus. It is the true repentance that the prodigal son experienced in his willingness to risk even humiliation to be restored. His repentance produced genuine change in his life. One word in the Hebrew language, *naham*, describes repentance as a "grieving for the evil a person has brought upon himself or another." This is the challenge for the abuser. The prodigal son knew, as did Judas, that he had sinned against heaven and against his father; however, the son felt that he was no longer worthy to be called a son. The journey from a distant land to his father's house was long and difficult, but he took responsibility and traveled the road.

The abuser also must travel the long road of recovery. This road is not an easy one; it requires a willingness to experience the humiliation of a complete confession of sin without excusing or defending his actions.

✎ **At the confrontation, is the perpetrator likely to blame you rather than accept responsibility? ❑ Yes ❑ No
How would you feel if the person who abused you blamed you for the abuse at a confrontation? How will you respond?**

_____

_____

_____

_____

If the abuser blames the victim for the abuse, it is a clear indication that he or she is not repentant. The survivor must be prepared to state the offense clearly and calmly, to stand firm in the fact that the behavior was abusive, and to refuse to take responsibility for it. Nothing short of genuine repentance on the part of the abuser is a legitimate basis for reconciliation. Even though you might wish for reconciliation, don't sacrifice the truth or yourself for it. Even though you might wish to retaliate, be careful to act wisely. State your feelings about the person's denial of responsibility, then act rather than react to any accusations of blame.

Assignment for the Lesson

➥ **Write on a card Psalm 32:3, the Scripture memory verse for this unit. Carry the card with you and regularly review the verse.**

➥ **Say aloud your affirmations. You may wish to repeat only once those you have been using. Repeat the new affirmations five times.**

> I accept God's love and kindness toward me.
> The truth will set me free!
> I am worthy to have God lead me and comfort me.
> I am clean.
> I am wonderfully made.
> I have permission to feel my anger and hurt.
> In Christ I am never alone.
> I can trust myself and others.
> Because God has forgiven me, I can forgive others.
> I can speak the truth. I can be free!

➥ **Pray for each member of your _Shelter from the Storm_ support group.**

When I kept silent, my bones wasted away through my groaning all day long.
–Psalm 32:3

LESSON 3

The abuser's request for forgiveness should not prevent the survivor from stating her feelings.

The Anatomy of Confrontation

Confronting the abuser is a normal part of a recovery process, but confrontations are difficult and should not be attempted without support and preparation. Confrontations may take place face to face with the person, or in simulated confrontations, to be described later in this chapter. In a confrontation the survivor expresses her feelings about the effects of the abuse and about the person who committed the abuse. Even though the person who committed the abuse may call, write a letter, or in person take responsibility for the abuse and seek forgiveness, the survivor still needs to confront. The abuser's confession and request for forgiveness is a positive step; however, it should not prevent the survivor from stating her feelings. Confrontation is especially important in the family setting, where, for reconciliation to take place, the victim may need to confront the abuser directly.

✎ **What are two types of confrontation?**

_____

_____

Remember that confrontations can be face to face or they can be simulated. In either case the primary objective is for the survivor to vent the pent-up feelings, get them out of his system, and move on.

✎ **What feelings do you have about the issue of confrontation?**

_____

_____

You may feel rage, a desire for vengeance, out of control, paralyzed by fear, or afraid of abandonment. Like many survivors you may still feel the need to protect the perpetrator or significant others that might be hurt if the abuse is revealed.

✎ **List any individuals that you are protecting by your silence. This person may be the wife of the person who abused you; the children; the husband; the person's position in the community, or in the ministry. You may want to write this list on a separate sheet of paper or use coded names.**

_____

_____

_____

_____

We encourage you to be honest with your support group about what happened to you. In addition, you can decide if you need to tell any agencies or authorities. You may think it is harsh to reveal this information, but consider these two reasons. First, the victim must be protected. Even when a perpetrator starts his or her recovery and is well into that process, it is not uncommon for a relapse to occur and for the perpetrator to try to revictimize you. The second reason is to protect all other potential victims.

✎ **List the two reasons that were stated in the previous section for revealing the abuse.**

1. _____

_____

2. _____

_____

The abuse needs to be revealed to 1) protect the victim from further abuse and 2) to protect other potential victims.

✎ **Can you think of any other reasons for revealing the abuse?**

_____

_____

_____

_____

Relationships have a chance to heal as the truth is known.

After the abuse is revealed, the abuser faces the choice to continue in denial or to seek help. Secrets in a system—a family, a church, a community, a workplace or any other system—create dysfunction. Relationships have a chance to heal as the truth is known.

✎ **List your reasons for continuing to keep your abuse a secret.**

_____

_____

_____

_____

_____

The abuse is difficult to talk about for many reasons. You may still be feeling shame and guilt. You may want to protect the image of the abuser. "It would hurt mother to know her dad would do that to me."

Only breaking the silence can stop the cycle.

In some families the pattern of sexual abuse is repeated through successive generations. Those who sexually abuse almost always abuse more than one victim. Only by breaking the silence can the cycle be stopped.

Disclosure also allows every family member to be a support to the recovery process of both the victim and the abuser. The purpose of disclosure is not to shame the perpetrator or to invade the privacy of the victim. Family members need to honor the victim's concern for privacy about the abuse. Recovery requires disclosure of some facts about the abuser and the nature of the abuse so that both the victim and others may process their anger and grief.

Don't try to do this alone!

Only confront the abuser with the help of a professional who has worked in the areas of sexual abuse and sexual addiction.

Confrontation also can be extremely emotional for both the person who committed the abuse and the person who suffered the abuse. We strongly recommend that you only confront the person who abused you with the help of a professional who has worked in the areas of sexual abuse and sexual addiction. Prepare yourself for possible rejection at the confrontation. Most abusers condemn those who confront them. In many states, children as young as five must face their perpetrators in court. This often revictimizes the young survivor, be very careful in preparing for confrontation.

A simulated confrontation is another way of dealing with the grief and pain. This method often is used in therapy sessions. This form of confrontation enables victims to release the painful emotions of abuse.

A safe environment in which to have a simulated confrontation is absolutely essential. In physical terms, the victim may confront an empty chair, a picture of the perpetrator, or any other association-producing object that will create a feeling of reality. This is a major step in the recovery of victims because it enables them to release the emotions stuffed inside and begin to regain the power lost to the abuser. Again, the need for the presence of a professional in this kind of confrontation is just as important as it is for direct confrontation. The emotional intensity a simulated confrontation generates demonstrates the need for a counselor to be present.

As you think about confronting the person or persons who abused you, which method do you believe would work best for you? Either a direct confrontation or a simulated confrontation can be effective. Your choice will depend on your own personal needs.

✎ **Circle your preference for a way to confront those who have abused you.**

Direct Confrontation   Simulated Confrontation

State your reasons for your choice.

_____

_____

_____

_____

✎ **Imagine a direct or a simulated confrontation with the person or persons who abused you. Consider the following questions.**

Limit your goals to the things you can control.

What are your goals for this confrontation? Limit your goals to the things you _can_ control.

_____

_____

_____

_____

How do you want the person you will confront to respond? These are matters you _cannot_ control.

_____

_____

_____

_____

How do you think the person will react to this confrontation?

_____

_____

_____

_____

Prepare for your confrontation under the guidance of a counselor. Discuss with your counselor your goals, hopes, fears, and the probable response of the person you will confront.

As she completed this exercise, Misty realized that she was not ready for a direct confrontation. She was still allowing her abuser to have too much power over her. She wanted her uncle to explain to her why he abused her instead of her sisters. Misty wanted to rescue her uncle by blaming herself. In a simulated confrontation Misty was able to verbalize her feelings toward her uncle and work through these feelings without accepting responsibility for the abuse. She was able to release herself from the need to understand her uncle's feelings. Misty was able to tell her uncle how angry, hurt, and disappointed she was.

Assignment for the Lesson

☞ **Below write three times Psalm 32:3, the Scripture memory verse for this unit.**

_____

_____

_____

_____

_____

☞ **Say aloud your affirmations. You may wish to repeat only once those you have been using. Repeat the new affirmation five times.**

I accept God's love and kindness toward me.
The truth will set me free!
I am worthy to have God lead me and comfort me.
I am clean.
I am wonderfully made.
I have permission to feel my anger and hurt.
In Christ I am never alone.
I can trust myself and others.
Because God has forgiven me, I can forgive others.
I can speak the truth. I can be free!

☞ **Pray for each member of your group.**

Reconciliation: Unity and Peace

LESSON 4

The Greek word for _reconcile_ means "to remove the cause that makes warring parties enemies or to remove the obstacle to unity and peace." When people are reconciled they are at peace with each other.

Joseph was reconciled with his brothers when they came to Egypt in search of grain. By the time Joseph's brothers reached Egypt, he was able to stand before them and to confront them because he had no inner feelings that would keep him from having a relationship of unity and peace with them. Forgiveness is unilateral. You can forgive even if the abuser never admits the abuse, is never sorry, and never changes. But reconciliation requires both people's commitment to recovery, honesty, repentance, forgiveness, and communication. Even then reconciliation is a long and difficult process of breaking down barriers and building trust.

I am sending you out like sheep among wolves. Therefore be as shrewd as snakes and as innocent as doves.
–Matthew 10:16

Jesus sent the disciples out to minister. Before they left He gave them the instructions in Matthew 10:16. Read the verse appearing in the margin. Another translation says be "as wise as serpents." If the perpetrator has truly begun to recover he will have asked God to forgive the sin committed against you. He will seek your forgiveness. He will want to make atonement by supporting your recovery financially; for example, by paying for your counseling. You can be assured that a person who is in genuine recovery will experience a deep grieving about what he or she has done to you. They will offer no excuses or rationalizations for the behavior and will take full responsibility for the abuse.

✎ **What do you need to do to be wise about dealing with the person who abused you?**

_____

_____

✎ **What would it mean to be "innocent as a dove" in relationship to the person who abused you? Check all that apply.**

- ❏ not to seek revenge
- ❏ not to be controlled by anger
- ❏ to be gentle
- ❏ to be manipulative and controlling
- ❏ to pretend that nothing ever happened

You can maintain your integrity while you break the silence.

One example of wisdom might be to make wise choices that protect you from being abused by this person again. Your behavior toward this person can be innocent even while you are honest about your anger and even as you confront the person. You can maintain your own integrity while you break the silence and assert your authority over your own life. The first three responses are evidence of innocent motives. The last two show a lack of healing. They are forms of aggression and denial.

Below you will read about some typical reactions of perpetrators to confrontation. As you read each reaction think about how you might feel if you were to be faced with that reaction. Respond in the space provided.

Typical Responses

In preparing to confront, understand that people who commit abuse typically react in one of three ways—remorse, denial, or rationalization.

Remorse—One kind of offender is extremely remorseful. This type of offender probably committed the offense only once or twice and may have been wanting for years to ask the victim for forgiveness. He or she is willing to accept responsibility for the actions and is aware of the possible damage the victim has suffered. These offenders probably have carried their guilt and shame for a long time. They usually are victims themselves, and usually are repentant. Confronting them generally results in a reconciliation and restoration of the relationship.

✎ **How do you think you would react if the person felt remorse that the abuse ever happened? Has that already happened? If so, what did he/she say? How did you feel?**

_____

_____

_____

_____

Ask God to lead you to truth and healing.

You may have a broad range of feelings in response to this exercise. Some survivors feel validated, even grateful, that their abuser has admitted and taken responsibility for the abuse. However, some survivors are angry when the abuser responds with remorse and repentance. Some survivors choose to avoid confrontation because they are afraid the abuse might be repented. Wherever you are on this journey, don't shame yourself. You will work through the confusing thoughts and feelings. Ask God to lead you to truth and healing.

Denial—Most commonly, offenders are in a state of denial and refuse to acknowledge that anything happened. After all, who wants to be labeled a "child molester" or "rapist"? Another obvious reason for the denial is that the abuse is a crime punishable by incarceration. Offenders also feel an intense need to justify and protect themselves from recognizing and feeling the extent of the evil that they have committed. Some abusers have sociopathic traits. This means they have little guilt, and quite loudly deny any involvement in the offense. Their denial is a powerful belief to which they cling tenaciously.

Ralph, an offender of the type just described, still denied committing child abuse even after all the authorities involved on the case explained that absolutely no one believed him; the physical evidence as well as his daughter's statements clearly pointed to him as the perpetrator. His daughter's hymen was not intact, and there was scarring in the vaginal area. She had also made several outcries that were a matter of public record. Ralph's response to overwhelming evidence was, finally, to admit that this "might have happened." He did not believe he had done anything to his daughter, and he certainly "didn't remember any such thing." But because the authorities, the therapists, and his daughter said so, he "guessed" he must have done it. Ralph never completed his recovery. This type of perpetrator is a great danger to society, as he will very likely victimize someone again.

Another offender, also in denial and having the same history, can be presented with the same set of facts that Ralph had to face but be relieved when the need for disclosure occurs. This individual wants the abuse to stop, even though it has been happening for some time. In no way, however, does his attitude indicate that he or she will not need an extensive recovery program. Quite the contrary—the denial in which this abuser has been gripped requires treatment just as urgently as someone like Ralph.

Paula's story

After a year of counseling, Paula confronted her uncle. Paula already had written a letter in which she and her husband asked her uncle and his wife to join them in her counselor's office. Paula and her counselor prepared a tape-recording that she played to her uncle at the meeting. Confronting a person by using a tape is very effective. The survivor is not forced to shut down if the abuser becomes verbally or emotionally abusive during the confrontation, and the survivor can include all that she wishes to say to the person. Another advantage is that if the confrontation becomes too emotional, the victim can shut off the tape and take time for things to settle down.

During the first part of the meeting, Paula's uncle began to apologize to Paula for what he had done to her. He explained that both he and his wife had been victims of sexual abuse. He took full responsibility for his actions and for the harm that they had done.

"I was just selfish and took what I wanted."

This confrontation was a very moving event that aided the healing process for both abuser and victim. He took responsibility for the offense and asked for her forgiveness. As far as Paula knows, her uncle is still in a recovery program along with his wife. Paula does not wish to have a close relationship with him, and in fact she doesn't care if she ever sees him again. But she counts her confrontation with him as positive and productive in her recovery process. One satisfaction was in being able to ask him why he had abused her. He seemed to have difficulty finding the words to answer, but finally said, "I was just selfish and took what I wanted."

Not every confrontation will be as productive as Paula's. In fact, ill-timed confrontation or confrontation with certain types of abusers may cause a serious setback for the victim, and in some cases may even be dangerous. If your offender blames the abuse on alcohol, drugs, or you, or minimizes the victimization, the confrontation still can be very profitable for you because you can see the stark, painful reality that the abuser will not accept responsibility. That realization may be very painful but it may be a stepping stone to reality and recovery. This is something you and a professional counselor will need to decide.

Alyssa's story

Alyssa, a mother of two, got a call that her father was in the hospital and about to die. She talked with her counselor who thought that confrontation might be a little premature but recognized the special circumstances. Alyssa flew out to see her father for the last time and to confront him. This was only a few weeks before his death, so she also prepared herself for the guilt that she might feel over this confrontation.

At the hospital, after a brief time of polite conversation, she asked him why he had molested her. He looked straight at her and said, "The reason I molested you is that from the time you were a baby I knew you wanted me. Whenever I would change your diaper, you would kick up your legs at me. You would just smile and I knew in my heart that you wanted to have sex with me." Venting her anger and disgust toward her father and toward his denial, she told him in considerable detail what she really experienced from his abuse.

Even in his terminal condition, her father did not accept responsibility or admit committing any offense. Alyssa's father did not respond as she hoped he would, but she says the confrontation aided her recovery. It helped her understand how sick and twisted he really was.

✎ **How do you think you would react if your perpetrator(s) denied that the abuse ever happened?**

_____

_____

_____

Has your abuser already denied that the abuse happened? ❑ **Yes** ❑ **No**
If so, what did the person say? How did you feel?

_____

_____

_____

_____

Your recovery does not depend on the abuser's admission of guilt.

Typical reactions to the perpetrator's denial of the abuse range from doubt and confusion to anger and rage. You may feel hurt, disconnected, and unimportant. These feelings are normal. Remember that your recovery does not depend on the abuser's admission of guilt. You know what happened to you. You can take responsibility for your recovery.

Rationalization—The person who admits to the offending behavior and without swerving protests that it was not wrong is the third type of offender. This person believes he actually was helping by teaching the child how to have sex, improving the quality of life for the child. People who have an impaired conscience are called *sociopaths* which means that these people wound others deeply and do not care.

Confrontation with this person is not effective in bringing about any reconciliation, because this person feels no remorse. Unless the survivor understands the situation and is prepared, she will be re-victimized in a confrontation. These abusers not only have no remorse, but often approve of those who participate in victimizing. Romans 1:29-32, which appears in the margin, may describe these individuals quite well.

...filled with all unrighteousness, wickedness, greed, evil; full of envy, murder, strife, deceit, malice; they are gossips, slanderers, haters of God, insolent, arrogant, boastful, inventors of evil, disobedient to parents, without understanding, untrustworthy, unloving, unmerciful; and although they know the ordinances of God, that those who practice such things are worthy of death, they do not only do the same, but also give hearty approval to those who practice them.
–Romans 1:29-32, NASB

✎ **Which description do you think best fits the person who abused you (remorseful, in denial, rationalizing)? Explain why you think so.**

_____

_____

_____

_____

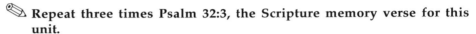 How does the possible attitude of your perpetrator affect your expectations of and preparations for a confrontation?

_____

_____

_____

Do not make your recovery depend on a response from another person.

Because you cannot know for certain the attitude or response of the person who abused you, you need to prepare wisely. Enlist the aid of an experienced counselor. Be prepared for whatever response you get from the abuser. Remember that you can grow even though the person who abused you may never respond appropriately. Do not make your recovery depend on a response from another person—especially not a sexually abusive person.

Assignment for the Lesson

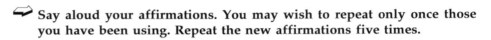 Repeat three times Psalm 32:3, the Scripture memory verse for this unit.

➥ Say aloud your affirmations. You may wish to repeat only once those you have been using. Repeat the new affirmations five times.

> I accept God's love and kindness toward me.
> The truth will set me free!
> I am worthy to have God lead me and comfort me.
> I am clean.
> I am wonderfully made.
> I have permission to feel my anger and hurt.
> In Christ I am never alone.
> I can trust myself and others.
> Because God has forgiven me, I can forgive others.
> I can speak the truth. I can be free!

➥ Pray for each member of your support group.

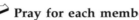

LESSON 5

The Decision to Confront

At the right time, in the right place, and with the right supervision and preparation, you can confront the person who abused you. You have the freedom to decide whether what you have learned points toward a personal confrontation or a simulated one. The purpose of confrontation is to release your feelings of hurt and anger.

We also strongly encourage you to seek the help of a professional to decide when to confront and whether the confrontation should be done personally or symbolically. Remember it is extremely important for the confrontation to take place in a safe environment. If possible you need to have support from other people. If more than one person abused you, confront each one of them individually. Don't rationalize, apologize, or make excuses for them, but directly confront the aggressor concerning the effects of the abuse in your life. Confront him or her with your honest feelings. Remember that each person who commits sexual abuse makes a choice to abuse. You make a choice to confront.

✎ **How would you prepare yourself for a possible confrontation?**

_____

_____

Listed below are some actions you will need to complete as you prepare. You may want to use the following as a preparation checklist.

A preparation checklist

❑ Find a good counselor to assist you.
❑ Establish clear goals for the confrontation.
❑ Anticipate the perpetrator's reaction.
❑ Anticipate your feelings in the heat of the confrontation.
❑ Determine the possible steps you will take depending on the person's response.
❑ Be prepared to process the pain produced by the confrontation.

✎ **What kind of support do you think you need to confront your abuser?**

_____

_____

✎ **What do you want to have happen when you confront? What will need to happen for your confrontation to be successful?**

_____

_____

✎ **If you expect an apology from your perpetrator, what would it be like?**

_____

_____

Define a successful confrontation to guarantee success.

✎ **If you do not receive an apology, will you feel like you have failed or can you give yourself the gift of success by defining a successful confrontation in such a way as to guarantee success?**

_____

_____

Jim decided to seek help from a professional counselor before he confronted his mother. He needed to explore his feelings, needs, and expectations. He also wanted to determine how to make the confrontation safe for himself and to prepare himself for the reaction of his family. He was concerned about several nieces and nephews. Jim really wants his mother to seek help. He wants the family to be safe. He is afraid. Jim knows he is not prepared to respond to denial from his mother or rejection from the family. He has images of his mother apologizing to him. Jim wants the counselor to help him evaluate his expectations and define a successful confrontation.

The Ideal Outcome

In some cases the offender recognizes his sin, asks for forgiveness, repents, and begins the long process of reconciliation. The confrontation is the first step in this process. The survivor and person who committed the abuse can meet with a professional and the victim can confront the abuser in a safe environment. The abuser at some point in the recovery process needs to meet with the entire family and ask forgiveness from each member. This is a very difficult occasion, and often the victim feels embarrassed by the disclosure. Also, other siblings may want to avoid the issues if they feel unable to cope with the situation.

As difficult as this process is, it may keep the spouse and siblings in an incestuous family from being second (and further) victims. An eight-year-old boy told how jealous he was of his dad for going into his sister's room so often. He wasn't quite sure why, but he felt confused and angry that she was getting all the attention. His 13-year-old brother says he just wants to forget about it, as it was too painful even to think about what his dad did with his sister.

These apology sessions require a great deal of effort on the part of each family member. But please remember that one of the primary blocks to recovery is "keeping the secret." Another block is denial. All the members of the family need to process their own individual forms of denial. This same principle applies within the alcoholic family, where each member must come to grips with what has actually happened within their family system. Such honesty can produce life if people respond.

✎ **How would you respond to an apology? Circle the feeling listed below which best depicts how you would respond.**

relief	anger
remorse	numb
gratitude	sadness
other _____	

✎ **What if there isn't an apology? Circle the feeling listed below which best depicts how you would respond.**

anger	frustration
resentment	remorse
numb	sadness
hate	bitterness
disappointment	hurt
other _____	

As we have stated earlier, sexual offenders are rarely strangers. They usually are family members, friends, or acquaintances. To have mixed feelings is normal. Do not criticize or ridicule yourself because of your feelings.

The Real Church

There are some who say
  The church is a sacred place—
And to let my feelings show
  Would be a real disgrace

So as I dressed for church
  And finished with my hair—
I glanced into the mirror
  To be sure my mask was there.

I heard the Lord so gently
  Speaking to my soul
"My child, I long to touch you—
  I want to make you whole..."

"I brought you here today—
  Not for you to hide—
But that others on life's journey
  Could help you see inside..."

"In the world, it's hard
  To let the real you show—
But here, my child, you're safe—
  It's where hurting people go.

"I long to help you children—
  That's why my church was born—
Come unto me, I'll help you mend
  When you feel tossed and torn..."

My tears began to flow—and
  My mask slipped to the floor—
But it's OK—I'm welcome here—
  I won't need it anymore.[2]

A confrontation is successful because it communicates truth.

Many abusers will not travel the road of the prodigal back to their father's house. They will not choose the difficult road to recovery. Some who start the process will not do the grueling work of recovery. Others will only pretend to start a recovery program to avoid prosecution. Still others will say a recovery process is not necessary because the abuse never happened. Do not allow your recovery to depend upon the response of the perpetrator to your confrontation. A confrontation is successful because it communicates truth—whether or not the person responds positively to that truth. The secret is revealed. You are no longer protecting a person who has hurt and confused you. You are no longer a victim under this person's power and control. That is success and victory. You may feel hurt and disappointed by the response. Do not let those feelings rob you of the reality that you have faced the biggest fear you will probably ever face. You finally have begun to learn how to experience the "serenity to accept the things you cannot change, the courage to change the things you can, and the wisdom to know the difference."

Unit Review

✎ **Look back over this unit. What statement or activity was most meaningful for you?**

_____

_____

✎ **Can you remember any statements or activities with which you were uncomfortable? Write those below.**

_____

_____

✎ **Write a prayer asking God to help you in your areas of struggle.**

_____

_____

_____

_____

_____

_____

_____

Notes
[1]Shannon L. Spradlin, *Does God Know About This?* (Henderson, Nevada, 1993), 46.
[2]Ibid., 75.

UNIT 12

Intimacy in Relationships

Focal Passage

Love is patient, love is kind. It does not envy, it does not boast, it is not proud. It is not rude, it is not self-seeking, it is not easily angered, it keeps no record of wrongs. Love does not delight in evil but rejoices with the truth. It always protects, always trusts, always hopes, always perseveres. Love never fails.

–1 Corinthians 13:4-8

This Unit's Affirmation:
I am loved
so I can risk loving you.

HIDDEN AND LONELY

Jacque struggled for many years with the issue of intimacy. She was aching to feel close to someone; however, to feel close meant relinquishing control. She was too afraid to trust that David really would not take advantage of her openness.

Jacque could not let him know she needed him. She felt safe and hidden behind her wall of self-sufficiency. Jacque also felt very alone.

In this final unit you will examine the issue of intimacy in relationships, including physical intimacy in marriage.

Growth goal

This week's goal
You will be challenged to evaluate your own need for intimacy and face the fact that you have a need for intimacy and take steps to find appropriate intimate supportive relationships.

From Isolation to Intimacy	The Nature of Intimacy	Unmet Needs for Intimacy	Ways We Avoid Intimacy	Why Is Intimacy So Difficult?
Lesson 1	Lesson 2	Lesson 3	Lesson 4	Lesson 5

Memory verse

This week's passage of Scripture to memorize
But If we walk in the light, as he is in the light, we have fellowship one with another, and the blood of Jesus, His Son purifies us from all sin.

–1 John 1:7

202

LESSON 1

From Isolation to Intimacy

As you began your recovery from sexual abuse, you may have been unable to experience intimacy with people. As you have worked at your recovery process, you have made many changes. The ultimate goal of recovery is to develop genuine intimacy with God and with others.

The purpose of this unit is to help you understand and begin to experience intimacy with yourself, with appropriate others, and with God. You will identify what intimacy is and what it is not and how to experience it.

Barriers to Intimacy

In previous units we discussed many of the potential barriers to achieving intimacy such as betrayal, lack of trust, fear, and dysfunctional family relationships. Victims are often violated in their families, which are the very relationships that God created to teach them the concept of intimacy. If this happened to you, you may have developed an intense fear of loving someone again. Loving became associated with pain and suffering.

 In the following paragraphs circle words or phrases that describe ways you have used to cope with the need for and fear of intimacy.

The sense of intimacy is a very fragile thing and can be damaged easily. Victims often attempt to cope by either becoming too isolated from others or by smothering family and friends with their need for intimacy. For example, you may have decided years ago that you absolutely do not want to risk the pain of attempting to connect with anyone in an intimate way. You chose to isolate yourself as a means of self-protection.

Other people try to cope by attaching themselves to anyone who expressed any interest in them. In doing so they overwhelm others with their desperate need to be accepted. They drive others away with their insatiable neediness. They try again and again to find someone to meet their aching need for closeness. Then they drain her and leave her feeling incapable of giving enough. When she pulls away, the needy victim feels more empty and alone than ever. People with this tendency find a friend and call him three or four times a day, drop by his house uninvited, or become angry when they hear he has participated in an activity with someone else. Their happiness depends on how someone else responds to them.

enmesh–v. When people lack a healthy sense of separateness, they have poorly developed boundaries and they confuse their own identities and responsibilities with those of others. This confusion of boundaries is called enmeshment.

Whatever your tendency—to isolate or to enmesh—if you are unable to be close to people, you still are living in the darkness of the storm. Fortunately, you can find an answer. You can learn how to have healthy boundaries for yourself and to respect the boundaries of others. You can find balance in your relationships with others. You can experience intimacy.

Three factors—the trauma of the abuse, your relationship to the abuser, and the rules and roles in your family system—affect your ability to express and receive healthy intimacy. As you embark on your journey from isolation to intimacy, remember that you will have to deal with each of these factors.

✎ **List the three factors that affect your ability to express and receive healthy intimacy.**

1. _____

2. _____

3. _____

✎ **Below or in your journal record your thoughts and feelings about how you think these factors have affected your ability to express intimacy.**

_____

_____

_____

_____

The more traumatic the abuse, the more it affected your ability to express healthy intimacy.

The level of trauma you experienced during the abuse depends upon factors such as age, duration, severity, and your own beliefs and expectations. The more traumatic the abuse, the more it affected your ability to express and receive healthy intimacy. The closer your relationship to the abuser, the more your ability to trust was affected as was your ability to express and receive healthy intimacy. Families have different rules and roles concerning the expression of verbal and physical affection. These also contribute to your needs and responses to intimacy.

✎ **What is your tendency in relationships? Below check the appropriate response.**

❑ I tend to isolate myself.
❑ I search for the person who will meet my need for a friend, then lose the relationship because I am too smothering or possessive.
❑ I have experienced both of these tendencies.

Explain your answer by describing your relationship tendency.

_____

_____

_____

Whether you isolate, smother, or both, you need to recognize that your behavior is for survival. The further you move on your recovery journey, the more appropriate your methods for connecting with others will become.

Embarking on the Journey from Isolation to Intimacy

Not only does God want us to be close to Him, He wants us to be close to others—mates, children, families, and friends. Our inability to be intimate affects all these relationships. The voyage from isolation to intimacy is difficult but rewarding. As you begin your journey, you can equip yourself for the challenges of the journey. We encourage you to make the journey. Our old patterns seem safer because they are familiar, but we miss the real joy of life if we remain in the false security of isolation or control.

As you learn to experience intimacy, you will find that some people in your life will not be able to respond to your new openness. This is disappointing, of course, but in time, as your own increased understanding and empathy become apparent to them, improved relationships may result. You do not have to stop growing just because they cannot participate in intimate relationships. Hopefully, your spouse, your children, and your family will be able to learn intimacy along with you.

You do not have to stop growing just because others cannot participate in intimate relationships.

Your need for intimacy is God-given. The need has always been there, but you may have never experienced the need being met in a healthy way or with any consistency. When the sexual abuse occurred, every boundary of intimacy was violated. The dilemma this creates is often overwhelming. The hunger for intimacy is like that of a starving child for food.

✎ **Underline the phrase or phrases that describe your need for intimacy.**

Afraid of it	Impossible
Don't want it	Why risk it?
Starving to death for it	Overwhelming
What is it?	
Too painful	Other _____

✎ **What are the greatest barriers to your ability to experience intimacy?**

_____

_____

_____

Jacque struggled for many years with the issue of intimacy. She was aching to feel close to someone; however, to feel close meant relinquishing control. She was too afraid to trust that David really would not take advantage of her openness. Jacque could not let him know she needed him. She felt safe and hidden behind her wall of self-sufficiency. Jacque also felt very alone.

✎ **Use the space below to draw a picture that symbolizes your struggle with intimacy.**

✎ **Describe what the picture means to you.**

_____

_____

Assignment for the Lesson

✎ **Write your own paraphrase of 1 John 1:7, this unit's Scripture memory verse.**

_____

_____

☞ **Say aloud your affirmations. You may wish to repeat only once those you have been using. Repeat the new affirmations five times.**

> I accept God's love and kindness toward me.
> The truth will set me free!
> I am worthy to have God lead me and comfort me.
> I am clean.
> I am wonderfully made.
> I have permission to feel my anger and hurt.
> In Christ I am never alone.
> I can trust myself and others.
> Because God has forgiven me, I can forgive others.
> I can speak the truth. I can be free!
> I am loved, so I can risk loving you.

☞ **Pray for yourself and for each member of your support group.**

But if we walk in the light, as he is in the light, we have fellowship one with another, and the blood of Jesus, His Son purifies us from all sin.

–1 John 1:7

LESSON 2

The Nature of Intimacy

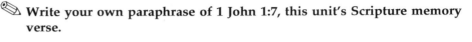

Webster's Dictionary defines _intimacy_ as "marked by a very close association with someone else; friendship that is marked by warmth and a long association; a very personal and private association with another individual." All of us should, and probably do, long for this kind of relationship.

Throughout the Bible, we find many examples of warmth and closeness in relationships. Paul continually encourages new Christians to love each other. Jesus' mother went to see her friend and relative Elizabeth to share the news of her pregnancy. She remained with Elizabeth three months. David trusted Jonathan, the son of King Saul, even though King Saul sought to kill David. But who desires intimacy with us more than Jesus? He deeply loves us. We are fully pleasing and acceptable to Jesus, and He would do anything to help us—even die for us. He knows everything about us. He cares about every detail, even to the number of hairs on our head. His deep, loving intimacy can be ours if only we can learn to respond to Him.

✎ **Write your own definition of intimacy.**

_____

_____

_____

Why do we need intimacy?

_____

_____

As you read Cindy's story in previous units, you learned that there was a time when she had to accept the fact that she was lonely and miserable in isolation. Cindy finally realized that she needed God. She needed people. She needed love. She needed intimacy. Cindy found that intimacy as she journeyed toward restoration and recovery.

Most of us who have been victims are afraid of intimacy because we fear it will mean violation of our boundaries. Remember this and get it firmly fixed in your mind—true intimacy respects boundaries.

True intimacy respects boundaries.

✎ **Mark the following statements _T_ (true) or _F_ (false).**

____ 1. Intimacy means that we blindly trust people.
____ 2. Intimacy means physical or emotional isolation.
____ 3. Intimacy means betrayal.
____ 4. Intimacy means agreeing with another person when you know that person is not right.
____ 5. Intimacy includes the element of freedom.
____ 6. Intimacy means disclosing private or personal information when you do not want or wish to.
____ 7. Intimacy means bondage and abuse.

Intimacy does not mean blind trust; isolation; betrayal; disconnecting your own opinions, values, or needs; or disclosing personal information. It does not mean emotional bondage or abuse. Intimacy may have become frightening to you because you have been taught that in order to become intimate you had to sacrifice your own needs. To experience intimacy, you must develop the skills necessary for healthy relationships. All of the answers were false except number 5.

Intimacy Is...

Intimacy is difficult for most of us who enter recovery, but over time we can develop the necessary skills. These skills include the ability to identify our feelings, to recognize whether or not another person is trustworthy, and to talk about our feelings. Intimacy requires the ability to set and maintain boundaries. Intimate relationships allow you to disclose personal and private matters when and if you choose. It allows for trusting those who are trustworthy and for forming long-term, meaningful relationships with others who desire intimacy. It is the ability to accept the fact that no one human being

Intimacy requires the ability to set and maintain boundaries.

will be able to meet all your needs. Intimacy is the ability to risk, to take the initiative of truly giving of yourself and allowing someone to know you— warts and all. It is the ability to keep secrets, but not be a secret. Intimacy is the ability to give and receive love.

✎ **From the previous paragraph list the characteristics of true intimacy.**

_____

_____

_____

✎ **Which of the characteristics do you most need to develop and why?**

_____

_____

Hopefully you have discovered that intimacy does not mean losing yourself in another person or having that other person lose herself in you. It is an interdependent relationship that acknowledges the value, meaning, needs, and worth of both individuals.

✎ **What would or does it mean to be intimate with God?**

_____

_____

God desires our praise, adoration, and confession. Intimacy with God does not mean performing for Him—it means being *with* Him. Acknowledge your needs, desires, and feelings to God. Listen to Him. He speaks by the Holy Spirit through the Bible, prayer, circumstances, and the church.

✎ **What would or does it mean to be intimate with other human beings?**

_____

_____

Assignment for the Lesson

✎ **On a card write 1 John 1:7, this unit's Scripture memory verse. Carry the card with you. Whenever you do some routine task like getting a drink of water or waiting at a stop light, review your memory verse.**

↪ **Say aloud your affirmations. You may wish to repeat only once those you have been using. Repeat the new affirmations five times.**

I accept God's love and kindness toward me.
The truth will set me free!
I am worthy to have God lead me and comfort me.
I am clean.

But if we walk in the light, as he is in the light, we have fellowship one with another, and the blood of Jesus, His Son purifies us from all sin.

–1 John 1:7

I am wonderfully made.
I have permission to feel my anger and hurt.
In Christ I am never alone.
I can trust myself and others.
Because God has forgiven me, I can forgive others.
I can speak the truth. I can be free!
I am loved, so I can risk loving you.

⇨ **Pray for yourself and for each member of your support group.**

LESSON 3

Unmet Needs for Intimacy

When we isolate ourselves, our intimacy needs are not met. Anytime a personal need is not met, we experience painful feelings.

In this lesson you will examine some feelings and related behaviors which result from a lack of intimacy. After each description you will have an opportunity to consider how you relate to the particular emotion or behavior.

Self-pity

Most of us don't like to admit when we practice self-pity. We feel sorry for ourselves, pout, and display oversensitivity. We say, "Why did this happen to me?" To feel sorry about the abuse is valid, but self-pity is a pit that we must crawl out of. Have a good cry as often as necessary, but pray to get past the stage of self-pity. Self-pity will not help your recovery, and it will not help you to be intimate. Prolonged self-pity will isolate you even more.

✎ **How often do you struggle with self-pity?**

❑ occasionally
❑ often
❑ never
❑ constantly

Do not think that we are saying it is wrong to feel your sorrow and grief. Grieving does not equal self-pity, but if you get mired down in painful emotions, you will be revictimizing yourself. Develop the ability to feel your pain and then respond appropriately to it. In time you will become more aware of how feelings of sorrow affect your capacity to experience healthy intimacy in relationships.

Anger

Anger is another reaction to unmet needs for intimacy. As discussed in a previous unit, we must deal with anger appropriately or it will lead to resentment, bitterness, or retaliation. To feel angry about the abuse you experienced is appropriate; however, anger can also become a barrier to intimacy.

To complete your grief-work, you must learn to express your anger and then get beyond the anger to a different stage of recovery. You hurt yourself if you remain stuck in the anger stage.

✎ **How do you typically deal with anger?**

- ❑ I "stuff" it, deny it exists, and pile something on the lid.
- ❑ I let it build up and then explode at somebody or something.
- ❑ I try to control it, but it seeps out at all the wrong people.
- ❑ I usually express it in an honest and appropriate manner.
- ❑ I do a "slow burn."
- ❑ Other: _____

"When my husband forgot to turn out the light, I went into a rage."

Julie described her struggle with anger. "No one was ever reliable. No one ever did what they said they would. I began to work through my anger when I realized how it was affecting my life. When my husband forgot to turn out the light, I went into a rage. I felt I'd been betrayed and that he'd done it on purpose. I knew this wasn't true, of course, because he had other things on his mind and had just forgotten it. I always expected so much of my friends that if they told me they'd do something and then didn't follow through, I would never want to see them again. I'd begin to withdraw from them and most of the time the relationships ended. I never allowed them any room just to be human. They had to be perfect.

"I really don't know how my husband managed for so many years. Once I asked him to bring me a candy bar. He forgot. I went into an out-and-out rage. At the moment it seemed he didn't care for me at all and that everything he stood for was a lie."

After counseling, Julie began to realize that she must learn to see people in the whole relationship, not just for one incident. Julie found that this kind of angry behavior was a fragment of her reaction to her betrayal as a child. It was still affecting all her relationships, and in order to overcome it, she would have to learn to see things in perspective and not to judge people based on one incident or on the past.

Hardness of Heart

Sometimes victims react by developing a hardness of heart, putting a shell around themselves or bullying weaker people. Ask God to give you a tender heart—a hard heart will only increase your pain. Even though you are an adult now and it may seem better to continue to protect yourself from intimacy, the continued isolation will result in more loneliness. Your involvement in this group says, "I want help, I need people." Take as long as you need to recover, but allow God to plow the fallow ground of your hard heart.

✎ **Check the appropriate box to rate yourself on the "hard-heart" index.**

- ❑ Diamond—my heart is made of the hardest substance known.
- ❑ Granite—hard, grey, and cold, but you can carve it.
- ❑ Sandstone—my shell is crumbling.
- ❑ Mica—my shell is coming off in layers, and it lets some light through.
- ❑ Clay—my heart is pliable, and God is shaping me.
- ❑ Other _____

Someone said, "the challenge in life is to develop a thick skin and a soft heart instead of a thin skin and a hard heart." An appropriately thick skin with a soft heart protects us from pain and makes life not only tolerable, but an adventure. A thin skin and a hard heart makes life difficult and painful.

A Judgmental Attitude

We sometimes test every aspect of a relationship, always hoping we won't be betrayed.

Another reaction to not having our needs met is a critical spirit. As survivors, we tend to be very critical of our spouses and children. We judge others because we fear betrayal. We sometimes test every aspect of a relationship, always hoping we won't be betrayed. We also tend to set standards that are unrealistic, thereby assuring that we do not have to get too close, because no one will be able to measure up to the standard. We keep everyone at a distance so we don't have to risk intimacy.

✎ **Describe a recent instance when you displayed a judgmental attitude.**

_____

_____

_____

Janice was occasionally very critical of other survivors. She angrily pounced on them when they were discouraged or withdrawn. She accused them of not wanting to get well. Janice was afraid to admit that she sometimes was discouraged. She was afraid of honesty and vulnerability in relationships.

The rejection we feel because of abuse causes us to develop many behaviors that destroy relationships. God will supply wisdom and strength, but we must do the work of replacing these old behaviors with Christ-honoring and life-enhancing behaviors. As we develop new relationship skills, we become free to experience genuine intimacy.

✎ **Review the behaviors you have studied in this lesson that grow out of the betrayal of sexual abuse. Below list the ones that you see at work in your life.**

_____

_____

_____

✎ **Describe how you display each behavior in your life and how these survival behaviors affect your life.**

_____

_____

_____

_____

Anger, self-pity, hardness of heart, and a judgmental attitude are survival behaviors. As you recover you will be able to express yourself appropriately when others offend you—without going to the extremes of isolation or manipulation. A healthy sense of self-respect will replace self-pity. You will be able to have healthy boundaries without rigidity or hard-heartedness. You will also develop a deep level of compassion and understanding for others as they struggle.

Matthew 22:39 records Jesus' words, "Love your neighbor as yourself." One reason we find it difficult to be intimate with others is because we find it difficult to be intimate with ourselves. You may avoid self-awareness because you will not give yourself permission to love yourself. You may not know what it means to love. In this passage Jesus said that we were to love ourselves and then to love others in the same way. What does it mean to love? We find the answer again in the Scriptures.

Love is patient, love is kind. It does not envy, it does not boast, it is not proud. It is not rude, it is not self-seeking, it is not easily angered, it keeps no record of wrongs. Love does not delight in evil but rejoices with the truth. It always protects, always trusts, always hopes, always perseveres. Love never fails.
–1 Corinthians 13:4-8

Read 1 Corinthians 13:4-8 appearing in the margin. We often read this passage and immediately attempt to apply it to loving others. Let's begin by applying these characteristics of love to how you treat yourself.

✎ **Are you able to be patient with yourself? Describe what specific actions you are taking to be patient and kind to yourself.**

_____

_____

Describe the last time you "beat yourself up" with anger at yourself.

_____

_____

✎ **Do you keep a record of your own wrongs long after God and others have forgiven you?** ❑ Yes ❑ No

If so, describe an instance where you continue to keep record.

_____

_____

✎ **Do you rejoice with the positive truths about yourself or do you look for things to cover yourself with shame?**

❑ I rejoice in my identity in Christ and my personal strengths.
❑ I tend to look first at my failures and shame myself.
❑ I tend to shame myself, but gradually I am changing the behavior.
❑ Other _____

Sometimes we are so hard on ourselves. We don't give ourselves a chance to succeed. If you keep a mental and emotional record of your failures, begin now to release that record. Romans 8:1 says, "There therefore now is no condemnation for those who are in Christ Jesus."

✎ Describe the last time you protected yourself. What are you doing to learn to treat yourself better?

_____

_____

Survivors tend to put everything and everyone else ahead of their own physical and emotional needs. Do you go to the doctor when you need to? Do you say no when someone asks for more than you can give? One way Brenda protected herself was to refuse to work unreasonable amounts of overtime to complete a project. The company hired a temporary employee to help her. Protect yourself by making wise choices in relationships. Say no to unhealthy friends and behaviors.

Assignment for the Lesson

✎ Below write 1 John 1:7, this unit's Scripture memory verse. Continue to work to memorize the verse.

_____

_____

☞ Say aloud your affirmations. You may wish to repeat only once those you have been using. Repeat the new affirmations five times.

I accept God's love and kindness toward me.
The truth will set me free!
I am worthy to have God lead me and comfort me.
I am clean.
I am wonderfully made.
I have permission to feel my anger and hurt.
In Christ I am never alone.
I can trust myself and others.
Because God has forgiven me, I can forgive others.
I can speak the truth. I can be free!
I am loved, so I can risk loving you.

☞ Pray for yourself and for each member of your group.

LESSON 4

Ways We Avoid Intimacy

Typically we change our expectations and behaviors to readjust to our inability to be intimate. If we cannot meet this God-given need in a healthy way, most of us will attempt to meet it in a dysfunctional way.

In this lesson you will examine several of those dysfunctional ways to avoid intimacy. After each description you will once again have an opportunity to identify if and how you relate to the emotion or behavior.

Substitutes for Intimacy

You may try perfectionism—setting standards too high so neither you nor anyone else can measure up. False compassion is another unfruitful way we compensate for a lack of intimacy. We help hurting people not for their sake but so that we can feel their pain. This may seem to meet our aching need inside, but it will not work forever. Some people adopt pets which they can safely love and depend upon to be loyal to them. Others readjust by demanding attention. You might act like a clown or show-off, or adopt extreme dress or a loud personality in order to get attention. Unfortunately, this does not meet the need for intimacy, and it often leads to rejection.

✎ **Do you recognize any of these behaviors in your life—**

❑ Yes ❑ No Perfectionism
❑ Yes ❑ No False Compassion
❑ Yes ❑ No Attention-Demanding Behavior
❑ Yes ❑ No Compulsive Behaviors
❑ Yes ❑ No Suppressing the Need for Intimacy
❑ Yes ❑ No Fantasy
❑ Yes ❑ No Unforgiveness

Compulsive Behaviors

Probably the most common method we use to fill the void left by a lack of intimacy is to practice some type of compulsive behavior. We use eating, smoking, drinking, spending money, promiscuity, compulsive religious activity, or many other types of behaviors. We feel lonely and depressed. In an attempt to compensate for our low self-worth we engage in some type of behavior that feels good. We may not see any other way to release the pain we feel, but the pain always comes back.

✎ **Compulsive behaviors are rituals that we use to avoid pain or to feel better. Rate yourself on the following list of common activities that we often use compulsively. Do you use these ordinary activities in a compulsive way?**

	normally	never	seldom	occasionally	often	compulsively
Eating	❑	❑	❑	❑	❑	❑
Smoking	❑	❑	❑	❑	❑	❑
Shopping	❑	❑	❑	❑	❑	❑
Watching TV	❑	❑	❑	❑	❑	❑
Reading	❑	❑	❑	❑	❑	❑
Sex	❑	❑	❑	❑	❑	❑
Work	❑	❑	❑	❑	❑	❑
Religious activities	❑	❑	❑	❑	❑	❑

"The only thing I really accomplished was to get fat and to get in debt. "

Leslie shares her story, "I felt empty. I was depressed, and I hurt inside. I didn't know what to do to stop the pain. I just wanted the pain to go away, even if only for a little while. I started eating, and it felt good. Many times I went shopping and overspent. At the time I felt happy, but later I hated myself. The only thing I really accomplished was to get fat and to get in debt. I hate it! And I hate myself!"

Perhaps you have tried to accumulate material things as a way of meeting your need for intimacy. You may feel better temporarily, but material things cannot fill the God-given need for close relationships.

Some survivors find themselves doing anything to avoid being alone.

Some victims give in to sexual lust. They feel that they must have someone there to hold, to sleep with, and to have sex with. Some survivors find themselves doing anything to avoid being alone. Their quest to stop the pain can lead to being revictimized or to sexual addiction.

Suppress the Need

Another common readjustment is to suppress the need for intimacy. Some people run out of ways to have their needs fulfilled, so they try to make themselves believe that they can live without intimacy. They try to believe that they are needless and wantless. They withdraw and live as if they do not need personal relationships.

Some people live out their suppressed needs by dominating everybody and everything around them. They have to be in control. They are tough, demanding, in charge, and often rise to the top of any organization.

Fantasy

Sometimes our fantasies keep us from intimacy. One victim, describing her fantasies of being raped, admits that she knows that rape would not be like her fantasies; it would be horrible. Her fantasies are full of helplessness and full of joy and of being overwhelmed. As the rape ends, she has an orgasm. She describes feeling full of shame and guilt over the fantasy, but in counseling resists dealing with her sexual dysfunction in her marriage. She gets pleasure out of the fantasy, but she is afraid to become intimate and commit to her husband sexually.

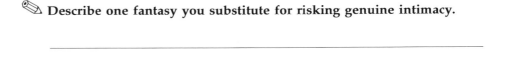 **Describe one fantasy you substitute for risking genuine intimacy.**

_____

_____

Genuine intimacy is more fulfilling than any fantasy. When tempted to fill your days with fantasy, chose a positive goal and take one small step toward accomplishing it.

Unforgiveness

Some people do not forgive because they are scared to death that, if they forgive, they will have to deal with people. A full unit has already been devoted to this subject, and that discussion applies here also. Dealing with unforgiveness is a normal part of recovery. But at some point, victims need to experience the freedom forgiveness brings. This will lead to the need to develop intimacy, because this need has temporarily been filled with the power of unforgiveness. As you forgive, you may feel empty, but that will produce the energy you need to grow in the Lord.

✏ **Review the dysfunctional attempts outlined in this lesson to meet or avoid our intimacy needs. Below list the ones you see affecting your life.**

_____

_____

_____

✏ **Describe how each of the methods you identified is affecting you.**

_____

_____

_____

_____

_____

_____

_____

Genuine intimacy is difficult, especially for survivors.

Substitutes for intimacy just do not meet the need. Substitutes provide false hope, resulting in more confusion and frustration. God created us with a need for intimacy that will not be met outside of healthy, personal relationships. Genuine intimacy is difficult, especially for survivors. You can learn to recognize when you are trying to fill your need for intimacy with compulsive behaviors. You can write about your feelings. You can call a supportive person and talk about what you are experiencing.

Assignment for the Lesson

✏ **Below write from memory this unit's Scripture verse. You may check your work on page 202.**

_____

_____

⬅ **Say aloud your affirmations. You may wish to repeat only once those you have been using. Repeat the new affirmations five times.**

I accept God's love and kindness toward me.
The truth will set me free!
I am worthy to have God lead me and comfort me.
I am clean.
I am wonderfully made.
I have permission to feel my anger and hurt.
In Christ I am never alone.
I can trust myself and others.

Because God has forgiven me, I can forgive others.
I can speak the truth. I can be free!
I am loved, so I can risk loving you.

☞ **Pray for yourself and for each member of your group.**

LESSON 5

Why Is Intimacy So Difficult?

The issues of neglect and abandonment profoundly affect our ability to achieve intimacy.

One survivor wrote, "Neglect . . . it is more painful than death. You are not allowed to live or to die. You are not allowed to join or to belong. You are alive—existing, but not living. You know you are not acceptable. You stare at people and things from a distance—observing, listening, and hurting. You see the pain, but you can't scream, because it isn't safe. It is not safe to cry, to want, to dream, to feel, to ask, or to desire. This is being abandoned."

As you can talk, write, and express your feelings with supportive people, you will be developing relationship skills. Intimacy involves sharing the private and personal things of your life, but it also includes the ability to ask for your private and personal needs to be met.

Knowing another and being known is to not only find shelter from the storm but to at last begin to scatter the clouds and let the sun shine through. This is intimacy; this is love as it is described in 1 Corinthians 13.

✎ **Describe areas in which you have felt neglected in the past.**

_____

_____

_____

You may have tried to talk to a friend about your abuse and she discounted your feelings. Maybe you had surgery and no one called or came to see you.

✎ **Describe areas in which you feel neglected in the present.**

_____

_____

_____

Worthy of concern

Everyone feels neglected occasionally. It just isn't possible for someone to be standing ready and available to meet your every need, however, it is important for someone to be there some of the time. You also need to talk about feelings of neglect and abandonment you have experienced in significant relationships. You are worthy of concern and attention.

Pray specifically about those areas of neglect, abandonment, and abuse that keep you from risking yourself in relationships. Again, be aware of any ways you have blamed yourself for the abandonment and neglect. Share your feelings with God. Write them in your journal as prayers for restoration and healing.

Victims who have experienced neglect have an especially difficult time dealing with the self-hatred that occurs in sexual abuse. Many victims of all kinds of abuse despise themselves, and consequently find it very difficult to receive the concern and affection of others. Confront those feelings with positive self-talk. Tell yourself the truth until you believe it.

Tell yourself the truth until you believe it.

Review the following list of probable causes for emotional isolation, and pray for specific understanding of how any of these causes have had an impact on your ability to be intimate. How did you learn to shut down emotionally? You will probably want to reread what we have said in previous chapters as you review the list. There may also be areas you need to deal with that are not on the list.

 Below is a list of probable causes for emotional isolation. Circle the items that apply to you.

Sexual abuse	Abandonment
Shame	Depression
Poor self-image	Neglect
Guilt	Inability to trust
Family messages	Others _____
Fear	_____

Go to your journal to pour out your feelings about each of these. Use the outline of "The Serenity Prayer" (see pages 157-161) to sort out how you want to respond to these issues in your life. For example, you cannot change the fact of the sexual abuse. It happened to you. You will find some items on the list which you can change. God can change them as you ask Him to grant you the peace to work through them. Right now you may feel overwhelmed. Relax and let God lead you to shelter from your storm.

Sexual Intimacy in Marriage after Sexual Abuse

Sexual abuse commonly damages the intimacy of sexual relations in a marriage. Often survivors confide that they never had a problem with sex until they got married. Some relate that they were sexually active before marriage and wonder if God is punishing them now in their marriage. The answer to that question is a hearty no! Marriage often appears to present the same problems for the victim that the abusive situation did, in that victims feel that they "have to" engage in sex. Consciously or unconsciously, they feel that their power of choice once again has been taken from them.

Survivors may have flashbacks while having sexual relations with their spouses. Other times spouses may do something similar to what the abuser did, and victims will be unable to respond. Sometimes, before starting in recovery, victims have been spared the common problem of dysfunction in the sexual area of their marriage. But during the recovery process, they may no longer desire to have sex with their partners because of emerging painful memories. All of these things are normal for survivors. The counseling professional may even advise the couple to abstain from sex for a period of time, but be assured that recovery does work.

✏ **Below you will find a list of attitudes and responses toward that are sex characteristic of sexual abuse victims. Some are gender specific, some are not. Check those that you have experienced at some time during your life. Place an asterisk beside the ones that you continue to experience.**

Attitudes toward sex

- ❑ Unable to enjoy kissing
- ❑ Guilt and dirty feelings after sex or about sex
- ❑ Problems concerning boundaries in sex
- ❑ Inability to tolerate own body
- ❑ Dissociation from own body during sex
- ❑ Feeling of worthlessness if unable to provide sex
- ❑ Wearing of seductive dress or asexual clothing
- ❑ Inability to look at a naked man/woman; feeling of revulsion
- ❑ Phobic avoidance of genitals
- ❑ Inability to tell whether or not men/women are "coming on"
- ❑ Effort to make life better with sex
- ❑ Avoidance of sexual activity or use of words associated with sex
- ❑ Compulsive sexual behavior
- ❑ Sexual acting out
- ❑ Lack of sexual desire
- ❑ Exhibitionism/lack of modesty
- ❑ Extreme modesty
- ❑ Alternation between compulsive sexual behavior and lack of sex drive
- ❑ Feeling of being caught during sex
- ❑ Fear of letting go during sex/stopping self in arousal and enjoyment
- ❑ Crying during or after sex
- ❑ Need for darkness during sex
- ❑ Feeling of being good only for sex; abandonment feared if victim refuses to participate in sex
- ❑ Lack of sensitivity in breasts
- ❑ Difficulty with or inability to achieve orgasm
- ❑ Need to feel helpless during sex
- ❑ Fantasizing of rape
- ❑ Aversion to parts of one's own body
- ❑ Pain in vaginal area during sex
- ❑ Nervousness at being stimulated
- ❑ Inability to have drug- or alcohol-free sex
- ❑ Desire to make partner responsible for sex
- ❑ Preoccupation with other concerns during sex
- ❑ Eagerness for sex to be over
- ❑ Feeling of having to perform during sex
- ❑ Inability to ask to have sexual needs met
- ❑ Anger during and after sex at having been exploited
- ❑ Inability to look at oneself nude
- ❑ Aversion to touching oneself
- ❑ Inability to be playful during sex
- ❑ View of self as sex object
- ❑ Need for sex to be dirty
- ❑ Feeling sexually inadequate
- ❑ Impotence

Certainly to have sexual relations is the most physically intimate action we experience with another person. We uncover our bodies and leave ourselves very vulnerable to another person. No one has to ponder too long to recognize the distortion that sexual abuse brings to this God-given act of marriage. But somehow, with God's help, we, as victims, must regain our dignity and learn to share that dignity with our mate.

With God's help both survivors and their spouses can learn how to provide the safety and nurture needed to recover this important part of themselves. Sometimes the couple must begin with holding hands until the survivor feels safe. Perhaps the couple must commit to only holding one another for a time. Often victims need to know from their partners that they would be loved by them even if they never had sex.

✎ **Describe how you feel when you think about the impact of the sexual abuse on your ability to respond sexually.**

_____

_____

_____

✎ **What would it mean for you to have the safety and nurture so that you could grow sexually?**

_____

_____

_____

✎ **If you are married, describe your sexual relationship to your spouse. What would make it more meaningful to you? What can you do to take the first step toward your goal?**

_____

_____

_____

Support each other through this struggle.

Anger is a perfectly acceptable response to the impact of the sexual abuse on your ability to respond sexually. You also may have listed hate, fear, resentment, and hopelessness. Survivors typically yearn for the freedom to respond sexually without experiencing survival barriers. As you and your spouse talk about what happens to you sexually, determine the steps you need to take to grow in this important area of your marriage. Together seek professional help. Support each other through this struggle. Remember this is a sensitive issue for everyone. Listen to your mate as he or she shares the personal impact your abuse and recovery has had. Mates need space to express and feel the intensity of the impact of your sexual abuse.

Martha had been avoidant and non-orgasmic for seven years of marriage. Doug, her husband, struggled with guilt, anger at himself, and inadequacy.

He thought he was an unsatisfactory partner. When Martha told him about the sexual abuse she had suffered from her brothers, Doug was angry at the brothers but relieved to know what was wrong. He was compassionate and prepared to support Martha in her healing process.

Survivors who are single may not face as many issues of intimacy because they are not dealing with a mate. Whether you are single or married, however, by working through your recovery process you will be better able to experience healthy intimacy in all types of relationships. The important part is to learn to replace unhealthy isolation with the joy of appropriate and healthy intimacy.

Commitment and Intimacy

Sarah, as a child, had been raped repeatedly by a neighbor. She and her husband struggled through years of hurt created by her abuse. Sexual issues troubled their marriage rather than blessing it.

As Sarah worked on recovery with the help of a counselor and a support group, she became more confident, communicative, and physically responsive to her husband. As she grew through recovery she was able to respond to him as a wife rather than as a victim of sexual abuse. For the first time in their marriage, they were able to experience both emotional and physical intimacy. She drew closer to him, not just physically, but in being able to give her heart to him.

God created us as whole persons. We are wonderfully-made physical, psychological, emotional, spiritual, and relational beings with a need for personal significance. God created us to be in relationships. We thrive in relationships that value and affirm us as whole persons. We die in isolation.

The Special Problems of the Single Person

The single person faces some unique challenges in recovery from sexual abuse. Often the single survivor is quite alone, perhaps too fearful to have married or perhaps having been in a marriage that ended in divorce. For a victim who is alone, becoming skilled in intimacy may be a somewhat more difficult path than he or she wants to follow. Obviously, circumstances for practicing the principles that will lead to a successful relationship do not present themselves as easily as they do for the married victim who is presently in a relationship. Remaining single may seem easier or better because many aspects of intimacy, including affection and sex as well as conflict, can be totally avoided.

There is no greater expression of love than the intimacy of knowing.

There are many challenges for the victim of abuse in the area of sexual relations, but God's Word is a place to start seeking for understanding. Genesis 4:1 says, "And Adam knew Eve his wife: and she conceived and bare Cain" (KJV). The word used here in the Hebrew to depict a sexual relationship is *knew*. Intimacy has the overwhelming challenge of commitment. There is no greater expression of love than the intimacy of knowing. It was God's intention for sex to be one expression of intimacy. Without knowing one another as people of value and worthy of respect and love, sex loses its meaning and purpose as God intended it.

Healthy relationships are a shelter from the storm. Your continued recovery journey is vital. Stay in touch with God and with others. Stay in touch with your own needs, desires, and feelings. You were harmed in a relationship. God will heal you as you relate to Him, yourself, and others. Keep your eyes on the Son as He shines His light through the clouds of the storm.

Recovery is a journey with peaks and valleys.

Recovery is a journey with peaks and valleys. You have begun and "He who began a good work in you will carry it on to completion" (Philippians 1:6). God created you and can re-create you. You can cooperate with God as He redeems and restores that which was lost.

Where Do You Go from Here?

We all need to grow. None of us has "arrived." As you have worked through *Shelter from the Storm*, we hope that you have come to understand yourself better. We hope that you have come to understand and to love God more. We hope that you have also discovered areas in which you need to grow.

The basic plan for *Shelter from the Storm* is for a member to cycle through the material more than once. Therefore, you may want to begin again, work through this book again, and participate in another group. If you do, you will find yourself understanding and applying your recovery at a deeper level in your life.

You may feel that you have done enough work in your recovery from sexual abuse, or that you need to leave this subject for a while and return at a later time. We have provided the following exercise and the information that accompanies it to help you plan for the next stage of your growth.

✎ **Think about areas in your life in which you need to grow. On the following list number your top three priorities.**

___ Understanding the Bible
___ Memorizing Scripture
___ Developing your prayer life
___ Overcoming either anorexia, bulimia, or compulsive overeating
___ Building witnessing skills
___ Changing unhealthy relationships
___ Conquering an addiction to alcohol or other drugs
___ Knowing God's will
___ Becoming a disciple maker
___ Caring for your physical needs
___ Other: _____

_____

Remember that character development and spiritual growth are not instantaneous. Worthwhile goals take time.

The following resources are written in the interactive format you have used as you studied *Shelter from the Storm*. All of these books are intended for group study along with daily, individual work. Determine a particular area in which you need to grow. Then use one or more of these resources to help you continue your spiritual growth.

To build your self-worth on the forgiveness and love of Jesus Christ:
- *Search for Significance* by Robert S. McGee, (Houston: Rapha Publishing). This study continues your work of replacing the four false beliefs with principles of truth from God's Word.

To understand a hurtful family history:
- *Breaking the Cycle of Hurtful Family Experiences* by Robert S. McGee, Pat Springle, Jim Craddock, and Dale W. McCleskey (Houston: Rapha Publishing). This study helps you to understand how parents shape their children and how they pass family dysfunction from generation to generation. It teaches you how to break the cycle of generational family dysfunction. Member's Book, product number 0805499814; Leader's Guide, 0805499822.

To identify and replace codependent behaviors:
- *Untangling Relationships: A Christian Perspective on Codependency* by Pat Springle and Susan A. Lanford (Houston: Rapha Publishing). This course helps individuals understand codependency and learn how to make relationships more healthy. Member's Book, product number 0805499733; Leader's Guide, 0805499741.

To apply a Christ-Centered 12-Step Process:
- *Conquering Codependency: A Christ-Centered 12-Step Process* by Pat Springle and Dale W. McCleskey (Houston: Rapha Publishing). The learned perceptions and behaviors called codependency—the compulsion to rescue, help, and fix others—often add to our addictive behaviors. *Conquering Codependency* applies the Christ-centered 12 Steps to these habits. Member's Book, product number 080549975X; Facilitator's Guide, product number 0805499768.

- *Conquering Chemical Dependency: A Christ-Centered 12-Step Process* by Robert S. McGee and Dale W. McCleskey (Houston: Rapha Publishing). Offers hope and healing for those who have developed a dependency on alcohol or other mood-altering drugs. *Conquering Chemical Dependency* applies the Christ-centered 12-Steps to help you overcome addiction. Member's Book, product number 0805499830; Facilitator's Guide, available for free download at www.lifeway.com/discipleplus/download.htm.

- *Conquering Eating Disorders: A Christ-Centered 12-Step Process* by Robert S. McGee, Wm. Drew Mountcastle and Jim Florence. (Houston: Rapha Publishing). Applies the proved Christ-centered 12-Step discipleship process to help you overcome either anorexia, bulimia, or compulsive overeating. Member's Book, product number 0805499784; Facilitator's Guide, product number 0805499776.

Remember—Recovery Is a Process

Life can be an exciting adventure. The options you have reviewed present some possibilities for a lifestyle of continued growth, health, and service.

Recovery is the process of victorious Christian living.

We heartily congratulate you for completing this workbook. Thank you for having the courage and tenacity to reach this point. This book ends, but the process of recovery continues. It is the process of victorious Christian living. If you feel some discouragement, pain, or fear about the process, remember the nature of the grieving/healing process. Your feelings are normal. Typically, we feel worse before we feel better. You can draw strength from God's promise: *You are from God, little children, and have overcome them; because greater is He who is in you than he who is in the world.* (1 John 4:4, NASB)

The False Beliefs and Scriptural Truths
from *Search for Significance*

False Beliefs	God's Truths
I must meet certain standards to feel good about myself. (This belief results in fear of failure.)	Because of *justification* I am completely forgiven by and fully pleasing to God. I no longer have to fear failure.
I must have the approval of certain others to feel good about myself. (This belief results in fear of rejection.)	Because of *reconciliation* I am totally accepted by God. I no longer have to fear rejection.
Those who fail (including myself) are unworthy of love and deserve to be punished. (This belief results in guilt.)	Because of *propitiation* I am deeply loved by God. I no longer have to fear punishment or punish others.
I am what I am. I cannot change. I am hopeless. (This belief results in shame.)	Because of **regeneration** I have been made brand-new, complete in Christ. I no longer need to experience the pain of shame.

Your Journey through the Storm

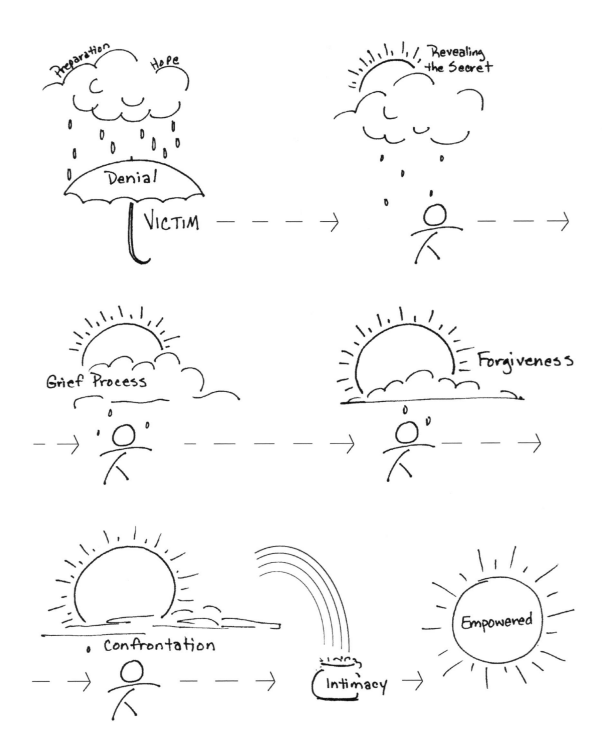

Untangling Relationships: A Christian Perspective on Codependency $15.50
- volume discounts also available

Codependency is the:
• Compulsion to please others.
• Feeling responsible to make others happy, successful and good.
• Feeling guilty when you don do everything just right - all the time.

Untangling Relationships: Leader's Guide $7.00

Conquering Chemical Dependency $15.50
- volume discounts also available

Whereas most other 12 step programs simply use an undefined understanding of God, this program presents the only true God. The person will be led to understand the following:

• What their real perception of God is and how it was created in their childhood.
• God's process for setting a person free from the power of sin.
• The origin of the pain in their life and what to do about it.
• The warning signs of chemical dependency.
• Who they are in Christ and how to deal with shame and guilt... and many other issues. This is simply the most extensive, Christ-centered proven program in existence.

Conquering Eating Disorders $15.50
- volume discounts also available

Here is an effective, proven program for everyone who has experienced the debilitating disorders of anorexia, bulimia, and compulsive overeating.

This 12-Step Program for Overcoming Eating Disorders tackles the compulsive-addictive patterns in which a person uses food in an emotionally or physically abusive way. The reader will learn what eating disorders are... and are not, and why they occur.

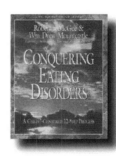

Breaking the Cycle of Hurtful Family Experiences $15.50
- volume discounts also available

Learn how your parents shape the way you feel about yourself, how you relate to others, even how you form your ideas about God.

Breaking the Cycle of Hurtful Family Experiences Leader's Guide $7.00

Conquering Codependency: A Christ Centered 12-Step Process $15.50
- volume discounts also available

Conquering Codependency: A Christ-Centered 12-Step
Process helps you recognize the painful problems of codependency, the compulsion to fix everyone and everything. It offers sound biblical strategies that give
hope and promise healing from the damage codependency can do to your life.

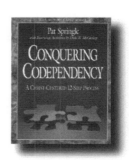

Shelter From The Storm $15.50
- volume discounts also available

From beyond her own darkness, author Cynthia Kubetin leads others to freedom.
"This was one of the most eye opening books I have ever read. After I read the book, I realized I wasn't crazy."

Codependency: A Christian Perspective $15.50
- volume discounts also available

Codependency is the:
- Compulsion to please others.
- Feeling responsible to make others happy, successful and good.
- Feeling guilty when you don't do everything just right - all the time.

Rapha's 12-Step Program for Overcoming Codependency $15.50
- volume discounts also available

Rapha's 12-Step Codependency manual is a complete work that introduces the reader to the processes they must go through to find freedom from the lifelong pattern of codependency. This manual not only allows the person to identify the specific ways their life has been impacted by this deception but takes them through the steps that will set them free. This manual was part of Rapha's Treatment programs that treated over 30,000 patients. There are no other books that have demonstrated the effectiveness and the attention to spiritual issues as this one.

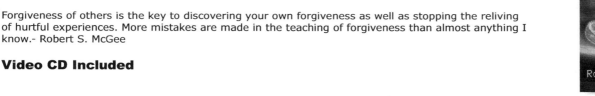

Rapha's 12-Step Program for Overcoming Chemical Dependency $15.50
- volume discounts also available

Includes what the other 12-Step programs leave out - how to deal with the foundational issues that allow the person to gain freedom.

The Search For Peace $12.50
- volume discounts also available

Forgiveness of others is the key to discovering your own forgiveness as well as stopping the reliving of hurtful experiences. More mistakes are made in the teaching of forgiveness than almost anything I know.- Robert S. McGee

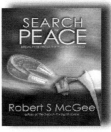

Video CD Included

The Search For Freedom $15.50
- volume discounts also available

As children we create strongholds which greatly influence the way we perceive life, respond and relate to others. Find out how to identify the strongholds and destroy them.

Rapha's 12-Step Program for Overcoming Eating Disorders $15.50
- volume discounts also available

Here is an effective, proven program for everyone who has experienced the debilitating disorders of anorexia, bulimia, and compulsive overeating. This 12-Step Program for Overcoming Eating Disorders tackles the compulsive-addictive patterns in which a person uses food in an emotionally or physically abusive way. The reader will learn what eating disorders are... and are not, and why these disorders occur.

Discipline With Love
- volume discounts also available

$10.00

A practical guide for establishing systematic discipline in your home. The principles offered here have helped many parents form a plan for discipline, so that their children can grow to be mature, responsible adults. These principles work because they are based on the truths of the Scriptures. With them, you can experience success in disciplining your children.

Rapha's Handbook for Group Leaders

$10.00

This book helps any group wanting to begin or improve on small groups. It contains the following:

- The Goals and Expectations of a Group
- Organization and Selection
- The Mechanics of a Group
- The Dynamics of a Group
- How to Get Started
- And more!

Right Step Christian Recovery Program

$50.00

In 1986, Rapha began. Over the next 12 years, over 30,000 patients were seen in this in-hospital program. During this time the presentations seen in this video series was presented to hundreds of thousands of people. This material comes from those who are in the best position to know what works and doesn't work. It contains the following video presentations:

- Functional & Dysfunctional Families
- The Addictive/Dysfunctional Personality
- Codependency
- Support Groups
- Leading Support Groups
- Getting Started/ Follow-Up Training

Would you like Robert McGee to speak to your group? Robert maintains a limited speaking schedule. However, if you would like to contact him about coming to your church or group, write to him at rmcgee@searchlife.org or call him at 1-800-460-4673.

To order call 1-800-460-4673 or go to www.searchlife.org